Alexandra Feodorowna

EMPRESS OF RUSSIA.

Grimm

GLK

Edinburgh : Printed by Thomas and Archibald Constable,

FOR

EDMONSTON AND DOUGLAS.

LONDON . . . . HAMILTON, ADAMS, AND CO.

CAMBRIDGE . . . . . . MACMILLAN AND CO.

GLASGOW . . . . JAMES MACLEHOSE.

FROM A BUST BY THE PRINCESS ROYAL OF ENGLAND, AND PUBLISHED
BY HER PERMISSION.

Alexandra Feodorowna

EMPRESS OF RUSSIA.

1

BY

A. TH. VON GRIMM.

TRANSLATED BY LADY WALLACE.

VOLUME FIRST.

Dum vetera extollimus, recentiorum incuriosi.—TACIT.

EDINBURGH:
EDMONSTON AND DOUGLAS.
1870.

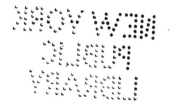

DEDICATED

TO HIS MAJESTY THE EMPEROR

ALEXANDER SECOND NIKOLAEWITSCH

WITH THE

MOST PROFOUND RESPECT AND HEARTFELT GRATITUDE.

PREFACE.

THE following pages, dedicated to the memory of the late Empress Alexandra Feodorowna, purport to give a sketch of the events of the period and the circumstances of the country in which her life was spent. The Imperial throne which for thirty years she adorned with the brightest feminine virtues, did not stand on her native soil. It was therefore above all imperative that the reader should be made acquainted with the peculiarities of the Imperial realm. Indeed, I considered this even more absolutely requisite for a thorough comprehension of the subject, from the fact that the empire of Russia, notwithstanding its high political importance, its adjacent situation, and its many connections with Germany, has attracted less attention in schools and universities than ancient Egypt or the Byzantine kingdom.

Both volumes of this work are indeed essentially the same in purport, and portray the life of the capital, the Court, and, more especially, that of the Imperial family, but their origin and sources of information are different. The second volume is almost exclusively written from my own personal observation and impressions as an eye-witness. Not only is this the case with all the incidents depicted in that volume, such as the visits to

Moscow and Palermo, the conflagration of the Winter
Palace, etc., but all the great personalities of the Court
and the capital are also delineated in accordance with the
direct impression made on me, and after many long years
of intercourse with them on my part. In the first volume
I am indebted to other sources than to my own diaries
or personal observation. The history of the events of
December 14th is faithfully transcribed from Baron
Modest Korf's work, *The Emperor Nicholas's Accession
to the Throne.* All particulars with regard to the Greek
Church are taken from a book written by Murawief—
Religious Services of the Northern Church, translated into
German by Muralt. But I am also indebted for many
details to the verbal information of various persons who
frequented the Petersburg Court in the reigns of Alexander the First, Paul the First, and even that of Catherine the Second. A considerable portion of that volume
has also been contributed by conversations with the
Empress herself, and with King William the First of
Prussia. I must publicly express my gratitude to my
friend and benefactor of thirty years' standing, Admiral
Frederick von Lütke, who was so kind as conscientiously
to read through my MS. and to make annotations on it.

   The chief aim of the book is to show that, after the
accession of Nicholas the First, the womanly charms of
the Empress Alexandra Feodorowna cast, for thirty years,
over the domestic life at the Winter Palace, a dignity and
a halo such as never previously existed in the Russian
Court,—above all, in the eighteenth century. She was
the soul of the Imperial House and society, and her
example, though quiet and almost imperceptible, yet

powerfully influenced the tone and ennobled the spirit of society in the capital. It must be deemed a step in advance in our century, that domestic life on almost all · European thrones is held in the honour it so well deserves; whereas in the eighteenth century it was ruthlessly trampled on by many brilliant Courts. Politics and military affairs are entirely excluded from this work, or at least only cursorily alluded to when influencing family life.

The public are too far removed from thrones and palaces to have any opportunity of closely observing them, and often imagine that in these golden halls and elevated heights uninterrupted happiness is to be found, and are not aware that those very storms that sweep harmlessly past the lowly huts in the valley, assail palaces fiercely, and fill them with alarm. How seldom do they know that the highest earthly dignity is too often inseparable from the most oppressive burdens, and that the peace and repose of a citizen's family are seldom vouchsafed to the splendours of a crown. Few persons of our time have passed through every cycle and phase of happiness and misery as thoroughly as Alexandra Feodorowna. The happiest wife, the happiest mother, she was not spared the most severe strokes of destiny, and some individual days in her career were more fruitful in sorrow and terror than the whole lifetime of a peaceful citizen. The history of our day can name no woman whose mission under peculiar circumstances has been more arduous, and at the same time none who have fulfilled their feminine vocation in similar perfection.

I feel that I still owe my readers an explanation
with regard to my own position in the family of the
Empress Alexandra. In the third chapter of my second
volume I have related that my office in the Winter
Palace first brought me, in the year 1834, into the
presence of her Majesty, who at that time bestowed
on me a degree of confidence that the next few years
were still to justify; but shortly the sphere of my
labours was extended, and the Empress often deigned
to hold long conversations with me, which at first
were confined to the subjects of art and literature,
but were gradually extended to every branch of the
interests of humanity. Her delicate health required
more tranquillity than a Court life permits, and greater
seclusion than the city was accustomed to see on her
part, and in the winter of 1838–39 she passed many
evenings in the circle of her children with only her
immediate suite. The Empress deeply regretted no
longer having the leisure time that she had devoted,
when Grand Duchess, at Anitschkow to reading and to
music, and it was now great compensation to her to be
able to pass some of these unoccupied hours in her
former pursuits. She often questioned me as to the
new literary productions, both of Germany and France,
telling me frankly the impression various works left on
her mind, but listening with the most entire equanimity
to any opposite opinions. When she was obliged to
pass the winter of 1845-46 in Palermo, I was invariably
included in her small circle, consisting only of her relations, the Grand Duchess of Mecklenburg, the Grand
Duchess Olga (now Queen of Würtemberg), and the

Grand Duke Constantine.. The conversation was very
animated, but always of a solid nature, and the subject of every work perused was the history of Italy and
its treasures. At that time she expressed a wish on
her return to Petersburg, that all the master-works of
German literature should be read aloud to her, in a
small and select circle. The Northern climate, and its
effects on her delicate health, were singularly favourable to this project, for in the early days of the autumn
of 1846 she was once more restricted to her cabinet,
and from that time I had the good fortune to be daily
in her presence, and while she only chose to appear in the
society of the Court and the capital, with the majesty,
dignity, and gracious condescension of an Empress,
I learned to know and admire this illustrious lady,
divested of all dazzling splendour in her pure womanly
dignity, and variety of culture, both of mind and heart,
and I was amazed how little her lofty and noble character was known to the general public.

In the year 1852 my own health compelled me to
leave Petersburg, and to pass some years in Dresden, in
the greatest retirement. This period seemed to me
well calculated to complete and to publish several
works that I had commenced in Petersburg. The
Oriental war compelled me to open my diaries sooner
than I intended, in order to communicate to the public
a portion of the travels I had undertaken with the
Grand Duke Constantine. In spite of my being so far
away, I did not seem to be forgotten by the Imperial
family, for in 1858 I was recalled to Petersburg, and in
spite of all the great changes, I found the Empress-

mother in the same cabinet, and with the same kindly
feeling towards myself.

She was at this time more delicate and fragile than
even formerly, but her sympathies as lively as ever.
At first she wished to hear the various events of my
life during my absence of six years, and also made
me depict the society of Dresden, and the various
individuals with whom I had been in the habit
of associating; she seemed to take the kindest and
warmest interest in my occupations, my mode of life in
Dresden, and my family.

The small social circles in her cabinet began in
the autumn, when two months were occupied by grave
but interesting conversations. When her strength permitted, she herself related the impressions of her
journey to Italy, and in spite of increasing years, with
lively power of memory, always continuing youthful
and fresh in her reminiscences.

In the course of fifteen months, however, she was
again forced to quit the North, and did not return there
till August 1860.

On the 8th and 20th September she invited me to
dinner in her cabinet, as her weakness did not admit of
her taking part in a family banquet, and on October
20th, at eight o'clock in the morning, kneeling by her
deathbed, I kissed the still warm hand of the dead
Empress. These facts will convince the reader that I
am both justified and entitled to furnish the details of
the whole life of Alexandra Feodorowna to the public.

THE AUTHOR.

BERLIN, *January* 1866.

CONTENTS OF VOL. I.

MEMOIRS

OF

ALEXANDRA EMPRESS OF RUSSIA.

CHAPTER I.

INTRODUCTION.

THE influence exercised by the female sex on the history of European civilisation is greater than at first sight may appear, and deserves to be recorded and commended as a memorable fact. We do not allude to the admirable energy displayed by individual women on the throne, to their political wisdom, nor to the brilliant genius that others have developed in art and literature, but more particularly to the quiet imperceptible sway exercised by the female sex over Christian Europe, and the civilisation and morality of society. A glance at the whole history of the world shows us, that the highest culture and the noblest moral excellence have only existed where the female sex have been permitted to assume a free and equal position and rank in society with that of the man. The more independent the condition, the more noble the rank assumed by woman, the more developed are the intellectual powers of man, the more exalted his whole aims, the more consummate the civilisation of a nation.

Islam has left the women of the East in their customary seclusion, in a position similar to that of a slave; thus the society of that nation has never attained the exalted and consummate structure of classical antiquity, far less the dignified forms of European systems. The Greeks and Romans allotted a higher rank to the fair sex, and there society displays more independent progress in grander types; still the life of the ancient classical world was a public one, from which woman was excluded, and the Roman father exercised with savage tyranny the power of life and death over the domestic hearth—for State and family life were never combined in stern Rome; and with the Greeks, when the higher cultivation and freer position of woman disappeared, the loftier phase of morality was destroyed also. The elevating, civilizing influence of woman first showed its wide-world historical significance by the spread of Christianity among the Germans. To the ancients, religion was an external worship of the gods, and philosophers esteemed every species false; to the people it was true in spite of its diversity; to governments a necessity, though indifferent as to its nature. The religion preached by the Cross was that of gentleness, humility, love to man, and the rights of humanity, and these doctrines struck root deeper and earlier into the heart of woman than into the stoical spirit of man; thus Christian mothers became the upholders of the new belief, and educating and fostering the rising generation in very different convictions, they founded domestic family life, where the barbarous rights of the Roman fathers yielded to the moral power of woman, whose gentleness and humility effected more than the edicts of the Roman Cæsars. Thus women transmitted the highest teaching and the most elevated sentiments from race to race, and their kindly nature achieved as much, if not more, than contemporaneous missionaries and apostles.

While Christianity pursued its course, misunderstood by the best Roman Emperors, it yet touched individual female hearts. Mammæa, the mother of Alexander Severus, comprehended and revered the spirit of Christianity, and owing to this new view of the world, her reign was truly beneficent in the midst of the decay of the kingdom, whilst it also seemed to proclaim to posterity the high historical mission of woman. Helena, mother of the great Constantine, openly professed Christianity, during the time of the most frightful persecutions, while her husband, Constantius Chlorus, had not courage to make an open confession of his faith.

History does not relate whether the women of Slavonic nations enjoyed equal reverence in ancient times, all social relations being on a different footing there, or at least differently developed from those of Western Europe. But a single glance at Russian history shows us the same susceptibility in female nature; for woman here also accepted sooner than men the lessons of meekness and humility. Olga, the wife of Igors, was baptized thirty years sooner than Wladimir, influenced solely by a receptive female heart. Many European complications seem to have arisen from the subsequent conversion of Wladimir. This prince married a Greek princess, Anna, sister of Theophania, and of rank equal to his own, who proved an ornament to the Imperial throne. Jaroslaw, like Theodoric, entered into relations with almost every crowned head of his time, but these could not take root in Russian soil; they did not produce sharply defined and strongly marked distinctions in society, nor that feudal State-edifice, chivalry, with its enthusiasm, nor could it boast of established cities, nor of established corporations; these things were only temporary in Russia; the succession to the throne itself depended rather on seniority, an arrangement emanating from Slavonic family and social life.

Equality of rank in the matrimonial alliances of the Grand Dukes gradually disappeared, and the whole female sex were condemned to a certain degree of seclusion, and seldom alluded to in history. We might conclude that women gained additional honour and respect from most of the Grand Dukes having chosen their wives from their own countrywomen and subjects; but this had not the smallest effect in obtaining a more independent life, or more chivalrous reverence for the gentler sex. The morality of men, who continued to live without acquiring influence or respect, thus deteriorated, and State life, as well as that of the people, progressed for centuries in another spirit and form, utterly estranged from European usages. The days of petty principalities, civil wars, and inward decay, could not supply what was originally wanting, and the Mongolian rule succeeded in utterly crushing the last European elements.

Still it was during this Mongolian period that the secluded Russian women of that day seem to have attained equally great importance, and the same imperceptible quiet influence, as those of Western Europe. The religion of meekness and humility penetrated into their pious minds, and their genuine fervour resisted every alien influence. The old Russian woman was the guardian and preserver of the Christian faith in that dreary time. The iron pressure, however, of the Mongolian rulers called forth in the people a craving for unity and more vital love for their Fatherland; thus an *undivided* Russia quickly progressed into a political power, and was victorious over Islam during the same century in which the standard of the Prophet was planted in ancient Byzantium, but social relations remained unchanged. In the newly constructed Russia woman's life was even more secluded than before, and every man shunned a woman if one by chance crossed his path; even in churches they sat apart. At home their occupations were limited to sewing and spinning, nor did they take any interest in domestic affairs. They did not even dine at the same table with their husbands, except on fête-days, and then only with the whole household. Nothing was accepted from their hands, as they were held to be unclean. Marriages were arranged by the fathers of the bride and bridegroom, in the form of a contract, while the bridegroom received his hitherto unknown bride with slavish submission from the hands of his father. Mean jealousy on the part of the man, and abject submission on that of the woman, took the place of love—thus neither of these natures could become ennobled; the need of social intercourse between the sexes was never felt; women and girls found the greatest charm of their lives in going a little way beyond the city, to enjoy the recreations of swinging and singing, but the simple amusement of walking for their amusement was denied them.

And yet the lives of the Princesses of the blood was even more restricted and monotonous. In Europe the brilliancy of Courts and the charm of life were derived from women, who, in many cases exchanging their feminine character for that of masculine vigour, conferred a crown by the free offer of their hands, and by means of their betrothal-ring often changed the destiny of countries and peoples, whereas the Russian Princesses withered and died in the palace in which they were born. They seldom married into any foreign country, as the orthodox Greek Church, to which they belonged, was considered heathenish in Europe, and no Russian Princess has ever proved faithless to her original creed; as little could they marry any subject, although the Czars chose their wives from that class. They were only visible to the people at public ceremonies, and even went to church by a covered passage. They rarely drove out, and always in close carriages, so that they could neither see nor be seen, surrounded and guarded by a legion of female attendants of every sort. Even the cavaliers attached to their Court household seldom knew their imperial ladies by sight,—in fact, only by name, thus serving invisible divinities.

The sole choice of these poor ladies lay between a palace and a cloister, but in the one, as in the other, they were doomed to languish and die a lingering death, both mentally and bodily.

The Czar, in whom all State-power was concentrated, to the most unlimited and absolute extent, and publicly manifested, was esteemed a god by the nation. From his lofty towers he rarely showed his face to the people kneeling in front of his palace; even the great dignitaries of his Court touched the ground with their heads when they met him within the palace. He was considered by the people the absolute lord and master of all the resources and revenues of the land. But the more highly they valued his power, his rights, and his authority, the greater were the demands made on him by his subjects. His cellars supplied daily for the benefit of the poor a hundred casks of brandy, and five hundred barrels of beer and mead; while three thousand dishes of food were distributed among the needy on week-days, but at festivals these alms were infinitely increased. The name-day of a Czar was a universal public festival, and rich as well as poor expected gifts from the generosity of their ruler; on such days even prisoners in dungeons were not forgotten.

When the monarch appeared in the street, he was preceded by a host of servants, with brooms in their hands, to sweep the path before him, and followed by guards and other soldiers and Boyars, all bareheaded, even in the most stormy weather. Those who met the Czar threw themselves on the ground, crossing themselves while gazing at the man delegated by Heaven to be their father and preserver.

He dined alone at his table, richly furnished with

countless dishes, served and guarded by a host of
chamberlains and servants. The great dignitaries of the
realm were obliged to appear before him daily by twelve
o'clock, and to remain in the palace awaiting his commands.

Dwarfs and Court-fools enlivened his winter evenings,
alternately with dice and draughts. His wife was distinguished as the " orthodox Czarina," and his daughters
as the "high-born Czarewne ;" yet this man, addressed
in petitions as on an equality with God, notwithstanding his omnipotence led a life devoid of all social
charm, while the mute, deathlike silence and desolation
of his palace could not possibly awaken sociability
among any class of his people. The same veneration
paid by his subjects to "Father Czar" was enjoyed
by the Patriarch, called "The Most Holy." On
Palm Sundays both these heads of Church and State
exhibited themselves together to the multitude. The
Patriarch, riding on an ass, traversed the square of the
palace to the door of the principal church, while the
Czar led by a red bridle the animal that had borne our
Saviour to Jerusalem.

The Court of this all-potent sovereign being destitute
of all sociability, it was of course useless to search for it
in other classes. But nobles, invested with high honours, did not even feel the want of spacious tasteful
dwellings. In the country, as well as in towns, they
were satisfied with mean log huts, the roofs covered
with shingles, but still more frequently thatched with
straw, and the interstices of the beams stuffed with
moss; the interior of these houses scarcely contained

anything beyond wooden benches and plain wooden
tables, the sole ornament being a picture of a saint.
It was by no means a universal custom to use knives
and forks at meals. Wooden spoons are not quite out
of use even to this day, though chiefly in memory of
the good old times, just as the earthenware vessels of
Agathocles still appear on the royal table.

Not till the commencement of the seventeenth century, when the house of Romanow ascended the Russian
throne, and the Church was no longer in a condition
to banish foreign customs and a foreign spirit beyond
the boundaries of the realm, were dawning symptoms
displayed of another code of morals, but first of all in
the female sex. Marriages indeed were still arranged
by parents, and often during the childhood and minor-
ity of the subsequent couples. The Cossacks of the
Don bought, sold, and pledged their women for the
price of from ten to twenty roubles, regarding them as
their actual goods and chattels; but the wives of the
Boyars gradually ventured to appear after dinner to
offer a wine-cup to the guests, and to exchange a few
words with them. The Czarina, who had lived, and
still lived, in equal seclusion with the other women,
sometimes dined alone with the Czar. This was a grand
step in advance towards the independence of women in
Russia. This first move towards the freedom of woman
led the men to European civilisation. The second
Romanow, Alexei Michailowitsch, authorized a foreign
physician to visit his invalid wife, but in a darkened
room, and to feel her pulse through a fine handkerchief.
This was not permitted in Turkey for two hundred

years later. This same prince was so delighted with
the accounts of the amusements of foreign Courts, that
he could not resist his inclination to introduce singing
and a ballet into his own Court, although Nicon, the
most influential and distinguished of all the Patriarchs,
had shortly before made an *auto-da-fé* of all musical
compositions.

At the same period the ancient Russian usages were
changed by the alteration in the circumstances hitherto
prévalent among the nobility, whose privileges not only
proved obstacles to systematic civil government, but
also by their continual dissensions with regard to precedence in rank, which rendered any strong army
impossible. For this reason the Czar Feodor, son and
successor of Alexei, by the advice of the enlightened
Prince Golitzin, caused all the books of precedence of
the nobility to be burned, announcing, in a solemn proclamation, that " dignities and offices were no longer
to be conferred on account of birth, or a long line of
ancestors, but to be achieved solely by personal merit."
This victory attained by the Sovereign over a society
benumbed by the most ridiculous forms, explains the
subsequent and speedy greatness and power of Russia,
and its rapid approximation to Europe. It proves not
only the propriety of Peter's reforms, but their actual
necessity. When the fetters that had obstructed all
progress for centuries past were broken, society was constituted in another and a freer form. The character of
buildings was also changed by the greater freedom in
social life.

So long as a nation remains in its original barbarous

condition its dwellings are hastily built of wood, to meet the first exigency. In the middle of the seventeenth century there were few towns in Russia worthy of the name from their architecture, for even Moscow itself numbered very few stone houses. Indeed, when the Czar Alexei wished to bestow a suitable residence on one of his most illustrious counsellors, Matweef, sufficient materials for the building could not be found in the city, and the people and Strelitzes were forced to demolish the sepulchres of their forefathers, to obtain the materials necessary to construct a dwelling in accordance with the rank of the individual. It was at this same period that Prince Golitzin first adorned Moscow with some hundreds of stone houses, for hitherto the palace of the Czars alone, and many of the churches, were of stone, though tasteless in exterior, and confined and gloomy within.

The spirit of Western enlightenment now penetrated in various guises into Russia, summoning the land to unite itself to Europe. Contact with Poland, Lithuania, and Sweden; an army organized, and commanded chiefly by foreigners; intercourse with Protestants, who had sought a refuge in Russia—a number of foreign artists, artisans, and merchants: all these combined could not fail to exercise due influence on Russian nature, so peculiarly impressible, teachable, and imitative.

Here also a woman was the first publicly to adopt European customs—the Czarina Sophie, daughter of the Czar Alexei, openly sought the society of learned men, instructing herself about foreign lands, and, contrary to all previous custom, she received State officials, gave public audience to foreign ambassadors, and appeared in the square before the troops; in the interior of her own apartments she occupied herself in reading, writing, and even with poetry, and her small rooms were often transformed into a stage, enlivened by the Muses. To her is due the glory of having liberated the female sex from Oriental chains, and it was she who first appeared among the people in all the dignity and independence of the European woman, calling forth her equals from the dusty recesses of their homes into social life, which races yet to come were destined to adorn, and thus leading the way to that dawning light which began with Peter. There is nothing enigmatical in a fact so fully explained by female nature. The Czarina was earlier and more deeply impressed with the new Western life than men were. Sophie plays the same part in European civilisation for Russia as the Empress-mothers Mammæa and Helena, the Queens Clotilde and Bertha, for Christianity, and, we may add, as the Grand Duchess Olga, for her new convictions. The irony of history, however, here also manifests itself: the antagonists of Sophie and of enlightenment—the old Russian party—upheld her brother Peter in opposition to this heroine, little anticipating that he would be the person finally to break off the last link of modern times that connected it with the past. The Czar Feodor and the Czarina Sophie prepared and facilitated Peter's undertaking.

Peter the Great, in the accomplishment of his work, unparalleled in history, found more assistance from previous events than from the nation whom he wished to raise to new life. The spirit of European progress had crept within the boundaries of the land, and began to be diffused through the army by the numerous foreigners it contained, and sustained by the impending wars with European Powers. This it was that compelled the Czar Feodor to sweep away the all-obstructive military privileges of the nobility, thus procuring for every species of talent the right and the opportunity to develop itself. Peter the Great could then with impunity select those who understood and manfully supported the new movement, without ascertaining the number of their ancestors, or their profession of faith. We therefore find among his adherents and followers, a motley assemblage of men of high talent. A man of obscure origin, said to be a Muscovite pastry-cook, Menschikof, adorned Peter's reign as a faithful friend and counsellor, both in the cabinet and the field, in the tranquil summer days of Peterhof, as well as during the dangers at Pruth, and the Czar elevated this trusty *parvenu* to the dignities of Field-Marshal and Prince. He caused a young Dutch Jew—Schaphirow—to be baptized into the Christian faith and educated, and subsequently appointed him Vice-Chancellor and Post-master-General. Lefort, from Geneva, first a merchant and then a soldier, became his ambassador, in whose train indeed the Emperor himself travelled incognito; and this same man, who succeeded in inspiring with enthusiasm Peter's susceptible mind, more especially in favour of European policy, died a minister, general, and admiral. A candidate of theology from Westphalia,

Ostermann by name, concluded the Peace of Nystadt
as Chancellor of the realm, and thus secured for the
land the rightful possession of two European provinces,
Esthonia and Livonia, which have since become seminaries for soldiers and statesmen. The son of a Lutheran
sacristan of Moscow, Jaguschinsky, became Procurator-
General in the newly established Senate, and under
the reign of the Empress Anna was buried a Cabinet
Minister in Newsky Cloister, with imperial honours.
A Portuguese of low birth, Devière, was made known
to the Czar in Holland on board a merchantman, and
we find him later in Petersburg head of the police,
and afterwards tutor to the Princesses Anna and Elisabeth. The young widow of a Swedish officer became
the wife and empress of Peter, and after his death was
adorned with the crown as an independent sovereign.
The Scotsman Gordon, the French Villebois, the
Dutch Brande, also belong to this succession of men
who lent a helping hand to the young Czar. But we
must not omit to say that Peter found among his own
nation also individuals who sympathized with the new
work as eagerly and perseveringly as himself. Conspicuous among these stands Boris Scheremetjew, whose
family had been celebrated for centuries past in early
history. This man conquered Esthonia and Livonia,
and decided the fate of the battle of Poltowa. At his
death, in 1719, the people exclaimed, " We have lost
a father!" By such names as those of Scheremetjew,
Ramadanovsky, Streschvew, Dolgorucki, and many others,
Peter's enterprise received national consecration; the
foreigners to whom we alluded—the most efficient tools

in Peter's hands—would only have caused Peter's reforms to be still more detested (as in fact they long continued to be by the public at large), had it not been for these great Russian names. We cannot but lament that the greatest man that Russia possessed before the accession of Peter the First, Prince Wassilewitsch Go-litzin, the friend and counsellor of Alexei and Sophie, was at that time pining away miserably in exile by the shores of the Arctic Ocean. Peter was constrained to have recourse to such expedients in a country, the condition of which rendered reforms indispensable, and where fatalistic indifference constituted the most prominent feature in the character of the people. Peter's peculiar and undisputed merit was that of having discovered the right means for his work, and most admirable of all was the thought of providing a fresh soil for the new policy, and only employing novel elements for that end. In Moscow, under the impression of memories of the olden time, the new spirit would have been stifled even had the aids been greater. That dungeon-like palace, the Terema, in that city, condemned the Czars to their ancient formal, secluded mode of life, whereas in the new capital, surrounded by a fresh and recently elevated society, the Czar himself gave the tone to the new epoch. The lower classes of the people felt more self-respect when they saw one of their own order in the vicinity of the all-potent Emperor, and the hitherto despised female sex were flattered and rendered more independent by the example of the Czarina Sophie, and still more by the maiden of Marienburg, who occupied the great Peter's throne with renown, though only for a short

time. The fair sex must have felt on a level with
the most superior men on learning that the Czar, the
boast and the pride of the whole realm, had been saved
at the Pruth by the counsels of a woman. Even distant
lands heard with astonishment that Peter's widow had
effectually carried out the plan of an Academy, suggested
by Leibnitz. The female sex appeared at Peter's Court
as the first visible result of European civilisation, and the
despotic Czar selected his Court ladies, like his generals
and ministers, from all ranks and nations, according to
their merits and attractions. Peter himself, with all his
admirable qualities as a ruler, never became European
or chivalrous towards the fair sex, and the knout was
inflicted on female shoulders, when simple banishment
from the palace would have been amply sufficient as a
punishment. It is however significant, that among
the Court ladies we find the daughter of a German
pastor, Frau von Villebois, *née* Gluck, and also the sister
of a French wine-merchant, Frau von Kaiserling, *née* de
la Croix, Anna Cramer, taken prisoner at Narva, who
was brought to Kasan, and then transferred to Petersburg, where she was placed at Court; and finally, a
beautiful Englishwoman, Lady Hamilton, of obscure
birth.

In Petersburg, as well as in Peterhof, the Empresses
and Grand Duchesses appeared in public in foreign
costume, tasteful but simple; their hair dressed in the
French style, accompanied by chamberlains and Court
ladies, but without the legion of inferior attendants, who
usually escorted even the Boyars. While the Court of
Catherine and her daughter recalled those of Europe,

Peter, the originator of all those changes, could not outwardly cast aside the old Muscovite. He was surrounded by common Denschtshicks (military men of inferior rank), as well as by generals and ministers, and the former were esteemed by him quite as much as the latter. The female sex adopted European customs with greater facility than the male, and supported Peter's plans with eager zeal. The foreign style of dress was highly approved, and liberty to appear and to shine in the society of men inspired the wish to adopt foreign languages likewise, and with it a European mode of thought. Peter wished also to enforce sociability on his people, and therefore commanded the introduction of assemblies, explaining that these were to include a company of both sexes, to meet together for pleasure and recreation. He appointed the hour and the duration of these meetings, and ordered the host to prepare chairs, lights, beverages, and games for his guests; he also gave permission to the company to *walk, sit, and stand* in this society. Still, even in the time of Peter, people gambled and danced in the European style. Blind-man's-buff was played by the ladies, and the feast generally ended by a good drinking-bout on the part of the men, which, however, the presence of ladies prevented being carried to the height of the old Russian fashion. Peter prohibited the Court cavaliers, invited to Peterhof, *going to bed with dirty boots on.*

Peter was well aware that, without ladies and their refining influence, his European work would never thrive, so in honour of his wife, and for the encouragement and emulation of the fair sex, he instituted

the order of Catherine. It seemed as if he had a presentiment that the supreme genius of history destined
female sovereigns after his reign, to rule the country almost exclusively till the close of the century,
in order that the sex whom we have designated
as the upholders of these novel customs, should be
honoured and acknowledged by the nation in its new
world-historical mission. The animosity to Peter's
reforms had not its chief source in women, but in his
own son, and also the clergy. If fate had so ordered it
that, after Peter's death, Alexei and his male heirs, so
inimical to Europe, had ruled in the next century, the
new arrangements would have perished for ever on
Peter's demise. It is a fact unparalleled in the annals
of the world, that eight centuries elapsed without women
having the smallest share in the history of nations,
and that the next century should close happily and
gloriously solely under female guidance. The alliance
of Alexei with a German Princess, Charlotte Christian
Sophie of Brunswick Wolfenbüttel, established the principle of equality of birth: a bold step for Russia, but
for the moment without any good effect on the bigoted
successor to the throne, and certainly equally unfavourable in its results to the old Russian party. The scion
of this marriage did not attain the age of his father, and
the newly-established throne by the Neva devolved on
a Russian princess, who had however passed the greater
portion of her life in Courland, and now transformed
the Petersburg Court into a German one. Peter's
daughter, Elisabeth, abolished capital punishment, established, through Ivan Schuwalow, the University of

Moscow, and by so doing transplanted European life
into the metropolis of ancient Russia; the French
language, and many Asiatic customs, prevailed in her
Court. The fourth Empress, however, shed a truly
European lustre on her Court and her kingdom, con-
ferring on her people greater independence and a higher
policy, and on the female sex such cultivation, that in
this respect they could compete with all the rest of
Europe, and a President could have been selected from
among them quite as easily as from the male sex.

The new capital however consisted in every respect of
foreign elements, and even in its cradle was a century
in advance of the elder sister. New men, new women,
new architecture! Everything indicated that the past
was swept away; it seemed not only as if by the
Neva people lived in a different century from that of
Moscow, but in a land far distant from Russia. The
number of great men in the field and the cabinet
suddenly brought to the surface, the distinguished
foreigners, the active sympathy of women, the bold
spirit of enterprise in every branch of State-policy, the
capricious good fortune, that boldly and blindly played
a prominent part in all things, could not fail to call
forth a peculiar spirit in social life by the Neva, dis-
tinguishing the city of Petersburg not only in Russia,
but making it differ from other European capitals. The
dreary winter and the northern summer, which the
poverty of nature there displays, constrain the inhabitants to domestic life and to pleasant sociability, and
as wealth from every source in the kingdom gradually
flowed thither, the charm of agreeable society soon vied

with that of foreign cities, and at the close of the century even surpassed these, in the splendour of households, and in the most liberal hospitality. The architecture of this city, suddenly called forth as if by magic, eclipsed the seven wonders of the ancient world, and travellers declared that you must not see Petersburg, like Naples, to *die*, but rather to *live* there. Princely palaces were pervaded by a freer atmosphere within; walls were adorned with the finest masterpieces of the Italian and Flemish school, and the strains of foreign orchestras were heard; plants from every part of the globe breathed their fragrance within doors, which the northern winter only saw reflected, through the windows, and, with the help of a stove, transplanted the guests into a southern climate. The winter palace of the Empress Catherine received the most distinguished men in Russia and in Europe. The Muses enlivened them with song and dance, with art and science, wit and humour, gravity and jest, and the sovereign lady, whom the people called "Mother Catherine," found time, with all her manifold cares of State, to attend at the Hermitage the performance of comedies written by herself, to give up an occasional hour to the claims of her heart, and to obtain public recognition for the man whose genius had created this new world, but who only saw it in its cradle. It is unnecessary to refer here to the political power attained by Russia at the end of the century; for not only did Russian military fame resound through Europe, but the recently established Academy could worthily enter the lists with others in Europe. This century brought to light a succession of families whose names had hitherto quietly slumbered in every class of the people, and yet who now eclipsed in energy and renown the ancient dormant Boyars. An aristocracy of. talent and merit (nay even of lucky upstarts) was formed in Petersburg, the spirit of which had nothing in common with old times. Women were now more powerful than the Czars Ivan the Third and Fourth had ever been; the subtlety and versatility of the gentler sex animated, incited, and urged forward on the one hand, while on the other it obstructed and paralysed energy, and women were esteemed a far from despicable secret power. The fame of those natives and foreigners, who before Elisabeth's time fostered and sustained the new world of ideas, awoke the emulation of the inhabitants of the soil, and thenceforward new Russian names shone with fresh lustre, and founded conspicuous families, who took their place beside the most ancient ones. The celebrated names of Rasumowsky, Besborodko, Sawadowsky, and the foreigners Lazarew and Kutaizou, all owe their origin to the eighteenth century.

But the ancient Russian nobility did not remain behind their time, and adorned it with the brilliant titles of Schuwalow, Woronzow, Orlof, Panin, Trubetzkoi, Wasiltschikof, and many others. With the Asiatic beard, the society of Petersburg also divested itself of old-fashioned prejudices and of old-established privileges, and the new ranks of the aristocracy were on a more democratic footing at that time than the republics of Switzerland and Holland. Men profited by the arts of women to procure advancement, though often devoid of understanding or education. Thus the most discrepant elements contended with each other, fermenting, and causing society to drift hither and thither, constantly imbibing new elements, working them out solely according to their own ideas, and in their own fashion. Slavonic nations do not possess the creative fancy of the Romans and the Germans, but they observe more keenly than the latter, shine rather by wit than by sagacity or profound judgment, and more quickly discover the deficiencies than the talents of others, the latter of which they coolly and unhesitatingly adopt. Petersburg therefore, even in the time of Catherine the Second, was already the highest and most finished school of social refinement, and the Empress herself considered that European the most accomplished in whom Petersburg found nothing to censure, and nothing to ridicule. Catherine herself was at that time esteemed in Europe the most finished model for society, while her charming and dignified deportment had a greater effect in refining the habits of a backward people, than volumes of Ukases. French and Germans, Italians and English, returned from her presence as if bewitched. At the time of her death Russia was closely interwoven with the history of the world, and the female sex shone forth in such brilliancy of knowledge, that it was only required of men to equal them in talent. The departing century beheld on the banks of the Neva a splendid capital, whereas at its commencement only a few fishermen's huts were to be seen ; a nation roused to thought, which formerly slumbered in Asiatic seclusion ; a number of glorious female names, where formerly the fair sex pined away in servile thraldom; a succession of military commanders and statesmen who could enter the lists even with those of Europe, and a kingdom that deservedly excited both surprise and admiration. It was the century of woman. Peter instituted the order of Catherine for women, and Catherine did the same for men, by founding the order of St. George for knightly prowess in the field, and the order of Wladimir for distinction in the state.

Notwithstanding all the lustre with which the four Empresses swayed the sceptre during seventy years, the most weighty element of refined life was wanting in the Petersburg Court: the domestic family hearth. The whole century was devoted to transplanting the Russian nation from an Asiatic soil to a European one, and causing it to take root there; the mission of the following one was to cultivate it into grandeur on the new soil. After their emancipation, women had shown as much talent and charm in their novel career as Germans and Romans; while history granted to them a certain license, in the intoxication of their newly-won freedom, which, however, time was shortly to terminate. The Empress Catherine bequeathed to her successors the important task of the systematic education of the female sex, in the European sense; she foresaw that the next generation must spring from mothers, educated not by chance, but by schools in the strictest meaning of the word, and that an Empress or a Princess of the blood must be at the head of such an establishment, to conduct it properly. She therefore at the very commencement of her reign founded a female Educational Institute in Petersburg, usually called the Maiden Cloister of Smolna, which was of no less importance to the kingdom than the Universities and Military Schools.

But here, too, prejudices were to be contended against and overcome. The domestic life of Russian families, even in Petersburg, alternated between severe fasts and richly-laden tables ; they clung to the one as much as to the other, but especially to fasting for the young. Under the supposition that these fasts might be diminished in this Educational Institute, parents at first were averse to allow their daughters to leave home. Peculiar gratitude is therefore due to ten or twelve families, who resolved to precede the others in setting a good example. Catherine often favoured the cloistered secluded young people with her presence and her Court state, and invited their parents to evening entertainments, so that in a short time the rooms at first so empty, scarcely sufficed for those who were anxious to receive instruction. Education and teaching were intrusted to foreign ladies, in whose society many an old fashion was obliterated, and the spirit of a new code of manners clearly and thoroughly imprinted. The Empress had the happiness, during twenty years of her reign, to receive ladies of the most cultivated refinement at her Court, whom she had herself educated in the first ten years. No stress requires to be laid on the fact, that such influence as theirs could not fail to ennoble men, and that very shortly ensued a reverence for the female sex similar to that of the Germans. The Empress watched as lovingly over the education of her grandson and granddaughters, who subsequently by their grace and wit excited the admiration of the Protestant Goethe, as well as that of the most distinguished Catholics of foreign countries.

After four Empresses, one of whom ruled as a maiden Queen, and three as widows, the father of a family, Emperor Paul the First, at length ascended the throne. Catherine's splendours were no more, the winter palace was silent, although the Autocrat and his numerous family lived there; all classes in the capital, and in the kingdom, felt as if the days of Ivan the Terrible had returned. At all events, female rule was at an end, and the sway of the sceptre doubly felt in the hands of a very different sovereign. Paul, however, bequeathed four sons to the new century, two of whom became glorious and mighty rulers, and his Imperial widow, who, though no daughter of the great realm, became a true mother to her sex. The European splendour of the Petersburg Court did not however again awake under the first Alexander, and the reign of this Emperor, so glorious in all respects, could not boast of the domestic life that from the throne of his brother Nicholas became so bright an example to the whole nation. The four Empresses and Paul the First never during their reign crossed the boundaries of their kingdom. The nineteenth century introduced a very different order of things; the tumult of war and the Peace Congress summoned the young Emperor into the heart of Europe, the boundaries of which Peter the Great a century before with difficulty reached. Alexander not only inspired admiration by his personal appearance, but also respect for the power of his kingdom, and for his own autocracy. He was satisfied with the fame of being the peace-maker of Europe, although his arms had penetrated from the ashes of Moscow into the centre of helpless Paris, and half Asiatic races, under his mild eye, displayed more discipline and better conduct than the civilized French in Germany. After Alexander had seen Europe, and left it in tranquillity, he returned to his northern capital. But even yet, in the most profound peace, the ancient pomp of the Court was not revived, and the man who entered Paris as a triumphant victor, lived in all the retirement of a private individual, alternately by the Neva, and in the secluded country residence of Zarskoe-Selò. The happiness granted by destiny to the Emperor Paul to so high a degree, that of a large and thriving family, was denied to Alexander and to his brother Constantine. Even during Paul's reign Alexander had already spoken of resigning his claims to the throne, desiring only a quiet country-seat on the banks of the Rhine, in the centre of Europe, and expressing the utmost dislike to a gay and stirring Court life; it was no wonder, therefore, that he now resolutely shunned and fled from it.

While Napoleon's arrogance in prosperity exceeded all bounds, and prepared his sure downfall, deep melancholy took possession of Alexander, who despised all earthly happiness, and gave himself up to mournful abstract contemplations. Napoleon in his imprisonment cherished only the one thought of escape; Alexander in the majestic solitude of Zarskoe-Selò cherished only the fair dream of abdication. His wife, the Empress Elisabeth, lived in similar seclusion from the world; her unassuming nature, and the force of circumstances, had inspired her with so much nervousness and timidity, that few ventured to approach this singular woman. Born the Princess of a petty German State, and a petty German Court, her pretensions were originally very modest, nay, limited, and they continued so in Russia; her spirit revolted from the splendour that she, as Empress, was bound to diffuse, and at length she was seized by the strange idea that her love and favour, on whomsoever they were bestowed, invariably brought misfortune in their train. Not having been blessed with a family like the Empress-mother especially preyed on her mind, and thus she felt herself a stranger in a strange land, like a fading flower. An English companion, Mademoiselle Pitt, the admirable historian Karamsin, and Mademoiselle Woluief, a maid of honour, formed the small circle of her quiet life. Few had the good fortune to frequent her society, and to discover in close and confidential conversation the treasures of her high culture and profound thought, hidden from the world. The Romanow gallery in the Hermitage of the winter palace, contains portraits of the above-named Empresses, all life-size, and executed by a superior hand; beside the shrewd Catherine the First stands the matronly Anna; next the vivacious Elisabeth, the autocratic Catherine the Second, Maria Feodorowna, youthful and charming; and at last, by the side of Alexander, the Elisabeth to whom we have alluded, resembling the others in majestic mien, but her expression that of hopeless resignation, and not

wholly without traces of some deep grief. All these
portraits attract, not only by the master hand that
executed them, but also by the character that speaks in
the features; and though Catherine the Second in her
portrait, as in life, excites our admiration, Elisabeth
awakens our quiet but enduring sympathy: we grant
to her in death what was denied to her in life.

The brilliancy of the Imperial Court in Petersburg,
as important as the *panem et circenses* of the Romans,
was only in some measure represented by the Empress-
mother, Maria Feodorowna. She showed herself daily
in the city in a carriage drawn by six horses, escorted
by hussars and pages, and so punctually did she appear
in the principal streets at the appointed hour, that the
passers-by could set their watches according to her
drives. The activity, however, of this mother of the
Emperor, and of the country, was without precedent.
The early morning saw her already seated in full dress
at her writing-table, occupied in reading herself all the
reports of the numerous female institutions under her
guidance, writing down remarks, and learning the wishes
of the parents and the views of the teachers; nay, she
did not even disdain to read the letters of the pupils,
and to supply their requirements with maternal love.
But with the exception of her daily visits to these
schools, there was little contact between the Empress
and the city; members of the reigning family rarely
attended the theatre, but when they did so the public
greeted their appearance as a festival, and received
them standing, and with music. The evening Court receptions were genial, and devoid of form, but small and

select, and could exercise no influence on the social life of the city.

The more retired the life of the Court at that period, the more gay and splendid was the society of the town, and the latter years of Alexander's reign display Petersburg not only in a European, but in a French aspect. The Russian language was entirely banished from the intercourse of the educated classes in office, and in petty trade and traffic, and the newest works from the Seine adorned the tables of the aristocracy. No wonder that in the year 1812, when only the mother tongue was spoken on the banks of the Neva, many were much embarrassed. Education and instruction were chiefly confided to foreign, and more particularly to French teachers; in some of the most admirable institutions of the whole country, all sciences were taught exclusively in French. A Count Orlof wrote memoirs of the Kingdom of Naples in the French language as fluently as Oulibischef the biography of Mozart. In many *salons* of the stately palace the classical music of German masters was heard, and among amateurs were to be found executants who could well vie with those of other lands. Music as well as French formed an important element in European education, and Russians have at all events taken precedence of the English and French in this respect. The susceptible nature of the Slavonic races for music is well known. The Emperor Alexander too was accustomed in his youth to occupy his evenings with the violin; his fondness for that instrument being so notorious that Beethoven dedicated three sonatas to him. This circumstance, after the restoration of peace

to Europe, attracted artists of every kind to the Neva.
Russian Princes and Counts proved liberal patrons of
the German Muses—among others, Bortujansky excited
the admiration of his countrymen and contemporaries
by his sacred music, so responsive to the spirit of the
Greek Church, and yet wearing the garb of the West.
The national literature also at that time broke vigor-
ously through the superficial French style, although the
early seeds of this movement were already springing up
in the time of Elisabeth.   The first to influence general
national culture seems to have been Sumarokof and
Dershawin, in the eighteenth century, whose ode to God
displays rather an Eastern tendency.   The man who
by his writings found at last an echo in the nation,
and consideration in foreign lands, was Karamsin, an
intimate associate of the Emperor Alexander, and the
constant companion of his consort Elisabeth.   His
historical work succeeded in attracting the attention
of his readers from the exclusive study of French literature, not only by its national import, but also by a
dignified form of narrative, and an easy flowing style.
Karamsin was no dry pedant, but had seen the world
with his own eyes, and visited France, as Anacharsis
did Greece; he combined a national spirit with European refinement, and, by his writings, inspired his
country with a certain degree of self-reliance.   Russian
society felt honoured on seeing this talented man
rewarded, and amply recognised by prince and people.
Nearly at the same time with Karamsin appeared
Krilof, a writer of fables, who, by his racy popular
style, produced a deeper and wider effect on the moral

INTRODUCTION. **31**

organization of his time than even the historian. He was assisted in his poetry by the curtness of Russian proverbs, in which the nation is peculiarly rich. Krilof's success was the greater, inasmuch as fables could venture to express many opinions in hidden guise, which the public censor and the secret police of an absolute Government would have prohibited. Irony, so peculiarly in accordance with the Russian character, found an opportunity in this form to display itself, and Krilof could take greater liberties from his character being genuinely national, while his manners and mode of life were certainly anything but European, thus estranging him from the higher ranks of society. He was the first really popular author who exercised an influence like that of Gellert in Germany. On the day of his interment an honest and candid preacher justly said to the assemblage present, decorated with stars and orders :—" You do not confer honour on him, it is he who confers honour on his fatherland."

Of still greater importance for that epoch of literature was Joukowsky. He had been already known to fame since the beginning of the century by the nation, and by his military songs and lyrics, but latterly he became so enthusiastic about German literature, that he strove to diffuse a knowledge through his native country, not only of the master works of Germany, but also of Greece, thus awakening a taste in his countrymen for universal literature, by showing the course that the German and English specially pursued, that of antiquity and the middle ages, in order to produce a national literature. Still the sphere of influence of these three men was limited, at least for a time, to certain classes in the society of both capitals.

While these men were conspicuous for their talents, the city itself shone in a peculiar light; the highest circles of society were thoroughly French on the surface, the ranks immediately beneath being wholly European, with very little national admixture; for national narrow-mindedness and provincialism disappeared before the flexible forms; the refined style of society, and the hospitality that attracted and captivated both natives and foreigners.   Petersburg vied with Paris in wit, sarcasm, and cheerful conversation, and surpassed Berlin in the wealth and splendour of its domestic and social arrangements. Russian ladies of the highest circles could challenge the rest of Europe in culture, genius, charm, taste, and dress, in versatility of varied talents, knowledge of languages, and attractive fascinations.   The heroes Miloradowitsch, Wasiltschikof, Tschernischew, Benkendorf, who had inscribed their names in France's genealogy, introduced a chivalrous element into society, and inspired in the far-famed charming Russian ladies a romantic interest in the distant times of the mediæval age. Such was the spirit of the capital which Princess Charlotte of Prussia entered in 1817, without any presentiment that she was destined to adorn the Russian throne for five-and-thirty years as Empress.

CHAPTER II.

CHILDHOOD AND YOUTH.

THE second marriage of the Emperor Paul, with Maria Feodorowna of Würtemberg, was blessed with nine children before he ascended to the throne; the two elder sons, the Grand Dukes Alexander and Constantine, were followed in unbroken succession by six daughters, and in the year 1796, shortly before Catherine's death, a third son, Nicholas, was born. The Empress superintended the education of her grandchildren not only with the care of a mother, but with the comprehensive spirit of a man. She daily visited the abodes of her grandchildren, and not the smallest fault in dress, manner, or speech escaped her quick eye. An hour's conversation with this Princess, so full of dignity, charm, and sparkling wit, sufficed to exhibit the *beau-idéal* of womanly accomplishments of that day. From her correspondence with German and French *savants*, she learned all the educational views of the period, considered them maturely, and herself acted on the maxim, that the heart, as well as the reason of man, should be cultivated in youth, instead of overloading the mind with dry knowledge.

In the year 1780 a work on female education ap-

peared in France, entitled *Émile*. The Empress found
her own views expressed in it, and therefore resolved
to make this book the basis of her grand-daughters'
education.   She must have been astonished, and not
a little proud, when, two years later, the French
Academy awarded the first prize to the work.   It
was also owing to this Empress that Basedow's im-
provements in the mode of female education in Germany
made their way at last through many struggles; for
she assisted that enthusiast both by her authority
and money.   She wrote with her own hand a scheme
of education for her two grandsons, Alexander and
Constantine, and selected Soltikow (subsequently a
prince) to carry out her plan, a man distinguished by
talent, benevolence, and knowledge, as well as by military
experience and travel; and with him a Swiss—Colonel
Laharpe.   For her grand-daughters, she selected the
future Princess Lieven, *née* von Posse, from Lithuania.
This lady by no means possessed that refined tone of
society which so highly distinguished the Court of
Russia; her appearance in that courtly world seemed
somewhat anomalous, but the Empress recognised in her
what she sought,—a sound understanding, mother wit,
a profound well-stored mind, faithful allegiance.   The
combination of such qualities gained the august lady's
entire confidence, which she possessed and deserved,
under four different reigns.   She was made a lady of
honour by Catherine, a countess by the Emperor Paul,
and finally raised to the rank of a princess by the
Emperor Nicholas.   During these reigns she continued
the object of universal respect, almost as great as that

due to the Imperial family. It was said of her that she never made an enemy, and never lost a friend.

The time when the most important development of her sons occurred, was the most brilliant and liberal period both in the society of the Empress and in that of Petersburg. Those who lived by the Neva regarded with secret approval the revolutions near the Seine, indeed a certain measure of rejoicing could not be suppressed at the tidings of the storming of the Bastille. Under the tutelage of such men, and the influence of contemporary events, the mission seemed to devolve of itself on the Grand Duke Alexander to realize from the throne the philanthropic views of the century. Prince Potemkin saw this young man in 1791, and said to the Empress, with tears in his eyes,—"He is an angel, he is the prince of my heart, born and educated to be a blessing to the kingdom." Alexander, however, was married at an age that in England and Germany would not be considered mature enough to enter a university, far less to form a household; the second grandson also, Constantine, married as early in life as his brother, two years afterwards. The only explanation of this singular conduct on the part of their admirable mother is, that she thought the future throne not sufficiently assured by only two sons. The greater was her joy and surprise when, in 1796, a third grandson, Nicholas, was born. She saw the vigorous nature of the child, and wrote to a friend in a prophetic spirit,—"This grandson seems born to the throne." But her eyes were not destined to watch over the education of this prince, for they closed for ever in the November of this year. The new Emperor, Paul, could now hope, on assuming the sceptre of the Russian realm, to assert his rights as a father, and to conduct the education of his children under the auspices of his noble-minded wife. The deeply mortified father, separated hitherto from his numerous children, had lived like an exile in Gatschina, a circumstance that had much contributed to embitter his character; for, in spite of the many vagaries that crossed his brain, Paul had originally been magnanimous and benevolent, and of varied acquirements; but his best feelings had been suppressed; estranged as a son from his mother, and equally so as a father from his children. The spirit of liberty with which the events of the world had been hitherto regarded, was replaced even before the commencement of his reign by gloomy views, and the few years of his absolute rule were passed by him in a state of feverish excitement. The education, therefore, of his children devolved on his admirable wife; and it would appear that his son Nicholas only on one occasion attracted the special notice of his father. On the evening before his death, the Emperor found this child of five, playing with the others, and was surprised by a strange question of the child's : " Papa ! " exclaimed the boy to his gloomy father, " why are you called Paul the First ? "

" Because no one of that name ruled before me," was the Emperor's answer.

" Oh ! then," continued the child, " I shall be called Nicholas the First ? "

" If you ever ascend the throne," interrupted the

Emperor suddenly. He then stood buried in thought, fixed his eyes long on his third son, and at last kissed him passionately, little thinking that it was for the last time. Although the despotic nature of the child and the boy cannot be denied, still his subsequent education and circumstances were not calculated to foster this disposition. In the education of all princes the opportunity fails for instruction by intercourse with companions of their own age in different classes of life, and thus acquiring the most valuable of all knowledge, that of mankind. The education in large public schools brings companions into contact with each other and excites a noble emulation, which a palace rather lulls to sleep than awakens, causes a youth to try to measure his own powers against those of others, to distinguish in early life the merits of one and the weaknesses of another; to know the wants and claims of life, to esteem men according to their value, and discloses in its true light the world in which the pupil must eventually live. The lot of princes is worthy of commiseration; their position, their palaces, separate them not only from the world at large, but they are specially guarded from all contact with other men, often on the absurd ground, that native dignity and princely self-confidence may be injured by the reverence of others being lessened. The seclusion of a palace benumbs the faculties, and shows men in hypocritical servility, and in a false light; princes are therefore educated and maintained in delusions, and at last like to be deceived. They are trained in narrow forms, remark every breach of these, hear very little that can enlighten their minds, take offence at every contradiction, and suspect independent-minded men as dangerous. They accustom themselves to enjoy the pleasures of this world, but are in no degree armed for the battle that must await them in life.

The education of Nicholas and his younger brother Michael formed no exception to this. The Empress Maria Feodorowna, as the head of the female seminaries, of the establishment in Smolna, of the Catherine Institution, and of the Foundling Hospital, was as highly regarded as the Emperor himself. She intrusted her two youngest sons to a distinguished German lady, Frau von Adlerberg, till the age of eight, when she appointed General Lambsdorf their governor; who, with four other officers, took charge of the two boys; for the purposes of instruction she selected Adelung and Storch, and other celebrated men. But the soldierly spirit of that day rushed like a tempest even through the school-rooms of these youths, and many blossoms that might have ripened into fruit never were unfolded. This by no means escaped the eye of the mother, and she resolved to educate her sons in a public school with boys of degree and of their own age; for this purpose a lyceum was established, and the new building added to the old palace in Zarskoe-Selò. Subsequently, however, we do not find the two youthful Grand Dukes in the lyceum, but in the gloomy Palace of Gatschina, where their father had lived in melancholy seclusion. Their abode here, where every encounter with men in the dreary desolate streets was prevented, resembled rather exile -from the capital than a visit to a seminary. According to the wish of their mother, they certainly were here withdrawn from all hurtful influences of either Court or capital; but, on the other hand, there was a deficiency of everything that could invigorate the youthful mind; intercourse with boys of their own age was wanting, and that useful emulation without which all development must be incomplete; neither did nature in this spot offer any captivating charm, nor the palace itself any elevating reminiscences. Meanwhile such active energy was developed in both natures, that they evaded the good-natured pedantry of their teacher, and the nominally strict discipline of General Lambsdorf. The eye of the Empress-mother detected various small deficiencies, but not the grand fault of the whole system of education—that of isolation.

One severe winter morning she visited the bedroom of her sons at an early hour and found it empty, the beds not having been slept in on the previous night; the adjacent rooms were also empty, and not one of the numerous suite to be found; a servant at last informed her that the Grand Dukes had disappeared on the previous evening after their tutors were gone. The alarmed mother searched every corner of the Palace of Gatschina, but in vain; another servant declared that the Princes had gone to the garden at ten o'clock the night before, and had not returned. The park was now searched in all directions, when the boys were discovered sound asleep in a sentry-box in full uniform, and muskets in their frozen hands. The mother was almost as benumbed from terror as the lads by the cold of the northern night, and only the conviction that both were uninjured restored her to composure.

Their stay in Gatschina continued till the year 1812, when the princes were brought back to Petersburg, and made their first acquaintance with life. They themselves felt freer and happier in their new atmosphere, and jestingly, in after years, thanked the Emperor Napoleon for having liberated them from their banishment. They both acknowledged that Gatschina had rather injured than developed their faculties, and it was long before the impression was effaced. On the first appearance of the Grand Duke Nicholas in public, in spite of his majestic mien, and his blue penetrating eyes, lofty forehead, and expressive mouth, he looked grave, reserved, and even gloomy.

The embarrassment that princes often show towards the public from want of intercourse with the world, is usually deemed pride, and public opinion entertained this prejudice against Nicholas, until he ascended the throne. In office his energy and method were fully appreciated, but his austerity and strict sense of duty were loudly proclaimed tyranny. Classical studies, that not only cultivate the understanding but animate the heart, bringing men nearer to each other, proved a failure in his case; and mathematics had given him a keenness of understanding that admirably assisted him in his sphere of work, but at the same time made him appear an inexorable judge. Mathematical ability has its drawback in life, a proficient in that science being too apt to treat the organization of men as dead mathematical problems; while the classics present to the student an endless variety in life and history. Official life in Petersburg was as little calculated as his abode in Gatschina to awaken and to develop the profound and fruitful mind of Nicholas; for official duties are never carried out by the heart. Court-life, too, is everywhere formal and cold, moving rather in a prescribed groove than in free shapes.

And yet the heart of Nicholas was his greatest treasure, and, indeed, perhaps even better than his understanding; but he was not himself aware of this rich possession. Not until his travels in England and Germany, when he laid aside the narrow garb of an imperial prince, did the depths of his character come to light; nature made as profound an impression on him as the friendship and love of men, and the arts of painting and music; he felt equally free and happy in the stately castle of an English nobleman, in the studio of an artist, or in the beech woods, where he listened dreamily for hours to the nightingales. He acquired knowledge of life and of the world in its endless fulness, and of himself also.

His relations with the Emperor Alexander had never been those of a brother, but of a child. Alexander ascended the throne while Nicholas was still playing with his sisters, and it appears that time did not bring them closer to each other. Gatschina, at all events, separated the brothers for years; and, in the latter days of the reign of Alexander, his brother Nicholas was nothing more than a brigadier, or a general of division, and not so near the Emperor's person as ministers, secretaries of state, and aides-de-camp. In later years, Nicholas, when Emperor, complained that his brother had not even deemed him worthy to be made Adjutant-General. Of the four brothers, his was certainly the

most remarkable disposition; he was a *thorough* man,
who either attracted or repulsed with irresistible force
—he was incapable of half measures or dissimulation ;
as Grand Duke, the first and most loyal subject of his
brother ; as Emperor, a born-ruler sent by Providence.
His elder brother, Constantine, looked on him in this
light; for though he was in more familiar intercourse
with the youngest of the brothers, Michael, and spent
many gay hours in his cheerful society, still he never
approached Nicholas without a certain measure of respect, even at a time when the latter had never ventured
to dream of ascending the throne.   France, with which
Nicholas became acquainted in 1814, after the taking
of Paris, did not make a favourable impression on his
mind, although the Emperor Alexander was the object of
universal reverence there.   Nicholas detested all flattery
through life, and the gravity and solidity of his character led him to dislike even such men as Talleyrand.

The education of Princess Charlotte of Prussia was in
progress at the same time, but the circumstances in which
she grew to womanhood were very unhappy for Prussia,
and must now be brought before the reader.

It was indeed a stormy time when King Frederick
William III. succeeded his father on the throne, on the
16th November 1797. He had seen the oldest Christian
throne in Europe overthrown, and the oldest republic
vanish before his eyes ; a Slavonic kingdom in the
north-east subjected to partition ; the left banks of the
Rhine yielded to the French Directory, the thousand-
fold foundations of all Europe shaken ; new relations,
new heroic names spring to the surface with volcanic

power, as the old ones disappeared. The wreath of victory that reposed on Frederick's brow after the Seven Years' War, and a glorious reign of five-and-twenty years, was appropriated by General Buonaparte after a campaign of eighteen months in Italy before he was eight-and-twenty, the age when Frederick first began his heroic career. The past, with all its slow developments and progress yielded to a new epoch, and to its stormy spirits and phenomena. The closing century loudly demanded the protection of states from without, and their progress from within; for every peaceful step of the young monarch, Frederick William, was accompanied by a military enterprise beyond his own territories. When in the May of 1798 he repaired to Königsberg to receive the oaths of allegiance there, Buonaparte sailed at the same time to Malta and Egypt, and Alexandria was in his hands before the King could return by Warsaw and Breslau to Berlin, from receiving homage in Königsberg. A few days after this peaceful affair, Queen Louise gave birth, on July the 13th, to her first daughter, Princess Charlotte, while Buonaparte appeared before the Pyramids and the Mamelukes. Three days after the battle of Aboukir, on August 3d, the Princess was baptized.

What profound peace prevailed in the world two-and-twenty years before, when Queen Louise, the mother, was born—and yet this princess, cradled by the muses and the graces, had a more trying lot than her eldest daughter, whose whole childhood and youth were startled by the thunder of cannon. For with the childhood of this Queen ended the fair peaceful times of

Germany and Europe. As a girl she first became acquainted with the chosen of her heart amid the tumult of war in Frankfort, shortly after the Prussians stormed that city and made it their head-quarters. When she had exchanged the betrothal-ring with her bridegroom, she knew more of his warlike life and deeds from the newspapers than from confidential letters, and their next meeting was in the camp, where the Crown Prince passed the whole of the year 1793 with his father. The marriage took place on the Christmas eve of that year in Berlin, and in the course of a few months the Polish war interrupted the happiness of this royal pair. Louise trembled for her far-distant husband, who, at the storming of Warsaw, was exposed like the soldiers to every danger. But her maternal prospects led her to think of maternal duties. Not till the last two years of the King's reign did this royal couple enjoy quiet domestic happiness. This continued too in the early years of their reign, and their inward repose and felicity seemed scarcely threatened even by the wars which at that time ravaged every quarter of Europe. The royal mother, as soon as her daughter Charlotte attained the age of seven, awakened her first religious feelings, and made known to her the history of her forefathers, sometimes even conversing with her about the great events of the day. But these very events smote with Titanic force the quiet royal house, inflicting wounds on the heart of the mother, and inscribing lessons on the childish mind of the young princess. She had scarcely attained her eighth birthday when she took leave of her father and

mother, who left the capital in September to advance to
Thuringia to meet the French army.

At the first thunder of cannon in Jena, the Queen
quitted Weimar on October 14th, and on the 17th the
news preceded her to Berlin of the entire defeat of the
whole Prussian army. She was herself the bearer of
these sad tidings to her children; there was scarcely
time to collect necessaries for flight, and to send the
children in advance to Stettin. The thoughtful young
princess learned history, by hard and indelible experiences; she saw her trembling mother, her sorrowing
father, and her brothers and sisters driven forth in hasty
flight, and heard from the lips of the Queen, Goethe's
much admired line, " He who never moistened his bread
with tears," etc. They reached Königsberg, where the
Queen was prostrated by illness. Separated from her husband, she yet found some consolation from the presence
of her children; but the enemy inexorably pursued his
course, and threatened the ancient coronation city, and ill
as she was, Louise was forced to flee to Memel. Indeed
they could all add to Goethe's verse the words, " No
one knew where to lay his head." Under these melancholy circumstances the Queen completed her thirtieth
year. The year 1807 indeed restored her to Königsberg, but only for a short time; for, after the battle
of Friedland, Königsberg was also occupied by the
enemy, and, in the prospect of increasing danger, the
Queen had already formed the plan of taking refuge in
Riga with her children.

The magnanimity of Alexander the Great towards
the Persian royal family forms one of the brightest

pages in the history of the world, whereas Napoleon's arrogance in Tilsit towards the Prussian King and Queen is one of the blackest features of later times. This highly admired hero, when a general in Italy, called his officers together on the field of battle, and pointed out to them a dog, whining beside the body of his master, saying, " Gentlemen ! learn fidelity from this dog !" Such genial sympathy seemed to have disappeared with the rank of general, and to be transformed into hard insolence, and petty suspicions, and distrust on the part of the Emperor ; for Alexander, in Tilsit, during a morning visit offered him a cup of tea, which the hero of Austerlitz declined, suspecting it to be poisoned. The deeply insulted Queen returned to Memel, and now began straits almost unexampled in history. Peace was concluded, but scarcely the half of his monarchy left to the King, who bore his misfortunes with much equanimity ; the capital and the most important fortresses remained in the hands of the enemy ; the royal family were restricted to Königsberg. Other German princes did not blush to adorn their brows with royal crowns bestowed on them by a hand stained with blood ; nay, they even suffered the youngest brother of the usurper to establish a throne in their midst, and in his Corsican-French dialect to rule over German territories.   No wonder that the hero, elated by victory, permitted these crowned heads to wait for hours in an ante-room with his domestics. While thus outwardly distributing royal prizes, he was unable to deprive the King and Queen of Prussia of their inborn royal dignity and noble independence.   No·

German kingdom, no German people existed at that time, and those German princes who basely bowed down before foreign splendour incurred the deepest ignominy.

The royal children travelled as fugitives with their parents for nearly two years, and their education was therefore much interrupted. In Memel, as well as in Königsberg, the deeply distressed mother occupied herself for hours in instructing her eldest daughter in religion, who declared in after days, that the feeling of piety that accompanied her in every circumstance of life was the fairest inheritance left by her mother. Princess Charlotte was nine years old when the sad peace of Tilsit was concluded ; she ought to have been regularly and earnestly instructed, but, in truth, the necessary means for that end were wanting for the royal family. A young man of the French colony, Chambeau, accompanied them in their flight, and bestowed on all the children some instruction to the best of his abilities. Their mode of living in damp, unhealthy Memel was not only simple as that of citizens, but scanty ; all outward show was abolished, and privations that would have been felt even by a *bourgeois* were the lot of the whole family. The royal mother thought that she saw in her eldest daughter a likeness to herself, and kept her constantly by her side, reading much with her, and, in their strange straits, sharing with her many a domestic occupation, like the German mother of a family. Every thing in the shape of royal plate that formerly adorned their table now disappeared from it, for the upright King had turned it all into coin, in order to lighten for his sub-

jects the burden that Napoleon had laid on the country.
The smallest sum of money was very differently considered now in the palace. Princess Charlotte required
a dress; the King could only give her five dollars
towards it, and this penury was extended even to
the education of the children. They avoided allowing
any stranger to witness their limited household means.
"And yet," relates a grey-haired man, who, as *chargé-
d'affaires* in Memel, once spent an evening with the
royal family, "I would not exchange my memories of
that spectacle for a thousand court festivals with their
golden uniforms and stars. A queen seated at a shabby
table, devoid, like herself, of all outward show, but in
charm, loveliness, and dignity forming the brighter contrast; next her the eldest princess, like the bud beside
the full-blown rose, sharing with her mother the
arrangement of house affairs: both enchanted me by
their graceful attention, and left on my mind a living picture that no subsequent occurrence could ever
efface." At the same time the Queen wrote to her
father, "Our children are our treasures," and after
portraying the characters of each, she says of the
princess, "My daughter Charlotte is reserved and
thoughtful, but, like her father, conceals by a seemingly
cold exterior a warm, sympathizing heart; she has
something stately in her appearance, and, if God spares
her life, I anticipate a brilliant future for her."

In the beginning of 1808, the whole family left
Memel for Königsberg, where they occupied the old
palace that possessed many a glorious memory for
them. Königsberg, the city of "pure reason," could

no longer indeed boast of her most celebrated citizen, the great philosopher Kant, but by his intellectual legacy means were found to call forth a new state from the ruins of the monarchy. " What a State loses in outward importance, must be replaced by inward greatness and development." Such was Kant's political wisdom, which men like Stein, Gneisenau, Hardenberg comprehended, and the State was reinvigorated in accordance with this maxim. But not in Prussia alone, throughout all Germany the truth of this aphorism was felt and understood ; for the generation of the nineteenth century, in contradistinction to the previous one, were peculiarly inspired by a national spirit, which, though unobserved by their princes, had sprung up since the year 1780 in the spirit of the German people. All classes of the new century, with the exception of most of the princes, had been trained and instructed in German literature, and the intellectual life of Germany underwent the same revolution as government and society in France. Poets, philosophers, critics, artists were the teachers of the new era, unsparingly rejecting all that was extraneous or borrowed, and rousing a genuine national spirit from its profound slumbers, while the new school of romantic poetry wafted it through the ravaged plains of Germany ; the Muse in national strains exhorted the oppressed people to unity and armed them for the gigantic struggle, pending before all eyes as the inevitable issue of this crisis. While German princes, decked with foreign crowns, formed a *parterre* for the French imperial throne, invisible spirits of vengeance sprung from the blood of Palm, inspiring stern resolve

in the new generation, founding the *Tugendbund*, and
calling on men of every class, and every German
district, to unite in one great aim, the liberty of their
fatherland. A German princess here also first understood the new spirit of the time, and instilled it into
those around her; she comprehended that strength for
her people was only to be found in their intellectual
progress. It must not be forgotten that the Hohenzol-
lerns and the Prussian nation, when both were overthrown, still remained strictly German, and served as
bright examples of endurance and courage, in their
mode of thought and energy, to the rest of their en-
slaved fatherland. This King and Queen, even soon
after their marriage, displayed a simple national spirit,
abolishing French court etiquette from the palace, and
those formal ceremonies that crushed all family life in
every court of the eighteenth century, but adorning the
interior of the palace with burgher ideas and burgher
virtues. They did not allow their family meetings to
depend on a mistress of the robes; their excursions were
not fettered by a cumbrous escort; they were simply a
married pair, who, whenever they appeared, attracted
the loving and reverential glances of the citizens, and
they had been regarded in this light for years past by
the Prussians and the German people, long before fate
deprived them of one-half of their monarchy, and of
their last vestiges of regal splendours. The German
youth, as well as grey-haired warriors, turned their
eyes justly towards this royal pair, who remained
faithful to German opinions amid raging storms, and
who, from their throne, still did homage in this century

to national usages. Louise inspired her daughter with these thoughts and dispositions, and circumstances only tended to confirm and strengthen them.

Their residence in Königsberg, devoid of all vain pomp, could not fail to warm and nourish the hearts and minds of the royal children, far more than any palace could have done. They all had the privilege of enjoying unmolested the happiness of childhood and tender youth. Princess Charlotte, even when Empress of Russia, numbered Königsberg as among the fairest memories of her life. In all the careless happiness of youth, she used to leave the palace to visit Busolt's country-seat, where a little garden afforded them all those games and recreations so natural to children, but prohibited at Court. They played at ball, gathered flowers, caught butterflies, and Princess Charlotte was thoroughly happy when she could bring her mother a wreath of blue cornflowers entwined by her own hands. Königsberg also brought the royal children into contact with companions from other classes, and at an early age trained them to observe the vast diversity of the human character in life. All this made a deep impression on the character of Princess Charlotte, contributing to the treasures of her nature, and to that rare womanliness which always continued the brightest ornament of her life. Example and intercourse with others form the youthful mind far more than dry lessons of morality, and the presence of her mother cultivated the heart and mind of the young princess for life. Her delicate, slender figure, her engaging appearance, her dignified deportment, and the charming expression of her eyes, already captivated all who saw her. Officers who, on guard at the palace, saw the royal children at play in the courtyards, when become old and grey-headed, spoke with enthusiasm of the easy, graceful movements, the kindly courtesy with which the Princess greeted them, yet tempered by a certain degree of reserve. During that year she first became acquainted, under the guidance of her mother, with the writings of those German authors who particularly attract and develop the youthful mind. The conversations of the Queen with learned men were listened to by her daughter attentively, though not always fully understanding the subject; but the sorely tried mother instilled into her daughter, with her earliest religious feelings, that trust in God inculcated by Paul Gerhardt, child-like submission to the inscrutable course of the world and its history, belief in the ennoblement of humanity, and the final triumph of the good and true, after the desperation of the combat. Thus three years elapsed far from Berlin, but they were fruitful in experiences and lessons for the young Princess, the impulses of whose mind were very early excited, ever continuing sympathetic and susceptible.

Queen Louise consulted with men at that time eminent for education in Königsberg; she attracted into her circle not only those who were amusing, but instructive also; men such as Hufeland, Professor Süvern, Prince Hohenzollern, Abt zu Oliva, and Fürst-Bischof of Ermeland, enlivened the evenings by their genial conversation, when the Queen, forsaken both by good fortune and courtiers, severed from friends and allies, became acquainted with life in a more modest, but inwardly more intellectual aspect. She pursued Pestalozzi's method of education, and by its aid she hoped to educate the rising generation in other views of life. Here therefore, too, the spirit of a new epoch was mirrored, while the love of country, liberty, and energy were first awakened in the well-stored mind of a distinguished lady—a German Princess. She understood the eager enthusiasm with which the poetical heroes of the day sung the freedom of the people, as a truth that must infallibly penetrate, encourage, and elevate the down-trodden nation. She felt this inspiration as a self-evident truth, not only as regarded the guileless good King, but for every class of the disorganized German people; in such universal excitement the gulf was disregarded that especially at that period divided the different ranks. There are no bounds to the extent of such a movement, but time alone makes it thrive.

Thus Queen Louise was the polar star in the miserable night of Germany. With what sensations did their faithful subjects flock from every quarter to the royal pair when at length, after three years of absence, the whole royal family, now increased in number, once more greeted their capital! The Queen, with her eldest daughter and Prince Karl, drove in the new equipage presented to them by the city of Berlin. It was on the 23d December 1809, the anniversary of the day when she first arrived there, the loveliest and happiest of brides. Did her poetical spirit augur that the coming year would not concede her many days? Did the shadow of a coming dark cloud already lie on her bright eyes? The impression she made in the theatre on the enthusiastic public was more touching than exciting. On her birthday, March 10th, she said, "This is the last celebration of this day;" and on the 19th July the brightest star of Germany was extinguished. Since the death of Frederick the Great, no such cry of grief had been heard in Germany, as at the time of Louise's death. Not only did the King lose his wife, but the whole Prussian nation its palladium, its guardian angel, and all Germany its highest *beau-idéal* of womanhood. She was the first truly national Princess. The *Hainbund* of Göttingen sung beside her cradle, and the most classical strains of the German language attended her youth: Jean Paul dedicated his "Titan" to her and her sisters. She was conducted on the path of life by German muses and graces; she adorned a throne with the fascination and dignity of womanhood; in storms of misfortune she shone more brightly by the virtues of her heart and mind than by royal splendours, and though stripped of all outward pomp, she ever continued the faith and hope of the entire nation.

The death of Louise was a most terrible stroke to the afflicted King, and the royal children lost the protecting, inspiring eye that had watched over their education. A letter of the Princess Charlotte's, written to her mother on July 13th, reached the sick-bed of the Queen only three days before her death, and its contents affected the sufferer so deeply, that she could not read it to the end. The Princess had written on her twelfth birthday, from the irresistible impulse of a filial heart, and the dying mother could leave the world with the consolation that her eldest daughter would fulfil her prophecy. Queen Louise, more than any other princess of her time, comprehended that history must assume a prominent part in the instruction of a princess, not only because it teaches the course nations have pursued to reach the present time, but also because historical contemplations, next to religion, both elevate and cultivate the mind in a way no other knowledge can effect. The blank in the family life of the King left by the death of his consort was very great, and equally felt by all, though the confidential relation between father and daughter was the best consolation to the afflicted man for his terrible bereavement. The hours thus lost for her education were amply compensated by loving intercourse with her father. She learned early in life how to appear before a great assemblage, with self-possession and dignity, to find something appropriate to say to each person, combining the most lofty manner with the most genuine goodness of heart. During these years of sorrow for the King, she stood by his side like an angel of consolation, inspiring the hope in the minds of the people that a deliverance at last from the political troubles of the time would bring about happier days.

The year of the Queen's demise was that of the blackest night for Prussia and Germany, for Napoleon was on the highest pinnacle of human greatness; his arrogance knew no bounds. German kings and princes were not only his vassals, but the daughter of a German emperor shared his throne, their nuptials receiving the blessing of the Church from the lips of a priest whose spiritual head a few months previously had excom-

municated Napoleon. The despotic will that sought to
unite the most opposite elements, grasping in its pride
the most distant objects, did not in its insolence foresee
that the next step was to entail destruction on his
head; in his blindness overlooking the first symptoms
of the destiny he had brought on himself.

On the 30th July, the mortal remains of the Queen
were deposited in a private manner, in the sacristy of
the Cathedral, a few days before the King's birthday,
August 3d, which the people intended to have celebrated
for the first time after their long separation from their
Monarch, but the universal mourning put an end to
this. When Princess Charlotte, with the other children,
came on the morning of that day to congratulate her
father, she found him silent and sorrowful; and when his
troubled eye first rested on his eldest daughter, after
having pressed her fondly to his heart, he said, " Your
dying mother could not give you her blessing, but the
star of my life will still shine brightly on you." In after
days the princess used to refer to this visit to her father
as one of the most touching episodes of her youthful
life. She also read in her father's heart, so lovingly
disposed towards her, the wish that she should help him
in bearing the cares that the Queen's presence formerly
lightened. The blessing of her royal mother followed
her through her life, which, amid much splendour and
happiness, had yet many terrors and much bitterness.

Her education was now conducted more regularly
than before, although nothing could subdue the grief of
the royal family caused by the death of the Queen. Indeed a heavy cloud hovered over Germany, obscuring by

its silent gloom the enthusiasm that animated the whole nation, who waited with eager desire but manly endurance the moment when the King should lead his oppressed but valiant people into the lists to struggle for liberty. The longer this moment was delayed, the better. prepared for it was the nation; and it came at the very time when least expected. Worldly events of the magnitude witnessed by Europe after the conflagration of Moscow affect every age, grey-haired men as well as children, in whose warlike sports this stormy, troubled time was reflected. What Napoleon's iron will had unnaturally soldered together, was rent asunder by the irresistible course of history, and nations, as well as dynasties, found their common weal in the strife for European freedom.

The epoch of national struggles and national liberty anticipated, nay invoked, by Queen Louise had arrived; the elements led the vanguard, and nations and heroes were to complete what they had begun. With the contest for freedom sprung up also trust in God, and confidence in their own strength. The Emperor Alexander took up the sword, King Frederick William summoned his people to arms. The friendship once sworn by both monarchs over the bier of Frederick the Great, and severed by Napoleon, stimulated both princes and people to an alliance, which was destined to humble the arrogance of the French Emperor. The two monarchs, accompanied by their staff, met in Breslau, where a banquet celebrated the new birth of European liberty. Queen Louise had witnessed the friendship sworn beside Frederick's coffin, and now the Princess Charlotte

was present at the new alliance. From the tears of
her mother fresh laurels were to spring up for prince
and people, which her virgin hand was to entwine and
to bestow. The universal enthusiasm powerfully affected
the youthful princess, cultivating her mind and leaving
memories for a lifetime. She saw the youth of Berlin
quit the University to repair to the seat of war, and
Lützow's volunteers flock together; fathers and mothers
separate from their sons; brides arm their betrothed,
to welcome them back as heroes; but she also saw the
danger that once more threatened Berlin happily warded
off by Prussian men of valour. Tidings of victory
reached the city in quick succession, filling every heart
with thankfulness, and with admiration for the heroes;
and before the princess attained her sixteenth birthday, the great work was completed, the Imperial throne,
erected by mighty power, overthrown, and Germany
and Europe free. The education of Princess Charlotte,
disturbed by the storms and terrors of war, and interrupted by the most severe losses, terminated happily
with this fortunate issue of events; the young princess
was now in all the bloom of loveliness. When she
celebrated her seventeenth birthday, Napoleon's throne
was, for the second time, demolished, and he himself cap-
tured in his flight from France. Princess Charlotte welcomed the returning warriors from France, from the grey-
haired Blücher to the most simple militia-man; once
more she saw the four bronze horses replaced over the
Brandenburg gate, and with millions gladly breathed
the spirit of peace that pervaded all Europe. Those
who saw the greetings of the returning heroes, the wel-

come they received, the joy pervading every breast at
the second overthrow of Napoleon, and public thanksgivings offered up to Heaven in every market-place, can
easily understand that thoughtful eyes should turn
aside from the smoke of the battle-fields, from these
sudden earthly vicissitudes, from the overthrow of a
throne, to an everlasting unchanging object, to faith in a
higher and Almighty Power. A new spirit arose with a
new epoch; a glance at the past caused amazement at the
course of events which had led to this change of scene.

But Princess Charlotte who first greeted, as a bloom-
ing girl, her liberated Fatherland, was not destined to
adorn a throne in her own country. We often silently
envy the lot of princes without reflecting that they are
subject to more severe restrictions than ourselves. No
great liberty is granted to them in the choice of their
hearts; and though recent times no longer ruthlessly
sacrifice their princesses to political considerations, still
certain limits remain, prescribed by the prejudices of
the times, and of their rank. For a royal princess of
Prussia, for Louise's daughter, a throne established by
Napoleon in Germany was no inviting position, even if
her feelings had impelled her towards it; but she had
already unconsciously given away her heart. Even
before the capture of Paris by the allied army, the two
Grand Dukes, Nicholas and Michael, had been ordered
to leave Petersburg to join the army in France. They
visited Berlin feverishly agitated by alternate fears and
hopes, and by the distant struggle. These young men
now, for the first time, passed the boundaries of the
kingdom, and escaped the confined limits of a court

life; their minds and hearts were appealed to, not only
by novelty, but by a sense of independence. Their
stay in Berlin was brief, but decisive for the whole life
of Nicholas; he saw and loved the princess, and left
Berlin with a heart no longer his own. The camp in
France did not efface the impression awakened in him
by the sight of Princess Charlotte. At last he confided
his wishes to his brother Alexander and King Frederick
William, Charlotte's father, neither of whom, however,
without an avowal on the part of the princess, would
either crush or encourage his hopes. The two monarchs ascertained Charlotte's wishes, and agreed not to
oppose a union that seemed destined by Heaven; for
the image of Nicholas had been constantly present
with the Princess since he quitted Berlin, and she ventured timidly to avow this in a letter to her brother
William. The Emperor Alexander, Autocrat of all the
Russias, and, after the downfall of Napoleon, beyond all
doubt the greatest Potentate of his time, did not, however, venture to sanction on his own authority such a
family connection, and awaited the consent of the Empress-mother, Maria Feodorowna. Meanwhile Europe
assumed another aspect, a King of France and Navarre
was seated on the throne at Paris, the victorious armies
had returned to their domestic hearths, and the Emperor
Alexander passed through Berlin on the way to his
northern capital.

Seven terrible years of trial for Prussia's King and
people were now closed; during this period the strains
of liberty and every pleasure had been silenced ; melancholy remembrances, gloomy feelings, had brooded like

black clouds over the usually gay city, and now, as the price of its courage and endurance, it saw the triumphal procession of the King and his victorious heroes. None of the European capitals had suffered more, none had made greater sacrifices; none had so great a right to enjoy the intoxication of victory. The unobtrusive monarch wished to avoid every pomp for himself, but he owed a festival of joy and gratitude to his capital, his generals, and his valiant warriors. On the 7th of August 1814, the wide space from the Brandenburg gate to the Palace bore the aspect of conquest and triumph, as the King slowly and solemnly traversed it with his brilliant staff. Between the Palace and the pleasure-grounds an altar was erected on a lofty pedestal, and higher still, a platform on which stood Princess Charlotte, with all the Princesses of the royal family; the whole priesthood of Berlin stood in front of the altar; the King and his heroes then ascended the elevation where the young and lovely Princess Charlotte stood high above all the rest—a symbol of peace—as if the King wished to typify that no victory could be attained without a struggle, and that woman's serene eyes confer the highest reward on the victor. The pealing of bells ceased, and prayer like incense ascended to heaven from every heart.

A few days afterwards, the same immense space was occupied by a banquet for the returning Russian troops, but the man chosen by Princess Charlotte was not among them.

The following year, when the warlike drama of a hundred days was played out, and the hero of European fame was pining away slowly in a distant rocky island,

and the King had entered his capital a second time
with the wreath of victory, arrived Nicholas, on a day
very memorable to the House of Hohenzollern. It was
on the 22d October, the anniversary of that day 400
years, when the dynasty had been first established as
rulers over the Electorate of Brandenburg. Two days
later, on the same day that the French had entered
Berlin in 1806, the Emperor Alexander also appeared,
and next day, his sister, the Grand Duchess Catherine,
the widowed Duchess of Oldenburg, and the Grand
Duchess of Weimar. Two brothers and two sisters of
Alexander's joined the royal family, and on November
4th, the Russian Grenadier Regiment, "the King of
Prussia," entered Berlin.

A banquet was held the same day in the Royal Palace
in Berlin, at which the two monarchs, and the members
of the Royal and Imperial families sat at one table, to
which only the grey-haired Blücher and Barclay de
Tolly were invited; the other Court guests, many in
number, were entertained in the adjoining room.

Suddenly the two monarchs rose and drank to the
health of the betrothed pair, the Grand Duke Nicholas
and Princess Charlotte. The heroes Blücher and Barclay de Tolly had heard of their betrothal before dinner,
to their great surprise, but it had been kept a secret
from the other guests, who now entered the hall, to
offer their congratulations to the future couple.

This intelligence spread rapidly through the town,
and the young Nicholas was now as much an object
of curiosity to the Berliners as his majestic brother
Alexander. On the following day, the Emperor and

the affianced pair visited the mausoleum of the Queen in Charlottenburg. Nicholas had only seen her as a child, but if he had not read on the lifeless marble the bright virtues of the deceased, the tears shed by the Princess on the tomb of her mother, and the silent sorrow of the Emperor, would have borne ample testimony to her merits. The Princess made a silent but solemn vow to be to her future husband what Queen Louise had been to her father, and implored strength from Heaven to carry out this resolve; to no one in our century has the mission of woman been more clear, and none have fulfilled it to their last breath more faithfully than herself. She required time to prepare for her future lot, and the claims made on her by the novel world into which she was about to enter, were by no means small. Indeed only three weeks were granted to enable her to become better acquainted with her intended husband, though even this short period for their first confidential intercourse, was constantly inter- rupted by festivities. On the next day there was a grand ball in the Opera House, which the society of Berlin saw opened by the distinguished couple. But the burghers also wished to celebrate this union, and in course of a few days gave a ball in the Theatre, at which Nicholas won for himself by his affability all those hearts that the Princess had already gained. This year closed with entertainments of every kind; shortly after the departure of the Emperor and his brother, the Empress Elisabeth arrived, the wife of Alexänder, who had passed two years in her native city, Karlsruhe; a variety of royal personages visited brilliant Berlin at

that time, when Princess Charlotte assumed the rôle of
the deceased Queen.   Her society became every day
more indispensable to the King, and he undertook no
expedition, even in the immediate vicinity of the city,
without her by his side.

The country and the city in which she was to assume
so prominent a position were at that time very little
known in Germany ; those who were not forced to
repair to Russia in order to gain a livelihood, were not
likely to travel thither from curiosity, and those who
settled there seldom returned.   From Russia also very
few expeditions were made to the West, and works
giving information on Russian life seldom appeared.
The Russian troops, by their good conduct and military
discipline, left behind them a better reputation than
the French and Bavarians ; the latter being everywhere
considered unusually rough and uncivilized.   Still
Princess Charlotte had time to prepare for her high
destiny, differing so materially from the course she had
hitherto pursued.   When we overstep the boundaries
of our native country, we cannot fail to feel, to a certain
extent, strange, even if it chance to be a land akin to
our own in morals, religion, and culture.   We give
up habits dear to us, and which have indeed formed
part of our lives ; we resemble a plant that takes root
slowly and with difficulty in a foreign soil.   A Protestant
Princess, even in Catholic Bavaria, could not feel quite
at home ; the difference in the mode of life would be
still more perceptible in France or England.   The
Russian Court, however, exacts from its foreign Empresses and Grand Duchesses in this foreign sphere the

adoption of the faith of the orthodox Greek Church, instead of the Protestant, for the Emperor, as the Head and Protector of his Church, must himself, as well as every member of his family, profess the same faith as the nation; so it was fortunate that the Princess had two years' time to make herself acquainted with these new doctrines. A Russian priest, named Musowsky, came to Berlin to explain to the Princess the dogmas and forms of the Orthodox Church, and to instruct her in the Russian tongue, and thus the years of her engagement passed even more rapidly than she herself wished. Nicholas, however, repeatedly visited Berlin during this period; the unaffected simplicity of Frederick William attracting him as strongly as love for the Princess; the example of familiar domestic life that Nicholas first saw here in all its magic charm, powerfully impressed itself on his mind; his complete mastery of the German language made him feel quite at home in Berlin, and the attractions of life, heightened by his being at the same time liberated from all official duties and classical studies, were thoroughly enjoyed by him. His predilection for military occupations found full satisfaction here; moreover, Berlin and Potsdam, with their treasures, reminiscences, and arrangements, excited his interest to the utmost. The intellectual atmosphere in which man lives, usually called by us circumstances, assumes the first and most important influence on his moral culture and development. Two unpretending men of science and learning, who were much with Nicholas, particularly in England, drew a sketch of him at that time, materially differing from

the individual whom Petersburg knew in his official
capacity later in life. At that period he was frank,
confiding, susceptible, indulgent, gay to an excess;
cramped, as he had hitherto been, by the Imperial
uniform in Petersburg, he was now awakened to self-
consciousness,—and such he was when Princess Charlotte first knew and loved him.

In later days, voices have not been wanting to proclaim that this alliance of the subsequent Emperor
Nicholas with a Princess of Prussia was merely a
hostage to the Holy Alliance, in which their hearts had
no concern; whereas, at the beginning of the year 1814,
Nicholas, then a youth of eighteen, as little thought of
ascending the Imperial throne as the three monarchs in
the French camp anticipated the subsequent importance
of the Holy Alliance. Nicholas and his bride were two
natures that would have been mutually attracted under
any circumstances; the Grand Duke, an accomplished
man—the Princess, a perfect woman. We must not,
however, overlook the fact, that Russia for the first time
now entered into an alliance with a great German State,
while no political results had ever been apprehended
with regard to the previous Empresses from Anhalt,
Baden, and Würtemberg. Both States had been added
to the list of independent European powers in the
eighteenth century, and quickly developed a degree of
energy which certainly astonished the world. Although
inimical to each other during the Seven Years' War,
they assimilated more closely in Polish affairs, and
divided the country that had hitherto severed the two
States; but it would seem that a family connection was

never intended. The Prussians under Frederick William the Second took an active part in the struggle against the French Revolution, whereas Catherine contented herself with menaces. When Paul subsequently was engaged in the French war, Prussia observed strict neutrality, but the final partition of Poland rendered both countries neighbouring States. The Emperor Alexander and Frederick William the Second now first formed a personal friendship, and political events united their interests more closely. A family connection under these circumstances could indeed only be welcome to both monarchs, but it was never treated as a deliberate political scheme.

When Princess Charlotte, in the course of two years, was sufficiently prepared for her vocation, her journey to Russia was fixed for 12th June 1817. It was the King's wish that her progress should be attended with every mark of outward dignity and pomp, and yet with the prudence necessarily imposed by the circumstances of the nation. The nineteenth century had renounced many customs of the previous one ; burgher and natural simplicity replacing empty splendour, without at all diminishing the love and respect of the people. Journeys of reigning families were formerly one of the most terrible scourges of the land. Denmark was forced to impose a number of new taxes in order to enable Christian the Seventh to travel. But even after abolishing all absurd precedents, a royal court must be properly represented, especially as the journey was to a country where externals played the same part as in previous centuries. After the wounds inflicted by war

on the Prussian land, the dowry of the royal bride was
a difficult problem for the ruined finances ; but the wise
King, with his admirable Grand Chamberlain, Baron
Von Schilden, found the right way to solve the enigma,
without at all impoverishing the country by the Princess's marriage portion.

In no circumstances of life are joy and sorrow so
closely united as in the heart of a father, when a bride
leaves a family circle, and, severed from her paternal
home, takes the first step towards an unknown future.
The reserved King now felt thus far more deeply than the
most fluent words could express.   He was about to lose
his eldest and most beloved daughter, who, since the
death of his incomparable consort, had always been by
his side.   With tears in his eyes, and a heart filled with
tender wishes, after embracing on June 12th his
cherished child, he conducted her to the carriage that
awaited her before the Palace.   Brothers and sisters
accompanied her to Freienwalde, where she spent the
first night ; Prince Wilhelm, her second brother, remained with her till she reached Petersburg and Moscow.
The immediate attendants of the Princess consisted
of Countess Haake, Mistress of the Robes, Countess
Truchsess, and the governess, Mademoiselle Wildermett ; the Grand Chamberlain, Baron Von Schilden,
Chamberlain Count Lottum, the secretaries Chambeau
and Schiller, Dr. Busse, the priest Musowsky, to whom
we have already alluded ; and, in addition to these, only
the necessary retinue of servants.

The whole procession consisted of twelve carriages,
containing the persons we have named, and also the

trousseau of the bride. The Princess herself was seated with her three ladies in a carriage drawn by eight horses, and eight fresh ones decorated with flowers awaited her at each stage. It was almost the same route the family had pursued eleven years before, when flying from Berlin to Königsberg. While at that time fear and dismay, and a heartless victorious enemy pursued them, now a loyal people, in the enjoyment of the most profound peace, came to welcome the Princess with joyous shouts. At the gates of every city, great or small, she was received by festively adorned young girls, and our German custom of welcoming distinguished guests in rhyme everywhere gave an impulse to the poetic vein. Her beauty and charm, her goodness of heart and dignity, recalled to many the image of Queen Louise, and every kindly glance of hers was long a topic of conversation, and to many a *souvenir* for life.

Beyond all other German countries these provinces had suffered from the yoke of the French. Danzig, the richest of their cities, remained in the hands of the French till the year 1814, and the closing of the Continent had impoverished its wealthy commercial resources. In other respects the mighty armies of the year 1813 had spared these countries; but they had not witnessed the great victory and the jubilation of Berlin, Leipzig, and other towns, though the wounds inflicted by war were still unhealed. Most of these cities are without any palaces, and were therefore busied for weeks in preparing a tolerable reception for the bride, even if not wholly worthy of her high rank. Freienwalde alone received the Princess in a palace; Stargard and Cöslin, as well as Lauenburg could only provide accommodation in private houses, and had nothing to show save loyalty to the royal family.

Danzig, the northern Genoa of Prussia, detained the Princess for two days within its walls; and from thence she visited Oliva, so important in the history of Prussia. The Prince Bishop of Ermeland also came to meet her, whom when a child she had so often seen with her mother, during three years of misfortune, in Memel and Königsberg, and who now initiated her into all the historical treasures of the abbey there. The journey was continued thence in two days by Braunsberg, to the ancient coronation city of Königsberg—what a revolution in destiny! Ten years before, the fugitive mother with her beloved child had taken refuge here, with feelings of misery and terror, nay, despair. Most of the inhabitants who had formerly witnessed the misfortunes of the land, and particularly those of the royal family, now enjoyed the spectacle of seeing the same Princess enter their city as a bride. No town in all this toilsome journey touched and affected the feelings of the Princess so deeply; but none other had such a right once more to see those who in the hour of their worst calamity had experienced their warmest sympathy when they used to traverse the narrow streets on which the pointed gable roofs looked down so sedately. In cities that we have not seen for long, we seem to live whole years in a few passing hours. But here, with the memorable past, and the happy present, the future was closely allied, bright with great and splendid prospects, a new world in which the Fatherland must be silently buried.

The Princess had the happy surprise of once more seeing her father at her first resting-place, and now at the last her chivalrous bridegroom met her, and thus she took her final farewell of home with him by her side. All Prussia regarded with sorrow their departing Princess, and everywhere beyond its boundaries she was received with eager curiosity.

No foreign Princess during this century had ever entered Russia as a bride, so the excitement in all these retired provinces was great. From Memel, Schründen, in Courland, was reached in one day, the outward aspect of which is not very different from that of Russia. The nobility there spring from the same stock as the Prussians, and the citizens, few in number, are little considered by their superiors, the original inhabitants of the country being treated like helots by their ancient conquerors. The smaller country towns have many wooden houses, a few only built of stone, and unpaved streets; they appear poverty-struck beside the innumerable country-seats of the old knightly families, reminding us of the Middle Ages. On the second day, preceded by her bridegroom, the Princess arrived at the Palace of Mittau, inhabited twelve years ago by King Louis XVIII. In this palace the Princess received all the nobility of Courland, and her charm and simplicity were praised on every side. She was welcomed with equal joy next day in Riga by the Governor-General Paulucci. In Mittau an exclusively aristocratic tone prevails, whereas Riga astonishes by the wealth of its energetic citizens. The town, thoroughly German at heart, recals German free cities, especially by its lofty church spires.

The wooden suburbs, however, show plainly that both
city and province have been longer subject to the
Russian sceptre than Courland, and through Russian
influence the separation between the classes is no longer
so marked as in Courland.   On the way from Riga
to Petersburg, Dorpat is worthy of attention.   At the
beginning of this century a German university was
established here by the Emperor Alexander ; with the
exception of this seat of the muses there is no town of
mark between Riga and Petersburg, and nature exhibits
as little variety ; the same flat plain is traversed to
Petersburg on the Neva, and the highways at that time
inured, nay compelled, travellers to patience and the
endurance of privations.   About sixty versts from Riga is
a little romantic valley, and an old ruined castle, called
the Lithuanian Switzerland.   The public road, however,
diverges some versts from it, so the Princess was obliged
to deny herself the pleasure of seeing it ; indeed, even
in the ensuing forty-three years of her stay in Russia,
she never visited it.   Her route in this long journey
never brought her into contact with actual Russia.   The
capital likewise is the work of Peter, and built in the
European style.   The reception, however, of a royal
bride there differs widely from our German usages.   In
Germany it is the privilege of the burgher guilds and
corporations to be the first to offer their greetings to a
crowned head or a royal bride on their formal entrance
into the city ; when all the respectable inhabitants, both
of city and country, appear, devoid indeed of external
pomp, but with feelings of the most sincere cordiality,
and all enjoying a certain degree of independence.   It

is otherwise in Russia; there the distinguished bride is received and escorted by the sovereign, and the most brilliant military suite, while the good-humoured but inquisitive populace only takes the share permitted by the police; even the actual Court, the chamberlains and lords in waiting, play very subordinate parts.

But notwithstanding the brilliant and cordial welcome bestowed by her bridegroom and the country on the Princess, she felt the burden of such heavy responsibility, and her modest doubts as to whether she were equal to the task caused her to shed many secret tears during her long fatiguing journey. The Empress-mother, though taking no part in government affairs, exercised, as head of the family, sovereign influence over them, and her approval was conclusive as to the future position of the youthful bride. She was the only one of the family to whom she had not been presented, and rumour depicted her as stern, and disposed to be arrogant towards her daughter-in-law. The close of the journey drew near, and the appearance of the Emperor Alexander at the last stage but one, forcibly reminded the Princess of the close vicinity of the northern capital. At length, on the eighteenth day they reached the first Imperial Palace, Gatschina, and drove thence past the gardens of Zarskoe-Selò to lovely Pawlowsk, the favourite abode of the Empress-mother. The Emperor received the Princess with the chivalrous grace for which he was so admired in Europe. The Empress-mother embraced her with cordial and sincere tenderness, and won the love and veneration of the bride from the first moment, and for the rest of her life. The Emperor

led Prince William to his mother with these words :—
" Allow me to present to you my new brother." On
which she embraced him, saying, " And I also gain a
son."

Maria Feodorowna was at that time fifty-eight years
of age, but still animated and slender, and she made a
striking impression on strangers by her energetic and
imperial aspect. The Princess was so agitated and
excited, that she did not distinguish one of the assemblage presented to her, not even the Empress Elisabeth,
till she came up to the young embarrassed bride, saying,
" Have you not a kind glance for me too ?"

The cordiality with which the Imperial family received
the Princess was great, and the reception was heightened
by the splendid roses that adorned Pawlowsk, and that
seemed also to greet her with home reminiscences.
They were the more welcome, being quite unexpected
in this northern region. Her future Court household
were presented to her, selected from the best families,
but their names and physiognomies were too strange,
the excitement and fatigue too great, and not till she
was once more in the solitude of her chamber could she
collect her thoughts, when, to her astonishment, without
being announced, a venerable lady walked into the
room, saying in the most familiar tone, " You are much
sunburnt, I will send you some water at once."

It was Princess Lieven, who, as the oldest lady at Court,
could alone presume to address the Princess in such an
unceremonious manner ; next to the two Empresses
she inspired the highest consideration at Court, and
although this, her first appearance, seemed very singular

to the Princess, she found, on further acquaintance, that she was worthy of the utmost respect. The Princess was expected to appear at the first family dinner, so, without waiting for her gala dresses, which were still on the way, she presented herself before the whole assembled Court, who observed every gesture and movement of the young bride, her mien and deportment, and her every word. Her appearance was so novel, and so different and singular to Russian ideas, and yet so lovely and charming, that they called her "the little dove." The evening was devoted exclusively to the family circle. Next morning ensued the formal entrance of the Princess into Petersburg, not less fatiguing for her than the journey thither. Early in the morning three German miles were traversed to reach the gates of Petersburg; the Princess rested at a country-house for breakfast, and then in full dress entered a gilt landau, in which the two Empresses and Princesses of Würtemberg sat with the bride, so that the public in the capital could see and welcome them. The different regiments of Guards lined the way for a mile, from the gates to the Winter Palace. Many of these troops were known to the Princess in the year 1813, when she was present at a review of the Guards. The procession passed through the Perspective, the longest and widest street in the city, to the Winter Palace, where they ascended the grand flight of steps, never permitted to be used except on some great festival. Their next progress was to the church, where the Princess for the first time kissed the cross, in accordance with the usage of true believers. From thence she was conducted to a

balcony in front of the great square, where subsequently
the Alexander pillar was erected. There all the regiments of Guards were stationed in their splendid
uniforms, and they, as well as the public at large,
received the bride with startling hurrahs. Dazzled and
deafened by so much brilliancy and noise, the Princess
at length, late in the afternoon, entered the apartments
destined for her, and decorated with imperial splendour.
She felt that she was now in an empire where all was
on a gigantic scale. She had only a few days for rest,
which, after a journey of nineteen days, on fatiguing
roads, and in distressing heat, she certainly greatly
required.

CHAPTER III.

In the life of many persons the change in events, the ups and downs of life, the transition from one position to another, are sudden and startling, while others live in incessant monotony, never leaving their homes, and perhaps not even the house in which they were born. The latter find their quiet state disturbed even by passing from one street to another.

How must the Princess have been excited by one change following another; town and country, human beings and skies, art and nature! indeed, even the season of the year, the month of June, appeared to her under a very different aspect. On the day of her arrival in Petersburg, June 30th, night seemed banished, and with it the repose of sleep; scarcely does a star of any magnitude appear in the sky in Petersburg at this season at midnight; instead of tranquil darkness, the morning dawn suddenly appears. The inhabitants of the north find compensation in this brightness for their late and brief springs, and enjoy these fine nights, like days, in the open air. The verdure of the north is at that time even more vivid than in Germany, being a month later in springing to the light. The birch trees,

so slender and delicate in Germany, adorn the gardens
and woods of Russia as grand forest trees, and the
most scientific skill has not succeeded in supplanting
them by our fruit trees. Our narrow streets, their
houses blackened by centuries, are not to be found in
Petersburg; and the Berlin of that day, in its newest
quarters, alone bore any resemblance to the never-
ending straight streets of the imperial city. Churches,
palaces, the costume and physiognomy of the inhabitants, all is new and all is different; we cannot recover
our astonishment when we enter Petersburg at sight of
the Neva and the islands. In Mittau, Riga, and Dorpat,
we may still believe that we are in Germany, at all
events in a late autumnal Germany, but in Petersburg
we find ourselves in a very different scene.

Yet this discrepancy in the external world was not
the greatest of all, for a change awaited the young bride
in the course of a few days that affected the deepest
emotions of her heart—her recognition of the Orthodox
Greek Church. Prepared as she had been for this step
by the priest Musowsky for the last two years, yet,
owing to her slender acquaintance with the Russian
tongue, she had been instructed chiefly in German, and
now her confession of faith was to be made publicly,
in the presence of the whole Court, in Russian. The
limited teaching of the same priest scarcely enabled her
to carry on an easy conversation; and of all the strange
things she encountered the Russian language was the
most strange. One of the first experiences, however, of
the fair bride was, that the Greek Church exercises a
far greater influence on the outer life of the people

than either the Catholic or Protestant, and that the
observance of religious customs and precepts is much
more strict in Russia than in other countries, and not
one even of the Imperial family can disobey these. The
orthodox Russian never enters a church, or passes the
house of God, without making the sign of the cross;
when he meets a funeral he stands still respectfully, and
bare-headed, till it is passed; on his entrance into any
dwelling he first of all greets the never-failing picture
of a saint; he says a prayer before and after dinner,
turning towards a picture of the patron saint; the most
casual glance convinces a traveller that the Church in
this country prescribes many rules common to all, and
conscientiously observed. The Greek Church justly
considers herself as the oldest of all, and in her construction, dogmas, and religious services, she is equally
independent of the Romish and of the Protestant Church,
although she has much in common with both. The
Bible and tradition are held in equal esteem. Her differences from the Protestant faith chiefly consist in
the invocation of saints, worship of images and relics,
prayers for the dead, the priesthood, monastic life, strict
fasts, the seven sacraments, and the mass as a blood-
less sacrifice. Divine service is performed standing, but
diversified by constant genuflexions and signs of the
cross. An organ is unknown in their churches, but is
replaced by the singing of a choir. The whole community partake of the bread and wine in our Lord's
Supper; the priests are married, but poor; the sacrament of ordination is bestowed by the laying on of
hands. There are three different orders in the priest-

hood, deacons, presbyters, and bishops, all strictly separated from worldly society, and recognised by their
costume, their smooth parted hair and long beards.   A
visible head of the Church, a Pope, is not acknowledged.   The Emperor is Defender of the Faith of the
Church.   The point of view in which the Russian people
accept Christianity seems nearly to assimilate to the
Apostolic age, by its humility, charity, and brotherly
kindness, diminished in Europe by the marked separation of classes, that evil enemy of European society.
The man of rank in Russia speaks to his inferior as his
equal, and calls him " brother;" the young address the
old as "father" or "uncle;" the cordial sympathy of
the people, and their truly Christian compassion, are so
great, that even a criminal is called " an unfortunate."
Ecclesiastical life has been in every century the chief
means of civilisation, a strong rock of refuge in misfortune, and to women is justly ascribed the merit of
having preserved the Christian faith in the land during
the Mongolian period.   Religious services are accompanied by surprising outward splendour; the solemn
nature of the ceremonies also displays a deep knowledge
of their hidden meaning, the length too not causing
weariness.   The progress of the Liturgy, the prayers,
the coming and going of the priests; the simple sublime
singing, the mystery of the holy office, is to the unini-
tiated an elevating mystic spectacle, even if unable to
divine its original significance; but every individual
ceremony has its own fixed import, and in the closest
connection with the most ancient usages of the Christian Church.

For the first five days after her arrival the Princess remained alone with one of her ladies, and the priest Musowsky, equally severed from the brilliancy of the Court, and the social pleasures of the Imperial family, in order once more to review in all its parts the spiritual fabric of the Church she was about to join, and to enable her to comprehend its whole signification, that she might not make her confession of faith without due consideration. She could do so with a clear conscience, never having been confirmed in the Protestant Church, and consequently not having received the Holy Sacrament in that form. On the 24th June she appeared, conducted by Alexander, before the assembled Court, in a white dress, with a cross on her breast, simple and unadorned, and with some timidity made her new religious profession in the Slavonic tongue. By her side stood, in striking contrast to herself, a nun clothed in black, which heightened the singular impression made on the foreign suite. They saw their much-loved Princess Charlotte for the last time, and greeted her after the Holy Communion as Grand Duchess Alexandra Feodorowna. The Greek Church sanctions no Christian names not included in her own Calendar, nor does she permit two, according to the customs of the West, but generally (and in former days universally) confers the name of the saint commemorated on the day of baptism, commending the newly baptized to the protection of this saint for life. The name-day is therefore of more importance all through Russia than the day of birth, as the Greek Church does not reckon the beginning of life from the date of birth, but from that of baptism.

Although in recent times this custom has not been strictly observed, and a name has been often selected not that of the patron-saint, still the name-day continues to be the greatest family festival. The previous name of Charlotte was exchanged for that of Alexandra on her being received into the Greek Church, no doubt as a compliment to the Emperor Alexander, who led the Princess to the holy ceremony. The second name, Feodorowna, in accordance with the ancient Greek *patronimicum*, denotes the Christian name of the father, and means the daughter of Frederick. The Greek Church, however, acknowledges the validity of Protestant baptism, and if any members of that faith wish to join the Orthodox Church, after changing their Christian name, as was here the case, they are then consecrated by the sacrament of being anointed with myrrh. " This is the seal of spiritual completeness for all the members and family of God who have come forth from the waters of baptism." If the Princess Charlotte had been much excited and agitated in setting out to perform this sacred duty, as the Grand Duchess Alexandra she remained tranquil and at peace with herself. She required rest of soul, as well as bodily strength, for her next step, and therefore passed this day also in perfect retirement and in earnest thought.

The following day, June 25th, was a double festival in the Imperial family, being the one-and-twentieth birth-day of Nicholas, and the betrothal of the illustrious couple in church. The bride appeared for the first time in Russian national costume, in a long bright pink dress and a crescent-shaped head-dress, the only distinc-

tive female costume in the Europe of the present day
which betokens the new life of a bride. A church
betrothal in the Greek Church is as indissoluble as
marriage, being rarely, and for six reasons alone dissolved; a second marriage is only tolerated, and for
a third, certain purifications and penances are enjoined.
The presbyter, after crossing himself three times, gives
a gold ring to the bridegroom, a symbol of the sun, with
the brightness of which he is to shine before his bride,
and a silver ring to the bride, a symbol of the moon,
that borrows her light from the sun; the attributes of
dependence and obedience being thus typified. He then
betrothes the pair in the name of the Trinity, when
they exchange rings. The bride had been hitherto
invisible to the public, except on the day of her entry
into the city; but from this day till her marriage the
people saw her daily in an open calèche, and the bright
nights prolonged the spectacle for the curious.

During the few days previous to the wedding Alexandra made her first temporary acquaintance with the
Winter Palace, which was only occasionally inhabited
during the fine summer days, and yet at this season the
view of the majestic Neva from the Palace, the Exchange, encompassed with columns, the golden tower of
the fortress, the bright green of the birch on the islands,
are unique in the world, and at night like Fairy-land.
The new Grand Duchess, however, was most surprised
by the gardens of the Winter Palace and the so-called
Hermitage, which, one storey high, rises to the level of
the other splendid halls and galleries. Here they dined
daily, surrounded by fine trees and flowers, and made

various promenades afterwards. One novel and enchanting picture replaced another; the bride felt not
only satisfied but proud, in the prospect of soon belonging wholly to a kingdom that welcomed her with so
much splendour and so much love. Her joy and delight
were beyond all bounds when, on the evening before
her marriage, she was surprised with gifts of pearls and
diamonds, to which the King's daughter had been as
unaccustomed as the most modest burgher family, for
we have already seen in what simplicity the good King
had brought up his daughter. As grand festivals are a
burden and a sacrifice to the Imperial family, they usually
assemble on the previous evening, when the gifts in honour both of name-days and birth-days are cordially presented. On this occasion also they all assembled at the
Empress-mother's. In addition to the members of the
family hitherto present the Grand Duke Constantine had
arrived from Warsaw; and some Prussian ladies of the
suite were also invited. The last evening was to be
spent in the Winter Palace, and on the ensuing one
Anitschkow was to throw open its doors. The circle
broke up early, out of consideration for the excitement
that awaited the bride on the ensuing day. When she
awoke next morning, the report of five cannons announced
to the city the eventful day, and the cloudless heavens
seemed to bestow their blessing on this union. The
Prussian ladies scattered red roses over the couch of the
bride, and the kind Mademoiselle Wildermett brought
her a nosegay of white roses, when, after being dressed,
she was conducted into what is called the diamond-
room, close to the bedroom of the Empress-mother;

there the lady of honour of the day decorated her with all the bridal jewels, placing on her shoulders a red velvet mantle bordered with ermine, and on her head a crown, and likewise such treasures of jewels, of every hue, that she was quite oppressed by their weight. To these gems, surpassing a kingdom in value, she added with her own hand only one white rose, the symbol of her life.

As she stood in all this splendour, so strange to her, a master of ceremonies announced the bridegroom, and from different sides, though at the same moment, both appeared in the hall of assembly, where the whole Imperial family greeted the illustrious couple. One-and-twenty cannon now proclaimed to the city that the grand pageant was about to set forth for the Court church. All the corridors and the rooms, from one end of the Palace, to the other where the church was, were filled by invited guests in full uniform, and even the ladies, on that occasion, were attired in the Russian national costume; but only privy councillors, grand dignitaries, and the diplomatic corps were permitted to enter the church itself. The procession was opened by Court *fouriers*, lords-in-waiting, chamberlains and masters of ceremonies, followed by the Emperor Alexander, with both the Empresses, and then came the bridal couple, and in their train a succession of royal personages. The superior clergy received their Majesties on their entrance into the church with the sacred cross and holy water, and the religious service commenced with the hymn, "*Domine fortitudine tua.*" At its close the Empress-mother conducted the bride and bridegroom

to an elevated dais prepared for them.   The ladies and
gentlemen present drew near.   The pomp and splendour
of the priests' vestments, the sublimity of the singing
executed by the celebrated Court choir, the odour of
incense, the striking decorations of the church, the distinguished assemblage, made a profound impression on
the strangers present.   The priest confers a benediction
on the betrothed, exhorting the bridegroom to shine
like the sun on his wife, and enforcing on the bride the
duty of obedience to her future husband.   Here rings
are exchanged.   The priest reminds the couple of the
patriarchal betrothal of Rebekah with Isaac, and implores the Lord to fortify this pair in faith, simplicity,
and truth.   Then follows the nuptial ceremony.   Bride
and bridegroom, with lighted candles in their hands,
follow the presbyter with the censer three times through
the nave of the church.   This progress represents their
path in life ; they are to follow the commands of the
Lord as they now follow the presbyter, and their good
works must ascend like incense to Heaven.   The choir
meanwhile sings, " Glory be to thee, O God !"   The
priest now appeals to the hearts of the betrothed once
more to vow mutual love and faith in the presence of
the whole assembled community, and, after having received their explicit assent, he confers on them the
blessing of the Holy Trinity.   Three long and solemn
prayers are said, in which an allusion is made to the
mysterious formation of the woman out of Adam's rib,
to their union in Paradise, a blessing which has thence
descended to all flesh.   He implores a similar divine
benediction on the young couple ; and also prays for

the preservation of their parents, who strengthen the foundations of a family. He then places crowns on the heads of the newly wedded pair, a sign that virgin chastity is crowned by Heaven, exclaiming, "Crown the servant and hand-maiden of God, in the name of the Trinity,—O Lord our God! crown them also with honour and renown!"

After this the priest fills a chalice with water and wine, and, blessing it, presents it to the newly-married couple; thus symbolizing that henceforth they are to drink out of one cup of joy and of sorrow, and mutually to bear the burden of life. He then joins their hands on his *epitrachalion* as a token of their indissoluble alliance, and leads them three times round the reading-desk while the choir sing a hymn. At the close of this solemn ceremony the presbyter removes the crowns from their heads, and says the following words:—"May you, O bridegroom! be reverenced like Abraham, and blessed like Isaac, and fruitful like Jacob; and may you, O bride! be beloved like Sarah, and comforted like Rebekah, and fruitful like Rachel!" The young couple bow their heads in all humility before God during the last prayer, which implores long life for them, and by desire of the priest they seal their alliance with a kiss. They then express their gratitude to their Majesties, and in the midst of a *Te Deum* and the firing of a hundred and one cannon, the stately procession returns in the same order to the Palace.

There is no church in the world where the marriage ceremony is more admirably performed than in that of Russia, and the rite we have described is precisely the same for the poorest person. The liturgy and the solemnities connected with it lasted three hours in the Court church. The young couple, in accordance with prescribed rules, fasted on this day till after the completion of divine service, the objects of more than ten thousand inquisitive eyes, and therefore could not be otherwise than exhausted in strength, and in a state of nervous excitement when they returned to their apartments. But even then they were not to rest; for a grand banquet was instantly held in the most spacious hall of the Winter Palace; to such feasts only three classes of the highest rank are invited, viz., adjutant-generals and imperial councillors, the senate and secretaries of state and privy councillors; and in addition those Court ladies who are adorned with the Order of Catherine.

From the galleries of the vast hall music resounded, while the spectators above, and on this occasion the Imperial family at one table, were served by the great dignitaries of the realm. In the midst of the thunder of cannon from the fortress, the first toast given was that of their Majesties and the King of Prussia; the second, the newly-married couple; and the third, the loyal subjects of the kingdom. After the banquet was over, there remained scarcely half-an-hour for rest to the assembled royal personages late in the afternoon, for at half-past eight o'clock another hall of the Palace was to be filled with the same guests, when the Imperial family, in pairs, walked formally several times round the hall to the music of a Polonaise, and an hour afterwards retired into their private apartments. About ten o'clock, in the

bright twilight of the North, the brilliant procession set
forth for the Palace of Anitschkow, to inaugurate it for
the young pair for whom it was destined.   The Emperor
Alexander and the Empress Elisabeth, escorted by
aides-de-camp and pages, had already preceded them.
Before the grand state entrance of the Winter Palace a
gilt carriage, drawn by eight horses, awaited them.   The
bride and bridegroom, conducted by their estimable
mother, were descending the spacious flight of stairs,
when suddenly a courier pressed forward to the Grand
Duchess and gave her a letter from Berlin, containing
the blessing of her father on this happy event.   Both
pressed the precious missive to their lips and hearts,
and hurried forward to their new abode.   For the first
time on this day they breathed fresh air, and enjoyed
the cool of evening in the singular soft light.   The
carriage was driven in slow and stately fashion, preceded by mounted Hussars of the Guard with drawn
sabres, and beside them the highest Court officials in
state uniforms, followed by the Horse Guards, and nine
equipages, containing the Court household and the suite
of the bride and bridegroom.   But all this splendour
was eclipsed by the hundreds of thousands crowding
the way from one palace to the other, all eager to see
the newly-wedded couple, expressing their good wishes
by loud hurrahs, and pressing round the gilt carriages
like the rushing waves of the sea round a vessel.   The
procession passed along the banks of the Neva, through
the largest and widest square in the city, and the
principal street, about two versts in width, to the
Anitschkow Palace, where the Emperor Alexander and

his consort Elisabeth received them with bread and salt. The same ladies of state as before divested the bride of her velvet and ermine mantle, her crown, and the oppressive burden of jewels, attiring her in bright pink gauze and Brussels lace. The day closed by a family supper, to which the Grand Duke invited his tutor, Count Lambsdorf, and the Grand Duchess her Prussian ladies and the excellent Mademoiselle Wildermett.

Thus was the first step accomplished in taking possession of a palace, which the young husband and wife inhabited for eight years, the happiest people in the world. The brightest day of their lives, although the most fatiguing one, had passed over solemnly but happily, the object of the distant journey was fulfilled, a new home was founded in a foreign land, and, after much harassing exertion, the hour of rest had come amid glorious scenery, and in full reliance on the love of him whom she had herself chosen three years before, for whose dear sake she had quitted her Fatherland, and to whom she had intrusted her whole existence in the most implicit confidence, and who never ceased to justify this confidence; for his whole life, public as well as private, proved to his people and to his wife that he was a true knight of noble nature. All the bells continued to peal for three successive days in the city, illuminated each evening by hundreds of thousands of lamps, and the people also did honour to the wedding in their own fashion by excursions in the vicinity of the town. In all the churches thanksgivings were offered up during divine service.

Next morning the Emperor Alexander came with

costly gifts that called forth much delight in the young
couple ; but both seemed to enjoy their greatest triumph
when they showed themselves first as husband and wife
in an open calèche, to pay their first visit to the two
Empresses. The populace from early morning besieged
the spacious court of the palace and the wide street, in
order to greet them with hurrahs. It was the same on
their first visit to the Winter Palace ; the Empress-
mother forthwith invited her children to a family feast,
with only the addition of old Princess Lieven and
the Prussian suite. After dinner Nicholas himself drove
with his young wife, through the town, pausing at
some of the finest points of view, always thickly beset
by the people. On the next day the bride and bridegroom received the congratulations of the highest civil
and military authorities, dined again on the same day
in the Winter Palace, and in the evening attended the
theatre in the Hermitage. This building, a continuation
of the Winter Palace, connected with it by arches and
covered arcades, is a museum of the fine arts, and the
furthest wing contains a small theatre, in which, once
on a time, comedies written by Catherine the Second
were performed.

Here that Empress used to appear divested of royal
purple and crown, but in the attractive aspect of the most
intellectual woman of her day, surrounded by a small
group of the *élite*, both native and foreign, who could
appreciate such a gem without the pomp of etiquette.
In Alexander's time it was chiefly the French, who
acted here before a limited and select audience ; the
public theatres at that time being rarely visited by the

Imperial family. The day after, a ball took place in the palace of the Empress-mother; on the fifth the illustrious assemblage dispersed to the different palaces, and the newly-married couple went to the Empress-mother at Pawlowsk, where Alexandra Feodorowna had passed the first night after her arrival. This country village lies a few versts farther than Zarskoe-Selò, but the gardens and the palace are widely different. A fine highway leads thither from the capital, but through a plain at that time boggy and uncultivated. After the oppressive splendours of Petersburg, the bride almost believed herself once more at home. All imperial pomp is here laid aside, and nature is not under military orders, as in Zarskoe-Selò. Trees and wild flowers of the field and the forest grow in freedom without any dread of the censure of the police. The gardens of the Zarskoe-Selò might be accosted as, " Your Imperial Highness ;" whereas, in the valley of Pawlowsk, we are embraced by artless nature. Even though the Palace, encompassed by verdure on every side, hidden almost as if in a wood, raises on high its cupola over the tops of the trees, it is very modest in its exterior. It was the country-seat of the Emperor Paul when Grand Duke, and subsequently celebrated as the abode of Maria Feodorowna, who never drove through the streets of Petersburg save with six horses, and lived here in summer divested of all pomp, as if in remembrance of Würtemberg. Just as she trained in various institutions thousands of young women for the kingdom, so here are thousands of roses surrounding a simple Swiss cottage, bearing the name

of the "Pavilion of Roses." Here she received her
third son, Nicholas, and his young bride, and herself
showed the latter the treasures contained in this unpretentious palace, and the beauties that a garden
can display even in the 60th degree of northern lati-
tude. Small lakes and rivulets alternately relieve the
obscurity of the forest, that stretches away from the
middle of the park.' Equally charming is a flowery
meadow, which enjoyed the cultivation of a loving
hand in addition to nature. A Swiss cottage with
pillars of birch, and a hermitage, offer coolness in
the heat, a ruin invites to reverie, a waterfall tempts
the listening ear. The Empress deplored the nightingales having ceased their songs before the arrival of her
daughter-in-law; but as a compensation she displayed
with pride her wealth of roses, which, once foreign
to this sky and this land, through her fostering care
bloomed in all the beauty and fragrancy of Germany
or France. After the most manifold diversity, a farm
is at last reached, so that the useful may be combined with the ornamental. And then come Russian
villages, with large corn-fields. The young couple
passed the first weeks of their marriage solely in the
enjoyment of golden freedom, and revelled in luxuriant
nature, under the protection of a mother's eye. The
Emperor Alexander inhabited the adjacent Zarskoe-
Seló, and, as often as time permitted, drove in a one-
horse droschky to Pawlowsk, to kiss the hand of his
venerated mother. The palace of that little town stands
higher than Pawlowsk, and this part of the country was
chosen by Peter the Great for a chateau. He planted

with his own hands fine maple-trees, which, like all
culture in his day, had hitherto been unknown to the
soil. The garden and palace have something majestic
in their aspect, whereas Pawlowsk is simply rural. The
palace makes a singular impression on those strangers
who view it on bright summer nights; its interminable
façade shining forth from under a green roof with gilt
spires, the grand front court leading to it, the majestic
stillness and solitude in the *chiaro-oscuro* of a blue and
starless sky,—all this transports the pilgrim into a
magic world. In this palace, the centre hall of which
is as lofty and spacious as a church, Alexander lived in
two plainly-furnished rooms, through the windows of
which a fragrant avenue of lime-trees cast their sha-
dows. It is the same alley where, in former days, his
grandmother, the Empress Catherine, used to walk,
leaning on her stick, with her greyhound, and where
she preserved a rose for her daughter. To the right and
left lie the other apartments, in all the pomp of amber,
porphyry pillars, marbles, Gobelin tapestry. A side
wing that Catherine particularly preferred, is furnished
entirely in the Chinese fashion. Alexander contented
himself with two rooms, which in no respect recalled an
imperial palace. He received the young couple here at
a banquet, and conducted Alexandra himself through
the quiet, unoccupied gardens, the keeping up and
dressing of which costs the Court large sums, and is
therefore unpopular with the public. The young pair
felt great love for Pawlowsk, the Empress-mother having shown greater gentleness towards them than was
her usual habit. The Court that surrounded them

was small. It consisted of the two aides-de-camp of
the Grand Duke, Adlerberg and Baron Frederichs—
the latter married to a youthful friend of Alexandra's,
Cecilia by name; two maids of honour, Countess
Schuwalof, and Mademoiselle von Uschakof, the Grand
Chamberlain, Kyrill Narischkln, and the Prussian suite.
Prince William especially attracted the attention and
won the liking of the old Empress, and one difference
between his training and that of her own sons and
daughters could not escape her. Prince William was
easy and active in all his movements, natural in his
intercourse with society, youthful joyousness animating his whole being, without causing him to lay aside
the dignity of a prince; whereas it was difficult, nay
impossible, for Nicholas and Michael, even in the
most intimate circle, to descend from their imperial
eminence, and to assume that genial tone which everywhere calls forth sympathy. In both the sons, indeed,
their mother's dignified, though rather formal, demeanour
was reflected. She, however, felt on her part how unsuitable ancient etiquette was to the present day, and
did not attempt to force it on her daughter-in-law.
She at once perceived that the unassuming and natural
graces of Alexandra, her frank mode of conversing,
her happy expression of countenance, won universal
approval even from the most fastidious and punc-
tilious circles, and that she thus brought forward to
the light the reserved spirit of her young husband.
It was not to be denied that the youthful bride,
during the first fortnight of her stay at Pawlowsk,
called forth a pleasing social tone, and that the old

Empress herself was so charmed with her that henceforth she was designated as the "darling" of the
Empress-mother. This small circle enjoyed the amusements of playing, dancing, driving, and walking, which
strict Court etiquette had hitherto prohibited. They
dined and supped where they pleased, and in different
parts of the gardens, which they rambled through on
foot afterwards, seeming thus to make up for what they
had been deprived of by the strict discipline of their
childhood; and every one of the family participated in
this môde of life, even the Emperor Alexander and his
sedate Empress. The blessings of peace, too, after so
much strife, were deeply felt by all.

An accident, however, disturbed for a few days the
gay spirit of the society. Prince William was bitten
by a chained mastiff, and, as no one could say what
the consequences might be, the wound was cauterized.
He submitted to this operation with a degree of coolness that caused the Empress-mother to exclaim, "No
wonder! he is a Prussian prince!" His absence was in
the meantime supplied by the arrival of Prince Radziwill, sent by King Frederick William III. as the bearer
of his congratulations to his daughter. This prince,
renowned as the most refined man of his time, and the
Mæcenas of the Berlin of that day, maintained in this
gay circle the same tone and deportment that had made
him the centre of aristocratic social life in Berlin. The
husband of a Prussian princess (sister of Prince Louis
Ferdinand), master of a large property, an accomplished
musician, his demeanour was distinguished by those easy
and high-bred manners in which the Slavonic races un-

doubtedly excel Germans. The society listened with
delight to the strains of his violoncello.

Thus passed a couple of weeks, which tended to heal
the first wounds of home-regrets for Alexandra, rendering her husband and his family daily dearer to her, and
obtaining for herself in these new circles not only a
secure, but an independent position. They proceeded
to visit the various country-seats by the sea ; Strelna,
Peterhof, and Oranienbaum, which, notwithstanding their
fine situation and splendours, were very little frequented
in Alexander's time. Although Potsdam by its fine ex-
panse of water, as well as by its monuments and grand
growth of trees, surpasses the Russian country places
we have already described, it must yield to those in
question ; as all three command an extensive view
over the Gulf of Finland and the city of Cronstadt, that
seems with its ships to swim in the water, and also
of the coast of Finland and the golden towers of the
capitol. The sea always offers fresh beauties to the
inhabitants of an inland country, and the spacious
watery mirror between Petersburg and Cronstadt fas-
cinates by its smooth surface and repose even those who
have seen the splendours of the ocean in the south.
Nicholas drove with his wife in an open calèche, from
Strelna to Peterhof, on a road parallel to the sea, occasionally hidden behind trees, and suddenly reappear-
ing. Alexandra exulted loudly at sight of such picturesque objects ; but greatest of all was her surprise
when, after a long drive through dark avenues of trees,
the carriage at last suddenly drew up before the exciting spectacle of a hundred fountains, in the spray of

VOL. I.   G

which every colour of the rainbow was reflected, emit-
ting wonderful coolness in the blazing heat of mid-
day. Above these water-works rises the palace on
a gentle elevation, commanding a view over the sea;
and in the rear lies a small but richly-cultivated garden,
which, by its ancient limes, elder-trees, and fantastic
figures on the fountains, transplants the beholder into
another land. Alexander celebrated his mother's name-
day in this palace on the 22d July, and it was the
more brilliant this year, the same day (August 3d), being,
according to the Romish calendar, also the birth-day of
the King of Prussia. A very ill-constructed road at
that time led from the capital to the site of this grand
fête, and the insignificant little town could not even
supply an inn to the public who took part in the
gaieties. Alexandra was deeply moved by celebrating
these two festivals in one day, and, in spite of all the
splendour that encompassed her, her heart was divided
between her former and present home. She commemorated her father's birth-day for the first time at a distance of more than three hundred miles from him. A
few days afterwards the whole Court adjourned to
Oranienbaum, where a display of fireworks welcomed
them.

The most novel and singular spectacle of all awaited
the bride in Cronstadt, where the Czar, attended by
his Court, reviewed the fleet. Alexandra learned both
to know and to revere the Empress-mother in Pawlowsk, and in those latter days she became more inti-
mately acquainted with the Emperor Alexander. She
first saw him in Berlin when a child of seven, but re-

peatedly since that time ; and with him was connected,
in her mind, the image of the greatest hero of his time,
and also that of her father's friend. Alexander, by
his inimitable courtesy, his chivalrous appearance, the
charm of his conversation, and his invariable goodness
of heart, was the *beau-idéal* of all ladies. Alexandra
thought the reverence in which he was held by all the
world fully justified.

In those days he disclosed the magic charm of his
nature; and all who approached him left him with
bright faces. Whether he appeared at the head of
his troops, in a brilliant *salon*, or in a small family
circle, everywhere he was felt to be imposing by those
around him. No one understood the disposition of his
sister-in-law so well as the Emperor, and he could, of
course, better than his mother or brothers, sympathize
with any *foreign element*; by his education, his intercourse with strangers, and his long stay in other countries. He became her friend in the noblest sense of the
word. The Court, in the beginning of August, returned
to Zarskoe and Pawlowsk, Nicholas and Alexandra,
with their small retinue, residing at the latter, with the
Empress-mother.

The young bride having thus made acquaintance
with the capital and its royal palaces, was now to
pay a visit with her husband to the ancient city of
Moscow. It was the intention of the whole Court
to pass the next winter in this metropolis, which
had arisen from its ashes so rapidly, and in greater
beauty than ever, and already busy preparations were
made for the journey. In the month of August night

quickly falls round Petersburg, the town is lit up
from eight o'clock at night, and a cold damp atmosphere
compels the inmates of Zarskoe-Selò and Pawlowsk to
forsake their gardens for· their town dwellings. The
little Court circle, however, persevered in their infor-
mal cheerful ways, now become a custom with them
in the *salons* of the palace. Prince Radziwill sometimes played on the violoncello, and Nicholas on the
trumpet.   On some evenings charades, or *tableaux
vivants*, enlivened the lengthening evenings, and, most
frequently of all, a merry dance, in which the fair bride
invariably excited the utmost admiration by· her extreme
grace.   An incident occurred, however, which, even
before the journey to Moscow, changed the character
of these social pleasures.   One day during mass Alexandra dropped down suddenly, and her husband carried her in his arms, breathless and senseless, into
an adjacent room, where she did not recover consciousness for ten minutes.   It was the first certain indication of her being likely to become a mother, so universal
joy succeeded the first alarm.   The whole company
quitted the church with her.

The reader has as yet made only a passing acquaintance with the Court and its country residences. Hitherto
it has been impossible to cast a glance on the society of
the capital and the kingdom, and on their connection with
the Imperial family and the Court.   More than in any
other land, the Russian Court since Peter the First has
been filled with persons of its own selection to enjoy its
confidence. Birth alone in Russia, since the Czars Feodor
and Alexiewitch, no longer confers the same privileges as

in the rest of Europe, and especially in the petty States of Germany.   The Russian nation at that time, like all Europe, was divided into nobility and burghers, free peasants and serfs; but not one of these entirely corresponds with this definition in other countries.   Burgher life at that period was very little represented in towns, and Alexander the First was therefore astonished at perceiving that the inhabitants of all European cities were composed almost exclusively of citizens, and that no "black people" (as the lowest class is called in Russia) were to be seen.   The numerous nobility in Russia are divided into personal and hereditary ranks, but the latter attain their greater privileges in no way through birth alone, but by their position in the State, and by individual services, promoting them to a more elevated rank and class of society.   Those who have not reached a high dignity in military or state service enjoy little respect, and those who have not served at all are almost despised.   Hereditary nobility without military or state precedence had at that time only one privilege, the possession of land and people; the position of the nobility at Court, and the right to be received there, certainly depends on the possession of the most illustrious rank, and so do all the highest offices at Court.   We remark, therefore, in Petersburg wonderfully strenuous efforts on the part of all servants of the State to attain advancement in rank, till at last the very highest is reached, so that they may draw nearer the Court.   Thus it is that, in the vicinity of the Imperial family, in addition to some of the most ancient and renowned names, many others are met with elevated solely by their talents and services. In the first half of Alexander's reign, we find his most confidential adviser and friend, the most influential man in the whole kingdom, to be the son of a poor village pastor, Michael Speransky; and in the second half of the same reign, General Araktscheef, raised to the dignity of Count, the son of an indigent major, and coupled with such men as Prince Galitzin, and Counts Kotschubei, and Strogonoff.

The society of the capital numbered at that time in its ranks a succession of families, who by their enormous wealth and the display of splendour in their palaces, were only to be equalled in England, or in republican ancient Rome, in the days of a Lucullus or a Crassus. To every large private palace belonged a church and choir, as one of its constitutional parts, and often an orchestra, consisting of serfs. The palaces themselves were furnished in a regal manner. In the ancient Roman spirit, he alone was esteemed rich who could not precisely count the number of his people or his estates, and could raise, arm, and clothe an army corps, consisting of the peasants on his property, and maintain it for a considerable time. Many of these palaces were adorned with picture galleries and other objects of art, which would have been considered treasures sufficient for German capitals such as at Stuttgardt, Hanover, and Darmstadt.

The domestic servants in such establishments amounted to hundreds, from the meanest stove and lamp-lighter up to the best trained valets, who could speak many different languages. Not only was a public table always kept, where uninvited guests were welcomed, but large sums were yearly contributed to certain fêtes, repeated at intervals, and attended not by hundreds, but by thousands. Russian hospitality such as this is greatly wanting in the rest of Europe.

Up to the time of Peter the Great, princely titles were only held by those families who could prove their descent from Rurik, and consequently vie with all other European families in the antiquity of their nobility. To the best known of this class belong the names of Odojewsky, Dolgorucki, Gortschakof, Barjatinsky, Obolensky, Wjasemsky, Labanof, Gagarin, Wolkonsky. Other princely families derive their origin from Ghedimin, the ruler of Lithuania, ancestor of the Polish Jagellons, and of these are the Galitzins, Kurakins, and Trubetzkois. Others are of foreign extraction, and trace their descent from Poland, the Caucasus, and even from the Khanate of Tartary. Till the reign of Peter the First the Czars appointed these princes and nobles to the highest Court and State charges, under the name of Boyars. This title by degrees disappeared in the eighteenth century, from the time that Peter began to confer on the men by whom he was surrounded the titles of princes, counts, and barons; the two latter being hitherto unknown to the Russians. The name of Boyar is now chiefly applied to any man of high degree whose house is kept up in the princely splendour of old times, even though not in the enjoyment of a title; for the great wealth we have alluded to is not always to be found among the princes of Rurik's race, and seldom descends through several generations. Since Peter's day the Court bankers all bear the title of Baron. One of these, in the time of Catherine, wrote as a motto over his door—" War feeds us, peace starves us."

The Court of Alexandra consisted of one Lady of State, Princess Wolkonsky. This office in Russia somewhat resembles that of a Mistress of the Robes; she wears on her breast as her badge the portrait of the Empress, set in brilliants. The two maids of honour were Countess Schuwaloff and Mademoiselle von Uschakof; besides these the suite consisted of Count Zacharias Tschernischew, two chamberlains, and one equerry; and also the Count Marshal Narischkin, of whom we shall speak more in detail in the next chapter. The aides-de-camp of Nicholas were Colonel von Adlerberg, who stood faithfully by his side from his youth to his death, and Baron Frederichs, married to a youthful playmate of Alexandra, Countess Gurowsky; we retain the name of " my friend Cecilia," for this lady was always so designated by Alexandra herself. With the exception of the above-named persons, very few had any intimate relations with the Grand Ducal family; of this number were the subsequent Field-Marshal Paskiewitch, Count Basil Perowsky, Count Orlof, and the poet Joukowsky.

CHAPTER IV.

MOSCOW.

THE stately Anitschkow Palace could not boast of harbouring for any length of time its Imperial guests. They passed a few days there after their marriage, and then quitted it for two months, subsequently returning for only a couple of nights to bid farewell to it for a long period. It was not only the preparations for the journey that induced the family to go there, but their desire to show themselves once more to the city and the public. The greater part of the society were invited to a masquerade, at which the Empress-mother appeared as a sorceress, the Empress Elisabeth as a bat, the Grand Duchess Alexandra as an Indian Prince; all the others were in masks chosen by themselves. Shortly afterwards, on the 18th September, the Court left Petersburg, in order to repair to Moscow by slow short stages, and in different divisions. The transference of the Court from the Neva to Moscow requires such an enormous number of horses that they cannot all be supplied at once, on which account the Imperial family travel in separate parties. The condition of Alexandra too required particular care, and on her account they were twelve days on the journey. The Empress Catherine, under similar circumstances, is said to have taken six weeks. The Court also avoids making their entry in any great pomp, but arrive quietly towards evening, without previous notice, and forthwith repair to the Kremlin.

The greater is the surprise next morning to one who views the city for the first time from the Kremlin, which includes within its circumference of six German miles several hundred churches, large and small, and as many palaces and gardens. Innumerable cupolas glitter in the most varied and lively colours, gold and silver, blue and red, while the motley roofs, by their diversity and the variety of individual objects, from the splendours of princely palaces to the poorest huts, cause Moscow to be esteemed the capital and national city of this colossal kingdom. Here, as in ancient Rome, families live in all the affluence of a Crœsus, in contact with the poverty of the original inhabitants of the Steppes, and yet in perfect good fellowship. The sight of this magnificence was the more surprising in those years, as the city had been rebuilt in a short time, and arisen out of its ashes as if by magic. For in the great conflagration of 1812, 14,800 houses became in a few days a prey to the flames, Napoleon's bold arrogance imagining that the narrow-souled egotism of Western Europe, particularly that of the French, had completely stifled in the Slavonic race all ideas of self-sacrifice. Alexandra, astonished and touched, stood long at the window sunk in a reverie, and could not tear herself away from the marvellous sight. The extensive inner space of the Kremlin had been crowded

since early morning, in order to see the Imperial
family, who proceeded from their modest abode amid
the ringing of bells, across the square into the churches
that adorn the Kremlin itself, which, like the Acropolis
of the ancients, is dedicated exclusively to God and the
Czar, and contains only churches, cloisters, and palaces.
Here is the church of the Ascension of the Virgin,
with its five golden cupolas, a work of the fifteenth
century, executed by a Bolognese architect, specially
devoted to the coronation of the Emperor. The walls
of the interior are decorated with rich colours, on a gold
ground; close by the entrance is the picture of our
blessed Saviour, by the Greek Emperor Manuel, at all
events taken from the Sophia Church in Constantinople in the sixteenth century; and likewise a picture
of the Virgin Mary, adorned with the most precious
stones, from the hand of the Evangelist St. Luke, an
object of the deepest reverence to the Russians; this
church is the receptacle of the holiest relics. Here
also stands the throne of the Emperor, the deserted
seat of the Patriarchs, and the graves of the most
ancient priests of the Russian Church, and that of
the Metropolitan of Moscow. Close beside it stands
forth in all its pomp the church of the Archangel
Michael, containing many sacred treasures; the tombs
of the Grand Dukes and Czars, from the thirteenth
to the seventeenth century, make this edifice a Russian
St. Denis. Instead of any more churches, we must
describe the great Bell Tower, called Iwan Weliki. It
stands alone, beside the churches we have mentioned,
in the centre of the Kremlin, and, with its golden

cupola, forms the highest object in the whole town, sur-
mounting it as a crown does the head it adorns.   The
colossal cross on the cupola glitters before all those who
approach from every part of the world, like the spire at
Athens on the Acropolis.   Iwan Weliki is the largest
bell in Europe, and peals forth only three times a year.

At that time the Imperial family inhabited an unpretending house in the midst of churches and treasures,
and thence repaired bareheaded along a path spread
with carpets, to the shrines of the different churches.
The spacious square seemed paved with heads, so great
was the crowd ; but when all the thousand bells in the
city rung out, and hundreds of thousands of people
broke out into hurrahs, it was like being in the midst
of the waves of a stormy and agitated sea.   The visits
of the Imperial family are specially to the saints and
martyrs, whom they greet by genuflexions.

Nicholas employed the first day in showing Alexandra the city, which, under this new aspect, was
strange even to himself.   The enthusiasm of the inhabitants is greater here, and more ardent than in
Petersburg, where they are accustomed to the daily
sight of the Court.   During these drives through this
interminable city, all eyes were directed to the liberator
of Europe—Alexander, and then to his youthful sister-
in-law, whose attractions surpassed all their expectations.   But the city did not offer many sources of
amusement to those accustomed to Europe ; the society
is much more proud and aristocratic than that of Petersburg, and though cordial, still formal as of old.   The most
distinguished families are frequently not in favour at

Court, and therefore resort to distant Moscow. One glance at a crowded assembly leads to the conviction that we are in another part of Russia, and far away from Petersburg.. The Court had various reasons for passing this winter quietly in Moscow. The wounds inflicted by conflagration and war were not yet healed, the damage to the city alone was reckoned at 200 millions of rubles; but in spite of this, the people were cheerful, because their sanctuary, the Kremlin, and their churches were saved. The news of the death of a brother of the Empress-mother placed the Court in mourning. Both Court and city therefore spent the months of October and November in the utmost retirement; Alexandra being the most secluded of all, for the visit to the Cathedral and the many genuflexions had fatigued her much, and the climate also necessitated great precautions, and yet the days passed very quickly, for she now began to collect her thoughts, and to occupy herself in earnest. In latter years, in Berlin, she had made more intimate acquaintance with the literature of her own country, which was, however, subsequently interrupted; one portion of the day was therefore again dedicated to the humoristic Jean Paul, who especially fascinated the youthful hearts of that day, and continued an object of peculiar admiration to Alexandra through life. But she devoted herself with still greater eagerness to learning the Russian language, under the guidance of Joukowsky. This poet, already renowned in his own nation, at that time entered more into lively conversations about Russia with Alexandra than into the regular study of

grammar, his illustrious pupil inspiring him with as
much interest in German literature as she felt for that
of Russia. Joukowsky's nature was simple and kindly,
shy as a girl, and his benevolence boundless; not
animated in intercourse with others, on the contrary,
absent and embarrassed; but his profound intellect
quickly displayed its superiority, especially in circles
with a kindred spirit, and free from the more recent
and artificial polish of the Court. Joukowsky was
the first who frequented the Court to discover the
eminent feminine qualities of Alexandra, and through
all ensuing years she continued the *beau-idéal* of this
poet. The day having passed in earnest but quiet
occupations, the small social circle assembled in the
evening in Alexandra's boudoir, that could not con-
tain more than a dozen people. The Emperor Alexander and the two Empresses seldom if ever appeared;
and therefore that free and unconstrained tone pervaded the little court which subsequently so highly
distinguished the Winter Palace in Nicholas's day
from all other European Courts. Instead of the stiff
etiquette of the Empress-mother, the most refined and
easy demeanour prevailed here; the most serious conversations, as well as the most playful jests and innocent
jeux de société, were carried on in the same good taste,
and made the evenings pass rapidly and pleasantly.
Among the few new members gradually attracted into
this small circle, particular mention must be made of
Countess Alexiewina Orlof, daughter of the great conqueror of Turkey. She was scarcely ten years old when
she came to the Court of Catherine the Second, but

although sole heiress to a prodigious fortune, and the richest bride in Russia, she refused all matrimonial overtures, and her great wealth was destined for the cloister. This lady felt a peculiar regard for Alexandra, perfectly understood her position, and showed her the most sincere friendship, enlivening the evening circle by anecdotes of earlier times. Princess Sophie Trubetzkoi assumed the second place, a German by birth, and of less illustrious descent than Countess Orlof; her disposition was gayer and more lively, and her conversation charming; being of the same age as Alexandra, she thought herself entitled to be intimate with her. A third lady was Frau von Kutusow, whose husband formerly accompanied Nicholas on his journey to England.

On Sundays the whole family assembled at the table of the Empress-mother, but in the most strict etiquette, long dresses and brilliant coiffures, and in the evening a succession of guests made their appearance; senators, retired generals, and many belonging to the time of Paul and Catherine; Alexandra now first learned fully to appreciate the freedom of her own home. Here also she saw the two men who at the time almost exclusively attended the Emperor Alexander; Count Araktscheef, and Prince Golitzin. The former, a man devoid of all European culture, and though highly prized and promoted by Alexander, hated and feared by the whole nation; in spite of his great wealth, he lived in an insignificant wooden house, in the old Russian style, but was devoted body and soul to the Emperor, an unwearied worker, and inexorably strict in carrying out any plans intrusted to him. His attachment to his master bordered on idolatry, and was the surest arrow in his quiver. Notwithstanding Imperial favour, his society was avoided by all, so he found his companions in circles that had not yet attained more noble views in a higher mode of life. Alexandra only saw him on those Sunday evenings when the Empress assembled her Court, according to their rank, treating them with the most uncompromising etiquette. Prince Alexander Nikolajewitsch Golitzin was of a very different nature; reared in the Court of the Empress Catherine, he had become the most refined and finished courtier, and by his animated conversation and noble deportment caused his ugliness to be forgotten. He was a friend of Alexander's from his earliest youth, which they had passed together, and although anything but a Stoic in those years, indeed rather an Epicurean under the mantle of Aristippus, he now practised the most ascetic piety. His influence over the Emperor was greater than that of Count Araktscheef, and to him in particular is ascribed the alteration in the tendencies of Alexander in the latter years of his life.

Thus passed the winter months in entire rest, so requisite for Alexandra, disturbed, however, by two incidents. Towards Christmas Prince William and the Prussian suite returned to Berlin, and thus Alexandra was left without any home element in a foreign country. The stay of this Prince for six months had not only been very cheering to her, but also encouraged the pleasant and unreserved tone of society which began to prevail in the little court. The parting

was painful, and Alexandra for the first time became
sensible of all the difficulty of her task; but she also
felt that the reverence and love of her husband every
day increased, that her nature met with more response,
and that she had already become strongly attached to
her new country and its customs. Nicholas counted
the minutes when he was obliged to be separated from
his wife, and both their hearts were more and more in
unison. One more change occurred in the little Court
at that time. The Grand Chamberlain, Kyrill Narischkin, was rather too dictatorial to the young couple in
virtue of his office, and, moreover, somewhat equivocal
in his conduct; he took the liberty to make remarks
unfavourable to Alexandra to her husband, and against
the latter to his young wife, which almost implied the
wish to undermine their mutual confidence, nay, even
to inspire mutual hostility. The Narischkin family are
held in the highest estimation in Russia, the mother
of Peter the Great having been a Narischkin. They
steadily refused all advancement in rank, and every
other patent of nobility, their pride fully satisfied by
being entitled to claim kinship with the mother of Peter
the Great. Their names, however, are to be met with
in the highest offices of Court and State, as, for example,
Chamberlain Narischkin at Alexandra's Court, renowned
for his wit, and father of the Kyrill Narischkin we have
already alluded to. His wife, the Princess Labanof,
one of the most attractive women of the Russia of that
day, never succeeded in controlling the violent passions
of her husband. Nicholas and his wife, feeling their
domestic peace disturbed by the tyrannical whims of one

of the officials of their Court, agreed to dismiss him. At first the youthful Alexandra was reproached with being capricious and impatient; but this opinion very soon changed, and the ensuing three-and-forty years amply proved to the world her indulgence and goodness towards her retinue. The vacant post was conferred on Count Modène, who continued to enjoy the confidence of both for many long years.

The feast of Christmas is, in Germany, the greatest of all, celebrated by special social and kindly family meetings, as well as the holy Christmas Eve, when both children and the poor are provided with gifts; but the festival passes very quietly in Russia, where Easter is considered a much greater church and national commemoration. Alexandra resolved to light up a home Christmas-tree in her little circle; its charm, however, was not then so well understood as in after years, when merry children played round it; she never gave up this German custom, and in succeeding years the Christmas-tree became as familiar in Petersburg as in German towns, and also Christmas displays, just as with us; indeed, the whole Court latterly assembled in the Winter Palace, in order to witness the little fête. As this season was devoid of all tumultuous gaiety, these cheerful domestic pleasures were a desirable change, transporting back Alexandra and the two Empresses to their homes, and the days of their childhood. The good city of Moscow also participated for the next two months in the quiet life of the Court, although, as we shall presently show, the two capitals usually display their most brilliant social life in January and February.

Nicholas now passed the evenings quite alone with his
wife, reading to her the novels of Walter Scott, which
from his intimate acquaintance with England and Scot-
land, particularly interested him. And thus time crept
on imperceptibly to the still more secluded and trying
period of Lent, which Alexandra spent chiefly at home,
as her delicate condition required the utmost cir-
cumspection. The preparations for Lent begin fully
three weeks previously; on the first Sunday is read the
parable of the Publican and the Pharisee, on the second
that of the Prodigal Son, on the third the Last Judgment,
and finally the Sin of Adam and Eve. Homilies about
the Day of Judgment continue all through the "butter[1]
week," and yet this is the most frolicsome of the whole
year. The Russians ascribe these turbulent festivities
to foreign influence, as they recall the carnival of Catholic
countries. In any Protestant land masked balls alone
are given at this time, and they occupy only the evenings,
whereas in Petersburg, during this week, the theatre is
open twice a day, and in the same way everything prohibited during the seven following weeks is enjoyed to
the uttermost. Before Peter's reforms, the "butter
week" was celebrated in a very different manner in
Moscow, the residence of the Czar. People paid each
other visits, mutually asking forgiveness, and taking
leave of each other till Lent was over. The contrast
between the last Sunday of the "butter week" and
the first Sunday of Lent is very striking. After the
most uproarious tumult in the streets, with the twelfth

[1] The week before Lent—the last in which meat and butter are eaten in
Russia; celebrated by great revels in eating and drinking.

stroke of the clock the most death-like silence prevails, and in the ensuing days as many brilliant equipages surround the churches as previously the theatre. Morning and evening prayers during Lent are distinguished by supplications and hymns of great sublimity. A penitential Canon of Andreas, Archbishop of Crete, dating from the beginning of the eighth century, is read in the first and fifth week. The hymns connected with it are deeply affecting; the heart of a Christian David being manifest in them. But during the whole time portions of the Bible, taken from the Old Testament, are read morning and evening, from the Books of Moses, and all through the Prophets. On Wednesday, when a vast throng of people assemble in the churches for the Liturgy, the account of the creation of our first parents is read, and on Friday their banishment from Paradise. On the first Sunday in Lent the orthodox are exhorted to commemorate the restoration of the holy pictures in Constantinople by the Patriarch Methodius, under the protection of the Empress Theodora. The remembrance of this great event is celebrated by prayers for the dead and living followers of the orthodox faith, and an anathema is also fulminated against all those who dare to attack the grounds of the true belief. The latter, however, has never at any period roused any fanatic zeal in the kindly nature of the people. The orthodox believer returns in a pious mood, and shows the same fidelity as before to his Master, whether Catholic or Protestant. The Church itself quotes the words of the apostle Paul, who says, " But though we or an angel from heaven preach any other gospel to you than that which we have preached to you, let him be accursed" (Galatians i. 8.) This first week is in every respect the quietest; many families attend the Holy Communion, and social intercourse ceases. In the second week, however, concerts begin again, and the brilliant *salons* are once more opened to smaller or larger circles, but not for dancing. The first Sunday commemorates the triumph of the Church over the Iconoclasts, while the second refers to St. Gregory, Archbishop of Thessalonica, who gained a similar victory over heretics. The next Sunday, and the ensuing fourth week, are devoted to the adoration of the Cross. The Church says, " The holy cross is to be planted in the middle of the toilsome path that pilgrims must traverse during Lent, for refreshment and rest, so that they may collect fresh strength for the second half." At the hymn " Holy Lord," the presbyter comes forth from the sanctuary, bearing the cross on his head; the deacon precedes him with a censer. The cross is decorated with flowers, to signify that the crown of thorns of our blessed Saviour blossoms with roses and lilies for believers. The presbyter at last lays it down flat in the centre of the church on the Analogicon, when he and the whole congregation fall on their knees, exclaiming, " O Lord, we honour Thy cross and glorify Thy resurrection." When the cross is once more uplifted, the congregation rise, and all nations are called on to adore it. The fourth Sunday is devoted to the memory of the hermit St. John, who lived till ninety years of age on Mount Sinai, and has left a sacred didactic poem called the " Klimax " (the ladder). On

the fifth Sunday Mary of Egypt is brought to remembrance, as a proof that by penitence and the grace of
God, even the greatest sinner may attain spiritual
perfection. The sixth week is a pause of rest, after
such severe fatigues; Lazarus Saturday and Palm
Sunday are also kept as festivals, when the city is
more thronged; and in celebration of the latter, the
first-fruits of the northern spring, willow catkins, are
exposed for sale in the market-place; the Friday of
that week is the last of concerts or society: all the
portions of the Bible read during this week are connected
with the advent of Christ.

Passion Week is celebrated by sublime singing and
significant types: each day corresponding with one of
Jesu's last days on earth. In the three first days the
four Gospels are read; the whole life of our Saviour,
even before his sacrifice, is commended to our devotion;
on the Thursday the Gospel on the institution of our
Lord's Supper, and the Prophecies of Isaiah concerning the sufferings of Christ, are read. When a bishop
holds the solemn service of Maundy Thursday he closes
the recital of the Holy Communion, after the Liturgy,
by a washing of feet. Surrounded by twelve priests in
the middle of the church, he divests himself of his
bishop's robes, pours water into a basin, and proceeds to
wash their feet. He then stands up again and says to
the priests, " For I have given you an example, that ye
should do as I have done to you." Good Friday, by the
singing and other church ceremonies, is the most profoundly affecting of all; but the streets are meanwhile
swarming with stirring life, as all are busily preparing

for Easter Sunday. The first week of Easter, therefore, deserves the name of "the silent week" far more than the last.

The sufferings of our Saviour are recited in twelve portions, taken from the Gospels. The Liturgy is not read on this day, not only owing to the state of contrition and grief of the Church, but also because the sacrifice once offered up by our Redeemer on Golgotha includes in itself the sacrifices of all altars. While the choir sings, " He hangs on the cross to-day, who set the earth above the sea," the Crucified One is heard saying, " What have I done unto thee, my people ?" and when at length the ninth hour is come, the bishop, escorted by his clergy, fills the church with incense, in remembrance of the spices with which Joseph of Arimathea anointed the Divine body. He then carries on his head from the communion-table the cloth, on which the entombment is painted, to the centre of the church —this spot representing the holy sepulchre till the hour of the resurrection. The faithful, however, follow the bishop, as the women followed Joseph, to see where the Lord lay. The day closes with a soft choral hymn.

The Saturday before Easter is called by the Church the "forerunner of the Passover." The whole day passes in mysterious expectation. Christ in his sepulchre in the centre of the church; the priests in black robes surrounding it; the holy doors, however, are open to receive the risen from the dead. The devout congregation hold lighted tapers in their hands, which diffuse a peculiar light; funeral chants alternate with

resurrection hymns. At the ninth ode, the Son calls
out of the grave to his mother, "Weep not, oh mother!
for I shall rise again in glory." In the evening the pall
is solemnly escorted with banners carried round the
church, signifying that the Lord shall yet conquer. It
is then borne back through the holy doors, and once
more laid on the bier. The Liturgy is given in the
evening, so that it concludes an hour after sunset.
The Sabbath closes with the reading of four portions of
the New, and four of the Old Testament, all referring to
the approaching resurrection, and exactly at midnight
begins the great day of redemption. Just as the first
rays of the sun glance on the highest summits of the
mountains before rejoicing the whole earth, so does the
mysterious light of the resurrection first shine on the
vestments of the priest highest in dignity, on whom,
being in closer contact with the Godhead, it is shed
before the others; suddenly his black robes are changed
into dazzling white ones, and also the coverings of
the altar and the communion-table. Four sub-deacons
in brilliant vestments come like the angels to relieve
the watch, to remove the pall, and to await the women
bearing spices. Another deacon now advances from the
sanctuary, and proclaims the resurrection of our Lord.
A splendour of light has meanwhile spread through the
church, and the same deacon announces the arrival of
women bringing spices to the empty tomb, their meeting
with the angels, and with Jesus himself. The close of
the Sabbath is also the commencement of the "Easter
Passover." No believer leaves the church; all are inspired with the wish to anticipate the bearers of the

myrrh, and with the angel to roll away the stone from the tomb. At the eleventh stroke of the clock the song within the sanctuary begins thus, " The angels in heaven sing the glory of Thy resurrection," while the priests walk round the church with the cross and with banners, singing amid the gloom, " We too do homage to Thy glory." The church is now forsaken by the congregation, who have followed the choir. Meanwhile from within the song bursts forth, " Christ is risen !" But at this first cry the door is not thrown open. The same cry is repeated during the singing of the psalms. At length the priest of the highest rank takes up the crucifix in one hand and the censer in the other, and swinging the latter, makes the sign of the cross before the closed door of the temple, which is at length thrown open. The entrance into the illuminated church out of gloomy midnight typifies the ascent of our Redeemer from the night of the grave into the heights of the bright heavens. The entire congregation now press forward through the church towards the sepulchre, that remains open the whole of the ensuing week. Thousands of voices in holy enthusiasm proceed vehemently to sing the enchanting hymn, " Oh ! glad day of the resurrection ; let us embrace each other, let us be brothers, let us forgive our enemies, for Christ is risen !" The mourning pall remains forty days on the same spot, as a sign that Christ remained on earth for that space before his ascension. The solemn cry of triumph, " Christ is risen !" resounds through the whole of the next Passover Week, both at morning and evening prayers. Before the termination of these great Easter services, the bread is consecrated in remembrance of our Lord, who is the Bread of Life.

Divine worship, such as we have described it, is more splendid and impressive in the Imperial Court church than in any other, owing to the well-trained Court singers; but the course of the ceremonies is the same in every church, from the grand Cathedral in the capital down to the most remote village structure. Indeed, since the first propagation of Christianity in Russia, no changes have, I believe, been made. The ceremonies have continued the same from the days of John of Damascus in 730.

With the Resurrection Day the populace of Moscow seem to come to life again, and carriages with four horses are seen in the streets, where the people throng together, swinging and exulting, when suddenly the thunder of cannon and the pealing of bells announced to the city that the Grand Duchess had given a son to the country ; tidings all the more important, as for twenty years (since the birth of Michael, Paul's youngest son) there had been no addition to the Imperial family No one anticipated at that time that this child, born in newly sprung up Moscow, on Resurrection Day, was destined to liberate his people from a yoke of two hundred years, and to set them free. Nicholas, not yet two-and-twenty, and already father of a son, filled with gratitude, wrote a letter as follows to the Archbishop Augustine of Moscow :—" I saw the decisive moment of my life approach with the dread of a mortal, but with the hope of a Christian, and prepared to submit to the will of God. Assist me, holy prelate, in the performance of a vow,—to build a chapel, dedicated to St. Alexander Newsky (tutelar saint of new-born infants), in the Church of New Jerusalem (a cloister in the vicinity of Moscow), as a thank-offering from a happy father. I entreat your blessing for mother, father, and child."

Alexandra no longer felt herself a stranger in her adopted family and country, like Elisabeth, through life; as the mother of a son she was now closely and inseparably connected with the history of the House of Romanow and their country. This happy family event caused the young parents to live in still greater seclusion; and they envied each other every moment that they could pass beside the cradle of their son. Twelve days after his birth, April 29th, the baptism and confirmation took place, which differed widely from the forms of our Protestant Church. This solemn ceremony begins by previous exorcisms against the wiles of the devil; the godfather and godmother take upon themselves the responsibilities of which the child is unconscious; they assume the office of spiritual parents, and enter into an alliance considered equally sacred with that of blood-relationship. Persons wholly unconnected, if they stand together as godfathers and godmothers, are prohibited from forming any matrimonial connection with each other. In a prayer the priest implores God the Father to bestow a guardian angel on the child, and breathes on its mouth, forehead, and breast, with the words, "All evil spirits avaunt!" He then turns the infant towards the west, and asks him three times, "Do you renounce Satan and all his works?" and the sponsors answer, "I renounce them all." He then again asks, "Have you renounced them?" and on receiving an affirmative answer, he turns the infant towards the east, and asks, "Are you united to Christ?" and one of the sponsors, in the place of the child, repeats his whole confession of faith. The infant is thus prepared for the rite of baptism, and now the priest proceeds to consecrate the water. "Be present Thyself, O King of kings!" he exclaims, "by the descent of Thy Holy Ghost, and bless this water." After pronouncing over it all the blessings of the Jordan, he makes the sign of the cross three times over the font, saying, "May all malignant influences vanish before the sign of the cross." Before the child is immersed in the water—a symbol of the death of Christ—the priest anoints him like a corpse for this mysterious burial, with oil—the oil of joy—on the forehead, breast, ears, back, hands, and feet. The baptismal water is consecrated by this oil with the sign of the cross. The priest takes the naked child into his arms, lays his hands on its head, and looking towards the east, he dips it three times into the water of redemption. It is then clothed in the raiment of righteousness, the white raiment of immortality; the sponsors have candles placed in their hands—a type of the spiritual light that has shone on the infant, and enabled it to receive the sacrament of anointing with the oil of myrrh, the visible symbol of the invisible Holy Ghost. The priest, while praying, makes the sign of the cross on the limbs of the child, saying, "This is the seal of the gift of the Holy Ghost! Amen!" And not till then is the Christian name bestowed on the infant.

The priest, with the child and the sponsors, walk three times round the baptismal font, the infant's face turned to the east, saying, " All those who have been baptized have been moved thereto by Christ. The believer must follow Christ the Saviour through life, as the son of truth, led by the teaching of faith." At the close of the sacred rite the priest implores for the new-born infant the maintenance of the gift of the Holy Ghost, and sprinkles him with water, adding these words, " Thou art enlightened and justified, sanctified and purified;" and finally he cuts his hair in the form of a cross, in the name of the Holy Trinity, after which the infant is carried back to his mother by a lady of honour and the Lord Chancellor.

A succession of festivals now took place in the gay city of Moscow, but the young mother continued for six weeks in the most entire seclusion, happy in holding her son to her heart, and happier still when at length she was able to go herself to church with her infant in her arms, and to pray at the tomb of St. Alexis. And now the joyful moment drew near when she could welcome and present to her revered father, King Frederick William the Second, his first grandchild, in Moscow, her new home.

While the Imperial Court had passed the last winter in Moscow, in the most quiet manner, the court and city of Berlin had celebrated one festival after another. In January, the newly married Princess Frederike made her state-entry into Berlin, welcomed by an ingenious masque—" The consecration of the marriage of Eros and Psyche." In February, the Duke of Dessau stayed

for some time in the Prussian capital, and in April married the Royal Princess Frederike. When in the midst of
these betrothal rejoicings the news came that the King
was a grandfather, he at once resolved to go to Moscow
in order to embrace his first grandchild, and his eldest
daughter. The King's route was through Posen, where
Prince Radziwill, to whom we have already alluded, received him in the most hospitable manner, celebrating the
presence of his illustrious guest by a grand banquet,
ball, and illumination. The young Crown Prince
accompanied his father. In Königsberg, the King
visited the Busolt gardens, now called " Louisenwohl."
Here, ten years ago, even in the midst of misfortune,
he had passed the happiest hours of his life, with
the incomparable Louise. The mightiest on this earth,
like the most insignificant, feel that time and circumstances inflict wounds that even the lustre of subsequent good fortune can never heal. The kingdom had
been restored and become more extensive and powerful
than before, but no victory could restore light to the
sweet eyes of Louise, for ever closed in death. The
King was received at the boundary of Poland by Prince
Trubetskoi, the husband of the Princess, so intimate
with Alexandra in Moscow. The name of this princely
race, their origin springing from the Lithuanian Prince
Ghedimin, is closely interwoven in every direction with
the history of Russia. In the year 1613, when the
Muscovite throne was vacant, the choice of the people
long vacillated between the Houses of Romanow and
Trubetskoi, whose arm aided in freeing the land from
the dominion of the Poles. In the course of his further

journey, the King visited all those places that had become renowned in 1812 by Napoleon's battles. In Orscha he was met by General Diebitsch, a Russian by birth, and, three miles from Moscow, by the Emperor Alexander and his brother Constantine, and at 10 o'clock at night on the 3d of June he embraced his daughter and his son-in-law, in a country seat of Narischkin's. The Crown Prince arrived next morning, when Alexandra, after having welcomed her brother, hurried back to the city, in order to witness from the Kremlin the festive entry of her father. The conflagration of Moscow had been to Frederick William the Third the dawn of the resurrection of Prussia and freedom of Germany. The King, the Emperor, and his brother passed through the Dorogomilsch gate on horseback, and at the moment when they entered the city thousands of bells pealed, and a hundred and one cannon-shots were fired. From the gate to the Kremlin, troops lined the streets, and the people climbed on roofs, trees, and towers, shouting out of the fulness of their hearts loud hurrahs. In after years Alexandra used often to declare that moment to be the most eventful of her life, when she, the young mother, saw the arrival at the Kremlin in Moscow of her father and her brother; for all who constituted the happiness of her life were here assembled—father and brother, husband and child, and her brothers-in-law, who all showed her equal affection. The three first days therefore were devoted to the family circle. Alexandra described to her father and brother the unvarying happiness of this whole past year, and her father listened with heartfelt sympathy. Let

any one who doubts the progress of mankind compare
the family circle of the rulers of Russia and Prussia, in
Moscow, in 1818, with that of the same year in the previous century, when Peter the Great condemned his son
Alexis to death, or with France, where the Regent
declared that domestic life and domestic virtues were
only fit for shopkeepers and peasants.

All the remarkable objects in Moscow are concentrated within the Sanctuary of the Kremlin. The town
consisted at that period of new houses and palaces
scarcely yet dry; but the physiognomy was no longer
that of the olden day. The King first inspected the
monuments to the memory of Minin and Pojarsky,
erected this year in the square of the Kremlin by the
Russian artist Martos. These statues are in bronze, and
stand on pedestals of granite, commemorating the time
when Russia, in the year 1612, groaned under the
dominion of the Poles, and those two men, summoning
their countrymen to the fight, liberated their fatherland
even before the Romanows ascended the throne. The
inscription is as follows: " Grateful Russia, in honour
of the Burgher Minin and Prince Pojarsky." Moscow
at that time contained many families, who still lived
in the style of the ancient Boyars in their palaces,
surrounded by hundreds of servants, and expending
lavishly their princely wealth. It was not uncommon
for such noblemen to possess upwards of 100,000
families of serfs on their landed property, which often
vied in extent with German kingdoms. Some of these
peasants had become millionaires as merchants in
Moscow. Count Scheremetief, in the year 1812, raised

several regiments on his property alone. Such wealth
might be equalled in England, Spain, and Austria, but
the hospitality of the Russians, more especially of the
Muscovites, is unrivalled in Europe, and the nobility
emulated each other in receiving the King, not only with
liberality, but with munificence. Within each of these
palaces, both within and without Moscow, is a church
with well-trained singers, a private orchestra, and treasures of art of every description. The fêtes in honour
of the King began with a ball at the Governor-General's
of Moscow—an entertainment that differed little from
a similar one in Petersburg; but a few days afterwards
Prince Jussupoff invited the whole Imperial and Royal
family, and also the society of Moscow, to a fête at his
country palace, Archangelsk, about two miles from the
ancient capital. This palace is picturesquely situated
on the Moskwa, surrounded by several villages with
churches; the gardens are adorned with the most splendid
trees, even cedars, and with orangeries, and it surpasses,
in the riches of its interior, most palaces of that date
in Germany. It contains a valuable library, with the
rarest selections of the ancient classics; natural history is enriched by important collections; antiquity
represented by a collection of marble statues; and
modern art by several masterpieces of Canova. The
picture-gallery contains the most celebrated names of
all periods. Adjoining the palace is a theatre, worthy
of a capital. When the Imperial procession approached
the palace, the population of its dependent villages,
amounting to nearly 40,000, came to meet the illustrious
guests, offering them bread and salt, and presents, and

fruit of all kinds; the clergy also, with cross and holy
water, greeted them. The anticipations of the King
were changed into amazement when he saw the
splendour of the gardens and the palace. During the
banquet the peasants strolled through the garden singing
and dancing, and the Prince's own orchestra played
national Russian airs, and likewise overtures of the
newest operas. In the evening, during the ball, all the
villages and gardens were illuminated, and also the way
back to Moscow for those guests who returned thither;
the people enlivening the fête the whole time by their
national songs and dances.

Prince Nicolai Jussupoff, the owner of this palace,
was of the date of Catherine's reign, whose ambassador
he had been in Turkey. Both palace and fête were
therefore reminiscences of the brilliant period in which
he formerly played a part. The Prince had been always
held in esteem on account of his liberality and noble
nature. He did not die till Nicholas was on the throne,
and thus survived to see four reigns.

A similar fête was given in the Palace Ostankino,
belonging to Prince Scheremetief, situated only a few
versts from Moscow; here also are a great many art
treasures, which unfortunately, like those in Archangelsk,
are too little known and valued. This palace attracts
the traveller more particularly by a church of the
sixteenth century; within its walls is a superb marble
statue of the Empress Catherine, and several pictures by Claude Lorraine. Count Scheremetief, whose
wealth was at that time a byword even in Russia
as a Crœsus, collected the whole population of his

villages and clothed them in very handsome new
national dresses, and made them perform a national
ballet in the palace. If the King was impressed by
these fêtes with an exalted idea of the riches and refinement of the Russian nobility, the institutions in the city
were equally well calculated to engage his attention.
The Foundling Hospital here is unequalled in the world,
its circumference being that of a city, with 2255
windows, a large church, and a garden; 1500 orphans
are received here, nursed and trained for some profession
or trade, or, if any special talent be developed, as
scholars or officials. The number of attendants, doctors,
and inspectors amounts to 500, including the foster-
mothers; several days are required to examine minutely
all the arrangements of this institution, founded by
Catherine the Second, and carefully sustained by the
Empress-mother. The interior of the city at that
period, by its modern palaces and streets, its straight
lines and avenues of trees, recalled modern Petersburg;
but on reviewing the whole town, especially looking
down on it from the Kremlin, with its innumerable
churches and thousands of little gay coloured cupolas, the
ancient physiognomy still predominates. The tone of
society bears a certain stamp of independence towards
the Court, and the people that of unvarying good-
humoured cheerfulness. The banquets of the Moscow
nobles rival those of Roman Imperial days, and foreign
delicacies are procured by the payment of large sums.
The son of the Count Scheremetief we have alluded to
granted freedom to one of his serfs, not for the thousands
offered him, but in return for a ton of oysters that the

latter presented to him at the right moment. We feel that the waves of two oceans here come into collision, and that old times and new are at variance.

In the midst of these festivities the King did not forget his Lutheran brothers in the faith, and he, as well as the Imperial Court, was present at laying the foundation-stone of a Lutheran church, burnt down during the war. It had been built in 1575, with the consent of the Czar John the Terrible, at a period therefore when the Protestants of the Netherlands were most persecuted by the fanatic Philip of Spain.

Eleven days after his arrival, the King accompanied the Prince to Zarskoe-Selò, where they were joined by the Imperial family at different times; the infant Alexander having preceded them. Thus this first year in Russia passed rapidly, and did not deceive the expectations of Alexandra. The grandest festivities, that could only be offered by such an Empire, had not abated her inclination for a retired domestic life, but, on the contrary, rather increased it; in the love of her husband she found again all that she had left in her own home, the memory of which had been revived by the visits of her father and her brother. She had adapted herself to the tone of the new Court without sacrificing any portion of her individuality; she was now on the most affectionate terms of intimacy with the reigning family, without being estranged from her own home; she had won new friends, without losing her former now distant ones.

CHAPTER V.

THE Court did not return at once to the city, but enjoyed some days of pleasant retirement, partly in Zarskoe-Selò and partly in Pawlowsk. The park of Zarskoe was quite new to the King, and the Emperor himself conducted his illustrious guest through the portion that bears a peculiar stamp, owing to Catherine's abode there. Here we see an artificial lake glitter, supplied by a brook with water pure enough to drink, and in the centre two islands, with summer-houses, and the Pillar of Count Orlow Tschesmensky; a handsome marble bridge, with marble colonnades, spans the mouth of the brook that supplies the lake; at the other end stands a Turkish kiosk; an Admiralty building adorns the third side, and thick avenues of trees the fourth. The walk round this smooth bright sheet of water is truly delightful; on one side you have a view of the colonnade adjoining the palace. At the lower end of the lake, concealed by a thicket of trees, are baths, and a fantastic building called the Hermitage, in which Catherine the Second used to dine with a select circle, without any attendants. The dining-hall is provided, like a theatre, with trap-doors, the tables vanish and reappear with fresh dishes without the presence of servants, who remain in the storey below. The arrangements of the table at that time in Petersburg were exclusively French, and consequently Russian servants entirely excluded—a precaution that cannot be too highly commended in certain families. In this garden the Emperor met a sentinel quite unexpectedly, whose pass-word was, "I guard a rose." As however there was not the vestige of a flower to be seen on the spot, the Emperor investigated the cause of the man's presence and pass-word, and found that a sentinel had been once appointed to keep watch over a rosebud by the Emperor's grandmother, and that to this day a sentinel is stationed here on the same nominal duty. When the King made his state-entry all the festivities of the previous year were renewed, but Alexandra, though pursuing the same route, in the same gilt carriage, did so with very different feelings. As she was passing the desolate-looking Anitschkow Palace, she saw her little son, two months old, in the arms of his nurse at the window. The pomp of the state-procession was forgotten, and maternal love, the strongest of all feelings, alone spoke in her heart, and her eyes filled with happy tears. When they stopped at the Kasan Church, the Emperor Alexander gave her his arm, and, observing that her eyes were still moist, he said, "Such tears are sweet to a mother, and pleasing to the King of Kings." The King of Prussia inhabited the apartment once occupied by the Emperor Paul, eventually named the Prussian apartment.

The fêtes very much resembled those of the previous
year. In Oranienbaum there were fireworks, consisting of 40,000 rockets, 200 fiery dragons, and a salvo
of 500 cannon. But the capital was never quitted for
more than one day, and the two crowned heads, surrounded by their whole family, were constantly seen
by the inhabitants of the capital and the islands. The
Empress-mother conducted the King and the Crown
Prince to the scene of her special labours; not only to
the Maiden Cloister of Smolna, but to all her institutions,
initiating the strangers into their most minute details.
They were astonished, not only by the extensive sphere
of the Empress's benevolence, but still more by the love
and child-like confidence with which the young girls
approached the illustrious lady. This same Empress,
who enforced the most strict etiquette, both in the
city and in the Court, was here the friend and maternal
confidant of this young world, where, instead of formal
Court etiquette, the most frank cordiality prevailed.
Once on a time the Boyars never appeared before their
Czars without bowed heads, fear dividing them by a
deep chasm from their rulers, but here a bond of love,
truth, and hope for the future united them to their
friend and mother. The ease and grace that specially
distinguish Russian ladies beyond those of England and
Germany, are to be explained chiefly by their habit of
frequenting the society of the highest personages without
constraint. The German Princes of that epoch were
devoted to the chase, but seldom indeed visited a school
or college. The Emperor Alexander also displayed to
his Royal connections the whole array of his troops, his

palaces in the city and on the islands, and thus the fine
summer days, with their bright clear nights, glided past
as if under a southern sky.

In the midst of this pleasant domestic life and the
festivities in the city an incident occurred that nearly
concerned Alexandra. Her husband was attacked by
measles, so she declined all gaieties, and even gave
up the society of her father and brother, in order to
nurse the invalid, sitting by his bed-side, and tending
him until she herself caught the malady. Their child
was taken to the Taurus Palace, that he might escape
infection, and intrusted to the care of the Empress-
mother. The name of this summer palace recalls the
time when the Taurus Peninsula was conquered by
Russia, and this palace built by the Empress for Prince
Potemkin. It is situated at the end of the town, close
to the Maiden Cloister and the Neva, and the passer-
by is only aware of its existence by a dome; but a
fine garden adjoins it, and this quarter of the town,
which lies rather higher than the other, and is less
populated, enjoys fresh, pure country air, even in the
height of summer.

Thus all these festivities, as well as the social charm
of family life, were suddenly transformed into the
anxieties of illness. It seems as if the mightiest on
this earth must be from time to time reminded of
human weakness and infirmity. Alexandra had only
sufficient strength to accompany her father as far as
Gatschina, where she took leave of him, and next day
was prostrate with fever. Happily the Crown Prince
remained a week longer, for his cheerful conversation,

full of Attic salt and wit, shortened the lingering days
to the two invalids.   It was also fortunate that an
upright and benevolent man was at the head of the
household, and maintained everything in the best order.
The physician, too, of the Grand Ducal house was an
Englishman, of the name of Crichton, whose intercourse
was most agreeable, and inspired confidence. The nurse
of Alexandra, Fräulein Klügel, originally from Berlin,
was equally trustworthy. The course of the malady
being favourable, convalescence ensued at the right
period; nevertheless this illness laid the seeds of a
weakness in the chest which Alexandra never entirely
got rid of. The Anitschkow Palace was inhabited by
the invalids at a time when the poorest seek fresh air
in the country. Their delight in the simple Pawlowsk was therefore the greater when they regained
health, enjoying the few remaining days of summer
in undisturbed repose. Nicholas and Alexandra, however, were destined to play a different part in the
autumn from that of the preceding year. The Emperor
Alexander and the two Empresses projected going
abroad, the former to attend the Congress at Aix-la-
Chapelle, the Empress Elisabeth to visit her home,
and Maria Feodorowna to visit her three daughters.
The youngest Grand Duke, Michael, undertook a journey
to Italy and to England, to finish his education. The
Grand Duke Constantine was Commander-in-Chief of
the new kingdom of Poland, and henceforth resided
there, in his little Palace of Belvedere. The Empress
lost three of her six daughters at different times, and
Katharina, the fourth, to the joy of her mother, two

years previously entered into a second marriage, and
ascended the throne of Würtemberg; a source of
especial happiness to the mother to see one of her
daughters adorn the throne of her own country, an
event scarcely ever paralleled in history. Three years
previously, this Princess, so distinguished by her talents,
married Duke George of Oldenburg, and remained in
Russia with her husband, in the vicinity of her mother.
Shortly after her marriage with the Crown Prince of
Würtemberg he was called to the throne of that kingdom,
and, by his wise laws, framed in the spirit of progress
of the day, he won in a short time the confidence of his
people, as he had previously done their respect by his
strategic talents as a military commander, and the young
Queen was equally beloved and revered. Anna Pawlowna, Paul's youngest daughter, had become Princess
of Orange, and was destined to fill the newly established
throne of the Netherlands. Maria Pawlowna married,
in 1804, the Hereditary Grand Duke of Saxe Weimar,
and was as well versed in the German spirit and German
affairs as if born in that country. Could a brighter fate
attend any mother than to visit three happy daughters
in their homes, accompanied in her journey by a son,
venerated by all Europe, and to know that she was
connected with most German thrones—for her eldest
daughter, Alexandra, was married to Archduke Joseph,
Palatine of Hungary, and her second, Helene, to Prince
Frederick of Mecklenburg Schwerin. Europe could not
at that time, on its many thrones, offer a more interesting sight than this energetic handsome old lady, who,
before entering her sixtieth year, wished once more to

witness the happiness that she had herself bestowed.
With the dignity of a high-priestess, when taking leave
of Nicholas and Alexandra, the only members of the
family remaining, she gave them instructions as to
their conduct. Although she granted them more independence of her maternal supremacy than to her other
sons of the same age, still she occasionally made her
authority felt, more from custom than from necessity,
and neither of her sons ventured to thwart her in this
respect. The young couple scarcely dared to ride or
to drive without previous notice to their mother, and
scarcely ever without a formal escort, such as the rules
of Imperial etiquette prescribe. Now they were to be
self-dependent, and on certain occasions to represent the
Court and throw open their Palace of Anitschkow to
society. Nicholas had been hitherto the happiest private
individual and husband, but never intermeddled with
State affairs; even in the military service his position
was merely that of chief-of a sapper guard battalion,
and he had only received this appointment since his
marriage; his responsibility was not greater than that
of any other colonel or major-general, and he was
further from the person of the Emperor in affairs of
State than any secretary or adjutant-general. He had
now passed a year with his young wife, in which he had
enjoyed all the charms of life, for there was nothing
wanting that the boldest fancy could imagine or aspire
to; but both sought and found their happiness chiefly
in quiet retirement from the world and the Court in
the gardens of Pawlowsk, where unknown they could
linger in the most solitary paths, or seat themselves

beside the cradle of their lovely child. Now they were
deprived of maternal counsels, and for the first time
must fulfil certain social duties, which the world
strictly exacts, especially in Petersburg, the capital of
all others most merciless in its criticisms. The character of Nicholas at that time by no means disposed
him towards intercourse with the world; there was
something peculiarly dignified in his appearance, more
suitable, in fact, to a man of mature age than to one of
three-and-twenty ; he was reserved towards others, indifferent and formal in society ; his wife alone possessed
the power to make him open his inmost heart; with the
highest feminine and imperial nobility of deportment
she combined a certain fascination and ease in conversation, that was reflected on all around her; she observed
the traditional rules of Court etiquette less strictly than
the Empress-mother, but was remarkable for her charms
of youth, beauty, and amiability, as well as heart-felt
benevolence, and Nicholas, inspired by such a wife, began
by degrees to be less formal.

Before the end of August they repaired for a length-
ened stay to Anitschkow Palace, situated in the hand-
somest street in the city, the Perspective, close to a bridge
of the same name, and about two versts from the great
Winter Palace.   Besides the latter, Petersburg could
count at that time five other Imperial palaces, only
inhabited at certain seasons, and sometimes not at all.
The former was built in 1748, in the reign of the Empress Elisabeth, by Count Rastrelli, and first occupied
by Count Alexis Rasumowsky, the favourite of Elisabeth, and subsequently by Potemkin. Owing to its

large court-yard and numerous out-buildings, it is, next
to the Winter Palace, the most splendid of all, and
though not possessing the immense space and valuable
treasures of the former, still it combines within its walls
every comfort for domestic life, in spite of its imposing
exterior. A small garden adorns it on one side, and
the adjacent buildings are large enough to lodge a great
Court retinue. The apartments overlooking the Perspective command a view of the most cheerful resort in
the whole city, while on the opposite side monastic
seclusion reigns.

The first occasion on which the illustrious pair were
forced to represent the Imperial family was on August
30th, the Alexander Newsky day. The mortal remains of
this hero, who gained a brilliant victory over the Swedes,
on the Neva, in the thirteenth century, were transferred
by Peter the Great from the Volga to the Neva, the scene
of his conquest, and deposited in a massive silver coffin.
The cloister named after the revered hero is adorned
with a splendid church, and surrounded by a spacious
garden. To the orthodox Russian this holy spot at the
end of the city is compensation for having no Kremlin.
Besides a collection of works of art, this is the last
resting-place of many Russian families. Here lie the
State Chancellor Besborodko, Field-Marshals Galitzin,
Rumäntzof, and the great Suworof, the Narischkins,
Panin, the wife of the Czar Iwan Alexeiwitsch, Natalie,
sister of Peter the Great, and, moreover, Paul's first
consort, and the two daughters of Alexander and Elisabeth. The Alexander Newsky Day, August 30th, is
celebrated as one of the most important Church festivals

by the whole country, for the memory of this heroic
victory recalls a land once possessed by heretics, but subsequently restored to the orthodox Church.   The whole
of the priesthood, therefore, of the Kasan Cathedral,
the chief church in Petersburg, walk in stately procession to the Cloister Church, and the Imperial family, as
well as the Court, attend divine service.

The young Grand Duke and Duchess on this occasion
represented their family, and afterwards were present
at a breakfast at the Metropolitan's.   Alexandra was
exhausted by such fatigue so shortly after her illness,
having stood for three hours, and also so nervous at
being the only lady at the breakfast (the company consisting solely of priests), that she could scarcely reach the
carriage, even supported by her husband's arm; her
long train too, and heavy head-dress, were very incon-
venient.   Nowhere is dignity so burdensome as in the
Court of Russia, and she stood in great need of refreshing country air, though there are few enjoyable days
in the beginning of September.   They went for a short
time to the Palace of Gatschina, not without having
received permission from their mother, who, though
laying down many rules for their guidance at the time
of parting, also granted them a good deal of liberty.
This palace offered no pleasant remembrances to
Nicholas, but the happy present chased away all that
was sad.   The little Court spent eight days there; the
gentlemen employed their time in sport, and the ladies
in promenades, while the evenings were devoted to
play and dancing.   A variety of new acquaintances
were invited to join the little circle, among whom M.

de Ribeaupierre was one of the most agreeable at that
time, and through life, to Alexandra. This gentleman,
subsequently a Count, was of French origin; a handsome man, of the most refined manners, sprightly and
vivacious, and by his talent in reading aloud he
eventually became almost indispensable to Alexandra
when Empress. In those days Ribeaupierre shone only
in society, his diplomatic career having commenced at
a later period. The acquaintance with the family of
Count Kotschubei seemed at the moment more important, for he played a higher part than the former, both
in State and Court, at that period. Count Kotschubei,
like Prince A. N. Galitzin, had formed part of Catherine's
brilliant Court, having accompanied her in her celebrated
journey to the Crimea, and been Alexander's most
intimate friend from his youth upwards. Letters are
still extant, written to him by Alexander when Grand
Duke, in which all his most secret wishes for the future,
all his complaints with regard to the present, are fully
expressed with a degree of confidence that usually exists
only between brothers. We learn from this correspondence that long before he ascended the throne, Alexander
cherished the wish to renounce the crown, and to retire
to the banks of the Rhine, there to live as a private
individual, with his charming wife. Kotschubei became
Russian Ambassador to the Sublime Porte before he
was five-and-twenty. This family, after an absence of
several years, had only recently returned to Petersburg,
and was therefore for the first time presented to Alexandra. Alexander himself, in taking leave of his
sister-in-law, had recommended his friend to her par-

ticular attention. No family, nor any of the older
courtiers, attracted her so much as this faithful friend
of the Emperor, and of his race. The house of Count
Kotschubei was one of the finest, richest, and most
hospitable in the city, fitted up with splendour, arranged with tasté, and enriched by works of art. The
principal persons of the Petersburg society were always
to be met there, both at dinner and in the evening, when
they were hospitably welcomed and intellectually entertained. On the education of only four or five of his children he spent from 40,000 to 50,000 francs, besides be-
stowing pensions for life on their tutors and governesses.
It was the first private house at which Alexandra
often and gladly visited ; the Count and Countess (née
Wasiltschikof), by their position and refined manners,
being well fitted to counsel her in the absence of her
husband and her mother-in-law. Their arrival at the
Anitschkow Palace was celebrated by a ball given on
the 15th of October (new style), the birthday of the
Crown Prince of Prussia. The company invited con-
siderably exceeded the hitherto small circle, and the
illustrious hosts were obliged to receive courteously a
number of persons whose names were as yet unknown
to them. But Alexandra was peculiarly skilled in a
duty of this kind, as since the death of her admirable mother she had been in the habit of receiving,
by her father's side, a vast variety of persons. She
found an appropriate word for every one, her charming courtesy animated the whole evening, her eye
quickly discovered any one apparently excluded from
the pleasures of the evening ; her graceful movements

in dancing, set all in motion, and although she devoted herself unreservedly on this occasion to joy and
pleasure, still she neglected none of the duties imposed
on her by society. This fête not only brought her into
closer proximity to the public, but likewise diffused and
confirmed a high opinion of her merits in the whole city,
hitherto only expressed by a limited number of persons ;
in short, all were delighted with this foreign Princess,
hitherto unknown to so many ; every one was charmed
with her manner, and she was praised and admired in
the town for weeks. After so brilliant an opening of
the winter gaieties, one ball followed another in the city ;
people vying with each other in securing the happiness
of receiving the young Grand Duchess. Wherever she
appeared, the house was adorned with masses of flowers
to welcome her. The way by which she drove from the
Palace was often illuminated ; indeed, in sledging-time
in winter the path was marked by fir-trees and torches.
The life of the capital was enlivened also in another
point of view : for Alexandra visited regularly once or
twice the various theatres in succession, whereas the
Imperial family had only appeared there on festive occasions in grand gala, received in state by the public with
music, and every token of the deepest reverence. This
was therefore a piece of good fortune for the German
company, whose crowded audiences had not hitherto, on
an average, consisted of the best classes of society. The
Emperor Paul alone had bestowed any attention on the
theatre, and it is well known that Kotzebue's comedy,
"The Body Coachman of Peter the Third," touched the
Emperor so much, that he despatched a courier on the

spot from the theatre, to recall its banished author from Siberia. In early winter, however, the situation of Alexandra prevented her attending balls, and so she often spent a few hours of the evening in the theatre. The first half of the winter season had been so brilliant, that still greater preparations were made in the city for the second.

At the close of the year all the Imperial family were once more together. The Empress-mother arrived on Sylvester evening, in such perfect health and activity that she attended the church ceremony in the' Palace on January 1, 1819. For the first few days the young couple visited their excellent mother, and listened with interest to all the details she gave them of the happiness of her daughters, and also to the Emperor Alexander's description of the brilliancy of the Congress of Aix-la-Chapelle; while the harmony of this young pair greatly heightened the joy of the mother. The time between Christmas and the 6th of January bears a quiet spiritual character, occupied by fasts, and evening prayers and masses. But as baptism, according to the views of the Orthodox Greek Church, stands higher than the day of birth, so the anniversary of our blessed Saviour's baptism on January 6th is celebrated by a procession attended by all the clergy, the Imperial family, and the Court, and with great military pomp, beside the Neva, though often in twenty degrees of cold. The Empress-mother was strong enough to be present.

None of the anecdotes of the Emperor and Empress-mother interested the young wife more than those about Berlin. Alexander had witnessed the laying of the foundation-stone of the Warriors' Monument on the Kreuzberg; the Empress had examined all the institutions in Berlin carefully with her experienced eye, and the praise she lavished on the royal family, the capital, and its society, was balm to the heart of Alexandra, and transported her back to the past. In foreign countries we feel doubly proud of the renown of our Fatherland. As Nicholas was kept at such a distance by his brother in affairs of the realm, the Emperor's political views met with very little interest or sympathy from his sister-in-law. The joy of a happy meeting, and everything having gone on to a wish on both sides, banished every other interest in those days. The Congress of Aix-la-Chapelle, so vividly described by the Emperor Alexander, gave rise to the desire in Alexandra to hear the most celebrated singer in Europe—Catalani. She was, however, quite indifferent to all the other splendours, and her sympathy with politics and diplomatic treaties only extended so far as they were combined with true humanity and patriotism.

In the early part of January the tidings of a death caused much grief to the Imperial family, and to the Empress-mother in particular. The highly esteemed Queen of Würtemberg, whom her mother so lately embraced, died suddenly, and the demise of this lovely and intellectual woman, only thirty years of age, seemed quite inexplicable. On the Emperor devolved the painful duty of announcing this sad news to his mother. He therefore repaired to her apartments at an unaccustomed hour, to await her return from her daily avocations; for in the Winter Palace not only the days and hours but even the minutes were exactly apportioned, and appropriated to the reception of different persons. The Empress was therefore astonished on her return to find the Emperor at a time when she expected her Secretary of State. The agitated face of her son at once betrayed to her that some grievous misfortune had brought him into the presence of his mother. When, however, the fact that he dared no longer withhold from her was told, she uttered a cry of horror, and stood motionless like a stone Niobe. This was the fourth daughter of whom she had been deprived by death. Next to the mother no one felt this loss more keenly than the Emperor, who held this sister in peculiar esteem, and formerly listened to her advice even in political matters. The whole Court went into mourning, and the festivities in the city at once came to an end. This period of rest and repose was most welcome to Alexandra, who felt that social duties, for a lady of her rank, deprived her of time and strength, when many other obligations were at least equally imperative.

She devoted the ensuing winter months entirely to study and intellectual conversation. She made great progress both in the Russian and French languages; and, after an interval of two years, resumed instruction in singing and the piano; and, in addition to Jean Paul, read the works of Madame de Staël, Walter Scott, and Chateaubriand. The evenings she spent almost exclusively in her boudoir, with her friend Cecilia and a maid of honour, while her husband filled up his time

with military duties. Alexandra, however, frequented
the circle of the two Empresses, who lived in the
most profound retirement, and saw only very few persons. At the receptions of the Empress-mother, our
German poet, Klinger, was an invariable guest; to the
Russian public, this author of *Faust* was only known
as a lieutenant-general; he had enjoyed the esteem
and confidence of the Imperial family since Catherine's
reign, as they highly prized his straightforward, manly
nature, which caused him to be much dreaded by
courtiers, and even by the society of the capital.
Alexandra never considered his society attractive, and
at that time she was not sufficiently inaugurated into
the spirit and tone of such men as Klinger, Schu-
bert, Storck, Adelung, Parrot; indeed, they were to be
met with less frequently in large Court entertainments than in the small and exclusive circles of the
two Empresses, who, as German Princesses, considered
it their duty to their adopted land not to show publicly
any particular favour to their own countrymen. The
struggle between the Russian and German element has
continued through every reign from the days of the
Regent Sophie, and though not open or vehement, it
is secret and subtle. Nicholas, never so happy in
society as in the quiet of domestic life, found, in the
course of this year, his occupations increased, and his
position altered, but not improved. He was now a
Brigadier-General and Chief of Engineers, his time therefore was fully employed, thus obliging him to be continually absent from his loving wife. It often happened
that the husband and wife did not meet till evening,

and that Alexandra sat alone at dinner with one of her
ladies.   These duties, too, were in no way calculated to
cultivate the mind of a young man of three-and-twenty,
except, indeed, in engineering, and least of all to prepare him one day to become an emperor.   To read aloud
and to sign and forward reports on daily barrack-life,
military exercises, and the short-comings of officers, ·
amply filled up his morning hours, leaving in their train
more dissatisfaction than contentment.   His expeditions
when he left home were to attend parades, exercises,
and inspections, a wearisome and exhausting task,
and the daily repetition of such monotony made him
reserved and severe to his dependants, nay, even gloomy
and morose.   How fortunate that the harassed and
exhausted man should find his good angel at home,
whose glance or smile could make him forget the burden
of the day, and transform the saturnine Grand Duke,
the grumbling Brigadier, into the most cordial and
amiable cavalier, and the most tender husband and
father.   His wife understood the art of making everything forgotten at home, except what belonged to
domestic life.

The strict period of fasting that we described in detail
in a previous chapter, passed on quietly and happily,
and after Easter all the world sought fresh air and freer
movement in the country.   The Grand-Ducal couple
now felt more than ever that the first golden year of
independence had vanished for ever, for Nicholas was
obliged, on official business, to drive daily back to the
city on a wearisome road, and forced to leave his beloved wife, even more than before, alone with her friend

Cecilia. The more highly did both prize the happy
moments of reunion, especially on Sundays and fête-
days. And ' yet, in spite of the subordinate part
Nicholas now played in the State, destiny had reserved a very different lot for him, in this same year
1819, of which we are speaking, and without his own
opinion having been consulted. After a stay of two
months at Pawlowsk, and of the Emperor in Zarskoe-
Selò, they repaired in June to the camp near Krasnoe ·
Selò. This place lies between Peterhof and Gatschina,
in the vicinity of a gentle richly wooded acclivity,
called the Duderhof Hill, and is only known by the
manœuvres that take place there every year. The
Palace, at that time belonging to the Empress-mother,
is small and insignificant in comparison with all the
other Imperial country residences; but the landscape,
embellished by lakes and rising ground, is romantic,
and recalls Potsdam. The Emperor and the Grand
Duke, like all the other officers, inhabit tents, and
the Imperial ladies the little palace. Alexandra for
the first time followed her husband to the camp of
Krasnoe-Selò, and took possession of a small wing of
the palace; but being accustomed from her youth
upwards to such displays, she took great delight in wit-
nessing all the military movements, sometimes accompanying her husband into his tent, that she might enjoy
every moment she was permitted to be with him. In
the district of Duderhof, she found a Matthisson landscape, which inspired her with the utmost enthusiasm
through life; she ascended, not without some difficulty,
the little height every morning, and watched from

thence the varied military spectacle, often exclaiming
with delight when she discovered her husband in the
tumult. These few weeks possessed a · double charm
for her, as, free from court and courtiers, and all wearisome etiquette, she could live solely for herself and her
husband, while at Pawlowsk both were obliged to
regard themselves as guests of the Empress-mother.

During this period of Arcadian life, the Emperor one
day offered to dine with his brother, and spoke in
high commendation of his services. Nicholas, much
gratified to have thus satisfied his Emperor and master,
nevertheless observed that this praise was spoken in
a dry, grave manner, which his brother indeed often
assumed on public occasions, but never in his own
family. After dinner he seated himself between the
husband and wife, and continued in the same tone,*
thus :—" Your zeal and conscientiousness, dear Nicholas,
more especially rejoice me, because at a future time far
heavier burdens and responsibilities will devolve on you
than you expect." Nicholas now conjectured that the
Emperor destined some higher military post or rank for
him, that would exact more time and strength, and thus
still further circumscribe his happy domestic life than
even during this last year. But both were thunder-struck
when Alexander, with increasing gravity, added,—" I
look upon you as my successor, and probably, too, in my
lifetime." The startled, and even alarmed young husband and wife sat motionless, and could scarcely believe
that the Emperor had really spoken in earnest. After
a pause, he continued,—" This seems to surprise you ; I
must therefore tell you, for your own information, that

my brother Constantine, who has never concerned himself about the throne, is now more than ever resolved to
renounce it, devolving all his rights on you, his younger
brother, and on your issue." The Emperor at once
perceived the agitating effect of his words, and purposely paused, in order that his two hearers might
collect their ideas, and thoroughly understand his communication. "As for myself," he continued, "I am
determined to give up the duties of government that
I have hitherto fulfilled, and to withdraw from the
world ; the Europe of the present day requires more
than ever younger and more energetic rulers, and, with
regard to myself, I feel that I am no longer what I was,
and therefore it is incumbent on me to retire in time.
The King of Prussia will probably do the same, and
your brother Fritz be summoned to replace him." Both
his auditors now passed from alarm into deep sorrow,
which showed itself by a burst of tears. When the
Emperor observed this he endeavoured to introduce a
few consolatory words : "But you must not be uneasy
lest this should soon occur ; years may elapse before it
comes to pass. Heaven, however, has blessed you in
your marriage differently from myself and my brother
Constantine, as neither of us have known the happiness
of having children ; and in the son whom God has
given you, I read His holy will that has appointed you
and your posterity for the preservation of the throne."
Nicholas now summoned up strength and courage to
answer, though his words were continually interrupted
by tears, saying,—"I have never had a wish except
to serve your Majesty faithfully and loyally ; I have

not been prepared for so high a calling, and never even
dreamt of such an ambitious project, and do not possess
the mental power it requires." The Emperor replied,
" I also was called to the throne suddenly and unprepared, and found the kingdom in the greatest confusion;
the former state of order in our grandmother's time had
vanished, and the new *régime* not yet introduced; were
you now to ascend the throne, you would not have to
contend with the difficulties I was forced to overcome."
After thus acquitting himself of his important task,
the features of the Emperor resumed their customary
serenity, for his own heart was lighter, and he took
leave of his brother and his sister-in-law with assurances
of the most heartfelt sympathy.

When the husband and wife were alone, and more composed, Nicholas declared that the whole conversation
must evidently be considered only a preliminary suggestion or hint; but that it was in his own power to accept
the proposal of the Emperor, or, like his brother Constantine, to decline it, and the latter was his deliberate
but immoveable resolution. The Emperor subsequently
made the same communication to Prince William of
Prussia, who hastened to congratulate his brother-
in-law and his sister on their golden prospects;
Nicholas, however, rejected all sympathy on the matter
in the most decided manner, declaring that he neither
knew anything on the subject, nor would he accept the
proposal. He earnestly entreated his brother-in-law
never again to recur to this affair. Alexander did not
discuss this most important of all questions a second
time with his brother Nicholas, who in turn always

avoided any reference to it, under the firm conviction that it had only been a passing thought of his brother's.

Nicholas and Alexandra quitted the noisy camp in July, and once more repaired to quiet Pawlowsk; the latter had been in delicate health before the birth of her second child; she had not strength to walk, so the anxious Empress-mother caused her to be carried down on a couch to the Pavilion of Roses, where she could breathe fresh air all day without leaving her resting-place. On the 6th August, the family happiness was increased by the birth of a daughter, the Grand Duchess Marie, who became subsequently the wife of the Duke of Leuchtenberg. Nicholas wished for a son, so his paternal joy was not so great on this occasion as on the former one. Little did he anticipate that two more daughters were to follow, still he did not the less tenderly love all three. In the autumn the Empress-mother with her son and daughter went for a short time to the Palace of Gatschina, which this year appeared under more favourable auspices to Nicholas. The recollections of the previous autumn entirely banished all former gloomy impressions. The presence of the Empress-mother, indeed, compelled them to observe particular forms, but we have already said that this highly estimable lady permitted her children to enjoy certain hours of golden freedom. As soon as the usual familiar society were assembled in a hall, called the Arsenal, youthful pleasure and gaiety swayed the circle with their magic wands. The Arsenal contained *Montagnes Russes*, billiards, pianos, and also space for playing, walking about, and dancing. The days passed partly in *chasses*, which the ladies often followed in *chars-à-banc*, and the evenings in the palace, that now, after a long and gloomy silence, resounded once more with singing, dancing, and gay society. Within these walls Prince Gregory Orlof had once on a time vented his rage, like a furious ape, on hearing that he had fallen into disgrace. The Emperor Paul, when Grand Duke, inhabited it from 1784, but it was devoid of the splendour his mother displayed in the Winter Palace. On his ascending the throne, he elevated this spot to the dignity of a town, and the Empress Maria Feodorowna adorned it with an institution, to which she devoted a large portion of her time. The acquaintances of Alexandra only included up to that time the families we have already named; and it was not till her stay here, on this occasion, that men like Benkendorf, Orlof, and Apraxin were presented to her. The name of the first of these was known to fame by the campaigns from 1812 to 1814, both in Russia and beyond it; he appeared one Sunday at the dinner-table of the Empress-mother, and stayed the evening for a ball. Sundays, however, were distinguished from week-days by strict etiquette. Benkendorf almost may be said to have made an epoch in the life of Alexandra, for he was the only person with whom she could converse in her mother-tongue. Her acquaintance with the family of Count Litta also dates from this period. The Countess, *née* Engelhardt, a niece of Prince Potemkin, once shone as a celebrated beauty at the Court of the Empress Catherine; she first married

Count Scavronsky, who, as Russian ambassador at Naples, distinguished himself by his regal expenditure. When a widow, she became acquainted with a Commander of the Order of Malta, at the time when Paul the First became Grand Master of the Knights. Count Litta first won fame as Admiral of the Russian Fleet, and subsequently became Lord High Chamberlain at Court; and last of all Treasurer, and husband of this highly extolled beauty. Even in the year 1819, the Grand Duchess could not resist expressing her admiration of this lady with her snow-white hair. At the end of October the whole Court returned to the city, and Nicholas and Alexandra to their beloved palace of Anitschkow.

The capital during the winter displayed itself in a most brilliant light, for the whole Imperial family were together; no melancholy death saddened the city as in the previous year; Alexandra, now the mother of two children, became daily more endeared to the country, her person daily unfolded greater beauties, and when she was seen in her carriage in the town, she met with the most respectful admiration. More and more did her warm maternal feelings, combined with grandeur of mien, beam from her charming countenance, enlivened by youthful freshness. A certain amount of timidity, that had clung to the stranger on her first appearance, was replaced by calm confidence, yet without depriving her of her original charm. This winter was distinguished by festivities in more than fifty houses, but Nicholas and his wife were forced to decline one invitation after another, as the health of the young mother was delicate, and the future was about to increase her mater-

nal duties. She joyfully lit up her Christmas-tree, and
allowed her little Saschinka to amuse herself by seeing
the bright lights; she occasionally also spent a few
hours in the theatre, but would not comply with the
wishes of those of high rank, that she should adorn their
entertainments with her presence; and this rest was
very grateful to her. Limited as were the hours she
and her husband could pass together in familiar intercourse, still they met daily; but in the month of May
Nicholas was obliged to leave his family for some time,
to inspect the fortresses as commander of artillery.
The winter passed quietly but pleasantly for the husband and wife, in domestic happiness; they occupied
their time not only by reading, but by cultivating
their favourite branches of art. Nicholas composed
marches, sang national melodies, accompanied on the
piano by Alexandra, and sketched and painted battle-
pieces with skill and correctness, under the tuition of
Sauerweid, a man distinguished both for his talents and
good character. He had made the acquaintance of
Nicholas when in England, and through life maintained the same independent but sincere tone in
his intercourse with him, and, subsequently, when
Emperor. This plain-spoken, simple artist was an un-
answerable proof to all courtiers, that straightforward
truth makes its way even with the most absolute
sovereign. He was often at the Anitschkow Palace;
for, in addition to the benefit Nicholas and Alexandra received from his talent, they thought Sauerweid witty, as well as amusing and instructive, in conversation. It was fortunate that Alexandra had been

so careful of her health during the winter, for in spring she became seriously ill; usually so gentle and calm, she was attacked by nervous irritability, for which she was repeatedly bled; it was with difficulty that she reached the wished-for Pawlowsk, and scarcely in the course of a few weeks had she in some degree regained her strength by country air, when she was obliged to repair to the camp at Krasnoe-Selò. She left it at the end of June, her feet so swollen, that during the fêtes in Peterhof she was visible only to her family and physicians. On the third day of her stay her recovery seemed so doubtful that on June 28th the family were prepared for her death. In the beginning of July, however, her illness took a favourable turn, and she was able to move to Pawlowsk, where in the course of a few days she had a dead child. The Empress-mother and the anxious husband during the next six weeks scarcely left her for a few minutes, and owing to their care and devotion, she was enabled in September once more to be in the open air, and to appear again at Court. She had given birth to three children in two years. She was still pale, but more lovely and charming than ever.

The joy and sympathy were sincere both in the Court and city when, towards the end of September, she went to Anitschkow; this time, however, not to pass the winter there, but to make preparations for a journey to Berlin, where the physicians recommended her to spend the winter. The thought of seeing again all her family, as well as the home scenes of her youth, where she had received her first impressions of life, was in itself truly delightful, and inspired the invalid with fresh strength. Change of air and scene are, under most circumstances, the best medicine, and her dearest treasure in Russia, her husband, was to accompany her. The farewell to her children, however, reminded her with irresistible force that her home was now for ever on the banks of the Neva. More than three years had passed rapidly far from her paternal home, a new domestic hearth had been established, new friends gained, and when she left these for some time to come, the love and good wishes both of Court and city, country and people, accompanied her.

CHAPTER VI.

BERLIN IN 1820.

BERLIN was at that time enjoying its fifth happy year
of peace, and the wounds inflicted by war had begun to
heal; but compared with Petersburg or Vïenna, it was
by no means a great capital, indeed, a provincial town
beside Prague or Venice. It could vie with the two
latter in the circumference of its walls, and in the length
and breadth of its streets, but these consisted of small
tasteless houses, indicating the quiet, unpretentious
citizen. No traces were visible of private houses such
as adorn every street in Petersburg like royal residences; it could not number as. many droschkys as
Petersburg daily carriages-and-four in the streets; no
vestige of hospitable mansions that received daily guests
at their table, or of aristocratic *salons* open every evening;
after ten o'clock at night the city seemed dead, and no
sound was heard in the streets but the cry of the night
watchmen, or the yawn of a sentry. There was no
very marked difference between the mode of living of
the noble and the citizen, although the two classes were
as strictly divided as in the previous century. The egotism of the Berliners was at that time quite a proverb
in the provinces and the rest of Germany; for the

usually pleasure-seeking social Berliners were unapproachable to strangers ; the city, too, was seldom visited, for, except its outward appearance, it offered nothing remarkable within its walls saving perhaps a parade. Vienna and Dresden possessed great treasures, which interested strangers, and the beauties of the environs of those cities constantly attracted foreigners ; but Berlin was surrounded by a frightful sandy desert, and within the city the clanking of warlike sabres on the pavement seemed to leave no place for the works of the Muses. In fact, Berlin in the year 1815 could not boast of as many art treasures as Prince Jussupoff alone in his Archangelsk Palace in Moscow. The military were predominant in society, the highest civil officials being at most only tolerated ; indeed General von Müffling allowed Alexander von Humboldt to stand half-an-hour before him while he remained seated in the presence of a man whom even the Emperor Alexander received with princely honours. The renown of the Prussian army was everywhere admitted and respected, but every officer proclaimed this loudly and with great eloquence, whereas Blücher himself spoke with modesty of his deeds, and the King with humility. The Berlin of that day was deficient both in means and taste, not yet called forth to imitate the richly furnished hospitable houses so universal in Petersburg and Moscow ; on the contrary, every worthy father of a family became a member of some public place of recreation, where, on Sundays and many other evenings, he found amusement away from his home, the care of which (as it still is in many German towns) he left to his wife. While the Berliners amused themselves in this inexpensive fashion, all that remained for strangers was the Thiergarten with its public restaurants, and in the evening the theatre. The King with his sound good sense had long been aware that a great capital must be provided with more intellectual resources, and thus, for the improvement of the people, the Berlin University was established, and the scientific men summoned thither diffused another spirit in every class of society. We may name as the first star in the new University that great philosopher of our Fatherland, the orator of the German nation, Fichte, who even in the previous century had the courage to demand from the German Princes freedom of speech and of the press. Fichte was not so much a teacher of students, as a man who appealed to the cultivated portion of the whole German nation, to endeavour to awaken in them at that dead period some interest in intellectual pursuits. By his lectures and writings he revived love for their Fatherland; he spoke of the rights of man and not of classes; he was a thorough popular instructor. During the few years of his academical career this man awakened the enthusiasm of the Berlin society for the more lofty aims of life. Fichte had at this period been dead for seven years; but Wilhelm von Humboldt, the true creator of the Berlin University, still lived, and although no longer a Minister of State, he exercised surpassing influence over the highest circles in Berlin; on others, however, the clever linguist, Frederick August Wolf, had much sway, not only by his comprehensive knowledge of antiquity, but also by his wit and refined sociable manners. Schleiermacher preached from the pulpit pure Christi-

anity, divested of superstition, as impressively as he
lectured from the professor's chair in the University ;
while in society, though combined with the strictest code
of morality, he was cheerful and amiable as well as
witty. Science and social life were more and more united
by men like Ancillon, Stägemann, Hardenberg, by the
celebrated physicians Hufeland and Heim, and above
all, by Prince Anton Radziwill. The King also provided
for the spirit gradually springing up in his capital by
other means. A new ornament of the city was the
Giustiniani Picture Gallery, purchased by the King in
Paris ; he also made a present of the choicest collection
of statues to his capital, the Collenberg cabinet of art
gems, and a set of plaster-of-Paris casts of the most
admirable works of antiquity. For the benefit of the
drama he built the new theatre in the Gens d'Arme
Market, a master-work of the talented Schinkel, who not
only contributed much directly to the embellishment of
the city, but also to the diffusion of good taste in architecture, by a succession of able pupils. The King likewise engaged the first actors in Germany to adorn his
stage, and this institution of the Muses soon became one
of the most esteemed in all Germany. He contributed
with still greater liberality to the ballet and to the opera,
which was not only as formerly open during the Carnival,
but during the whole year. Spontini developed his genius
in operas ; and the brilliancy of the orchestra, the scenery,
and the ballet began to vie with those of Paris and
Petersburg. In short, under the rule of Frederick William the Third, Berlin seemed to emulate the lustre of
artistic Dresden, and of those seats of the Muses, Weimar

and Jena. In the consciousness of a new epoch, the citizens, like the students of the Wartburg, began to abolish the old fashions, jackets, queues, and ratans, appreciating now the more elevated pleasures of life. Berlin gradually became a great city, less by its material resources than by its awakening intellectual powers.

The full importance of Russia is not properly estimated until, after a prolonged stay there, we revisit Germany, when the contrast forces itself on an impartial eye. All the treasures that the King had so munificently bestowed on his capital did not amount in value to the collections of individual Russian princes, far less to the objects of art in the Hermitage, recently adorned by the Emperor with the finest specimens of Claude Lorraine and Paul Potter. The Prussian nobility could, indeed, boast of the most chivalrous deeds and the most heroic self-sacrifice at all times, but the nobles in a whole province could not in wealth be compared with one single Scheremetief, Jussupof, Demidow, or Woronzow, while the munificence and hospitality of these nobles, and the grand princely style in which they lived, were utterly foreign to our German character. In Berlin only *one* house was celebrated for its reception of all, and especially open to the Muses, that of Prince Anton Radziwill. This Polish family has been numbered from the sixteenth century among the German princes of the empire, but Anton did not appear at the Court of Berlin till his Fatherland had been erased from the political map of Europe, in the time of Frederick William the Second; his handsome person, his stately chivalrous bearing, his German cultivation and conspicuous talents,

caused him to be the cynosure of all eyes.   Prince
Adam Czartoryski arrived at the same period at the
Court of Russia, and proved its scourge, though he gained
the friendship of Alexander. Prince Anton Radziwill,
however, accomplished an infinitely greater triumph in
Berlin, as he not only won the favour of the whole
Court, but also the hand and heart of Princess Louise, a
niece of Frederick the Great.   He fled with the Prussian
Court to Königsberg in those disastrous days when his
countryman, Adam Czartoryski, had again resigned the
brilliant post of Minister for Foreign Affairs for Russia.
Anton Radziwill strove to banish his sorrow for the
misfortunes of his Fatherland by the influence of the
Muses, and remained faithful to them even as Stadtholder
of the Prussian province of Posen, where he used every
effort to win his countrymen for the Prussian reigning
family. . In Berlin, his house was the earliest and only.
one where were to be met the members of the royal family
and the dignitaries of the country, along with Zel-
ter, Bernhard Romberg, Rauch, Schinkel, and Spontini,
and where the ten years' old Felix Mendelssohn performed his first attempts at composition.   The Prince
was a Mæcenas, an artist both in theory and practice ;
an aristocrat of the most refined manners and of the
most pure benevolence, never to be forgotten by those
who conversed even once with him.

The other houses open to society and entertaining
handsomely were those of Duke Carl of Mecklenburg,
the State Chancellor, Prince of Hardenberg, and Rose, the
English ambassador of that day.   The etiquette of the
Prussian Court only sanctions the members of the royal

family appearing at the houses of foreign ministers
when princes belonging to their own Court are present.
As the Duke of Cumberland was then living in Berlin,
the royal family could visit the hospitable and brilliant
house of the English ambassador, which very much
tended to promote the new life in Berlin. The King,
an enemy of all pomp, led a patriarchal life, equally
revered by his family circle and by the bulk of his
people, engaged in quiet but useful occupations; his
children were growing up to his entire satisfaction, while
his oldest and more distant relatives were gradually
falling like withered leaves from the stem.   In this year
too the sister of the late King, the widowed Princess of
Orange, and likewise the Duchess of York, the Queen's
step-sister, both died. His second daughter, Alexandrina, was, however, betrothed, and his eldest, the
Grand Duchess of Russia, was to join him in a few
days in the Palace, which she and her husband were to
adorn the whole winter.

The journey ôf this year awakened in the King the
most cherished remembrances. He saw in Prenzlau
the house where his mother was born, and heard with
emotion every word about her from the people, in whose
memory she still lived. He also visited Hohenzieritz
where Queen Louise died. The love of his people daily
increased, especially when they met him walking in the
Thiergarten, in a simple uniform, with his daughter,
sometimes stopping to converse with a passer-by, or
(which occurred this summer) buying the stock of a
poor lad, sending his aide-de-camp to the mother, and
providing for his future lot. He went with his children

to meet Nicholas and Alexandra at Friedrichsfelde; and now followed a succession of those happy family days, which form the brightest moments of life, particularly for crowned heads, granting repose to the delicate Alexandra, thus enabling her to regain health and strength. All festivities were therefore easily avoided for the first two months, though the Grand Duchess received all the friends of her youth. Family festivities, however, are very fleeting for monarchs; and scarcely had his beloved daughter and son-in-law arrived from Petersburg, when the Congress of Troppau demanded the presence of the King. The two Emperors, Alexander and Francis the First, were already there, awaiting their ally, who shortly arrived, and after a stay of several weeks, without any result, returned to Berlin at the end of November, when Nicholas also went there, and only returned about Christmas. A series of Court and family fêtes now took place in honour of the King's daughter and her restoration to health. The Berlin Court did not shine much in those days by lavish expenditure, but by the numerous intellectual minds that surrounded the King; but still, when the question was to receive an illustrious guest in a proper manner, Frederick William the Third perfectly understood how to combine royal splendour with good taste and good sense, as well as the utmost simplicity; he surprised the strangers in a very unexpected manner; and the Empress-mother was fully justified in saying of him, "He always does more than any one could think or expect." Some unusual festivity was at this time to be devised and accomplished for the amusement of his daughter.

Although the Berlin Court could not approach that of
Russia in the magnificence of its gifts, on the other hand,
the sphere of art in Berlin was far more varied and
imaginative than in Petersburg, and the Muses, in alliance with the Court, were capable of organizing a fête,
novel in its idea, rich in splendour, charming all by
its *tableaux- vivants*, and intellectual in its signification.
The theatre was undoubtedly the first in Germany,
and also the opera; in the former, by the aid of the
celebrated artist, Mademoiselle Händel-Schütz, *poses plas-
tiques*, or living representations of pictures and poems,
were introduced, which not only met with the most
unequivocal applause in public, but found many eager
imitators in domestic circles. At the suggestion of Duke
Carl of Mecklenburg, the celebrated poem of Thomas
Moore, " Lalla Rookh," was selected for the subjects of
these *tableaux*.

There was an ample personality to co-operate in the
scheme, and all the Royal Princes, the King and Court,
art and science, combined to enliven the fête. The
management of the whole was intrusted to Count
Brühl, Intendant of the Royal Theatre; the scenery and
arrangement of the groups to the talented Schinkel;
all the explanatory verses were set to music by the
Chevalier Spontini, and executed in the most masterly
manner by the great singers, Madames Milder, Schulz,
Seidler, and Bader. The substance of the poem contained a delicate allusion to the illustrious guests present
—the Grand-Ducal pair. The King of Bucharia (Abdallah) goes to Delhi, to visit the ruler of India, Arungzebe. The Bucharian monarch wooes Lalla Rookh, the

" tulip-cheeked" daughter of the Indian Sultan, for his
son, Prince Alexis. She is promised to him, and they
are first to see and meet each other in Cashmere, and
to be married there. They set out on their journey.
The bride, however, is accompanied by a Bucharian
court retinue, and among them is a young poet, who
beguiles the length and fatigue of the journey by stories,
to be represented by *tableaux*, displaying the different
acts of the whole poem. During the *tableaux* a song
behind the scenes explains the picture. The first was
the " veiled Prophet of Khorassan," the second " Paradise and the Peri," the third a tale of the " Ghebers"
(or Fire-worshippers), the last the " Feast of Roses at
Cashmere." Each *tableau* denotes that the Princess
has accomplished part of her journey. At the close
of the last tale Lalla Rookh arrives at a lake, and a
barque bears her across. On the other side stands a
palace. Her bridegroom, Prince Alexis, descends the
lofty flight of steps to meet her, and she recognises in
him the poet and minstrel who had enlivened her journey
by so much play of fancy. The preparations for the
fête were completed in fourteen days, and splendid Oriental dresses also procured. They succeeded in learning
thoroughly the proper costumes, translating the verses
into German, and having them practised by the singers
already named, besides distributing 123 parts in the
festive entertainment to the right persons. The whole
society was divided into two camps, Indians and Bucha-
rians. The ladies all wore their hair smooth, and
hanging down, without any ornament, but the head was
encircled with rows of pearls and delicate chains of pure

gold; the dresses were of the finest muslin, fastened by a girdle in front with two long broad floating ends, the arms bare and richly decked with gold and pearls. The Queen of the Fête was also that of this brilliant plastic representation. Alexandra was at that time three-and-twenty, in the most perfect bloom of her rare beauty; her waist and figure majestic and full of regal dignity; her features did not bear the stamp of the cold regular forms of the antique Greek, but rather the rounded contours that usually characterize a genuine German type in the charming luxuriance of youth; it was not the pride of a Juno, but the sensibility of woman's soul that glanced from her lustrous eyes; love for her husband and children brightened her aspect, and every portion of her being displayed the fascination and charm of happy youth. On this occasion she appeared with a crown on her head; her long hair drooping on each side in curls on her shoulders. She wore a white dress with a body of gold-cloth, while the ends of her girdle hung down; pearls and jewels vied with each other in beauty, and even her Oriental slippers were em-broidered with emeralds. A rose-coloured veil, worked in silver thread, floated over her graceful form. Alexis (the Grand Duke Nicholas), equally conspicuous among the male characters, selected his own costume. A close-fitting blue coat, in accordance with the Circassian dress, a broad girdle with long ends, yellow Oriental shoes, and a green turban, in the shape of a Tartar cap, distinguished the Prince of Bucharia. The significance of the tale was evident to both.

The remaining parts of the Indian and Bucharian

royal families were distributed to Royal Princes and
Princesses. Arungzebe was Prince William, brother of
King Frederick William the Third. The sisters of the
Sultan were represented by the Duchess of Cumberland,
and the Princesses William and Alexandrina; the sons
of the Sultan, by the Crown Prince and Prince William
(the present King of Prussia), and the youngest son of
Prince Albert, Adalbert, and Princes Solms and Radziwill. Abdallah, father of Alexis, was the Duke of
Cumberland, and the mother, Princess Louise Radziwill.

This interesting fête took place in the royal Palace
on the 27th of January 1821. The suite of rooms
selected overlooked the pleasure-grounds. In the largest
hall a theatrical stage was erected for the *tableaux*.
The singers were stationed behind the scenes, and accompanied each *tableau* with an explanatory song;
between the spectators and the theatre there was space
left for dancing, which occupied the time between the
acts. Never had the calm countenance of the King
betrayed so much emotion as on that memorable
evening, in the joy of seeing the bright happiness of
his daughter, and while glancing unperceived at her fine
features, no doubt many a furtive memory of his Queen
stole into his heart, who in former years had so embellished his existence, but whose loyal heart had been
broken by the hard strokes of fate.

The King by no means wished selfishly to reserve
this remarkable fête for the Court and the favoured few;
he desired that the greater part of the educated public
in Berlin should likewise enjoy it; thus it was repeated

on February 11th, and more than 3000 people invited
A few days previously, the handsome hall of the new
theatre had been opened by a ball, and the stage itself
some months later. A large portion of the Berlin public
could not reconcile the King's delight in operas and
ballets, and more especially in light comedy, with his grave
and devout character; foolish ignorance, not to comprehend that kings, in particular, must vary the grave
monotony of their existence by descending from such
heights into the exuberance of life, and that they require
recreation as much as other men: The development,
too, of every civilized nation has invariably pursued its
course by means of dramatic literature, and to this
belongs the light civic comedy, and even farces, just as
thistles, nettles, and marsh plants belong to the realm
of vegetation. The tastes of the German people at that
period were very still very coarse, and they rejoiced in
passing their evenings in beer-houses, and very often
in fighting. The first and best method of rescuing the
people from such debasing practices is the theatre; for
in farces they see their own defects ridiculed, and begin
to think of their own follies. Kotzebué and Iffland
succeeded in sweeping away much mischief that formerly existed in popular life. The King placed at the
head of his theatre as its superintendent a refined and
educated man, Count Brühl, who, in friendly connection
with Goethe, inspired good taste and talent into the
undertaking. Artists now began no longer to be excluded from society, but, on the contrary, were sought
after and invited; and the King, especially in Potsdam,
was in the habit of conversing with them in the most

friendly manner. There were very few evenings that
the King did not visit the theatre, although such was
not his custom till after the close of the war. Thus
Berlin daily more and more divested itself of its old
provincial "peruke and pigtail" ways, and the King
contributed most of all to remove the prejudices of the
German *Philister*. Berlin became the capital of Germany,
not owing to the wealth of its inhabitants, like Petersburg and Moscow, where all sources flowed together in
harmony, but by the alliances and relationships of the
Court with so many others in Germany and Europe,
and by the vast number of men of intellectual capacity, who, without always being natives of Prussia, had
distinguished themselves in the Liberation War, and
subsequently settled in Berlin, and also by its being a
place of rendezvous for royal personages of every
country. Although the homely simplicity of the King
was highly to be commended, still it did not suffice to
meet the new state of things; of this the monarch was
fully aware, and, thanks to his foresight, he laid the
foundation of the present art-loving Berlin. But this
was only the beginning. At that time the King could
not show his foreign guests the wealth and pomp of
museums similar to those in Petersburg, Vienna, and
Dresden; fêtes, such as Augustus the Strong formerly
gave in Saxony, were contrary to his pious ideas, and
nature will never even now attract any one to Berlin.

But the theatre at least was on so great a scale in
every branch, that people came from the country solely
to attend a performance; it was the central point of
union for the King and his people, for native and foreign

visitors, and for emulation of talent from all German districts. Frederick William was not only the King of his people, but, more than any other sovereign, a genuine German King. The Berliners took the liberty of discussing him very freely, because they loved and venerated him both as a king and father, and perhaps from his showing more sympathy with his subjects than the Great Frederick ever did.

After a quiet but enjoyable winter, Nicholas and Alexandra accompanied the King to the country; to Potsdam, Sans Souci, Paretz, and the Peacock's Island. Potsdam, like Zarskoe-Selò, once the abode of the great Catherine, has become renowned by Frederick the Great having inhabited it, and also by its fine palaces and gardens. Just as Alexander the First only lived in two simple rooms in the enormous Palace of Zarskoe-Selò, so Frederick William the Third also preferred the most remote and unadorned apartments, and liked to stroll about constantly in the adjacent lime-tree avenues in solitude, like his ally Alexander. Neither of these sovereigns, however, excluded the public from their gardens, and were therefore often disturbed in their contemplations. Frederick William the Third on this account preferred the village of Paretz, particularly in the spring, to royal Potsdam or Sans Souci. That secluded village, situated about two miles from Potsdam, bears a good deal the character of one of Van der Velde's Dutch landscapes; the church projects over the whole scene, and green meadows, enlivened by rich flocks, surround it on every side. All that might recall royal pomp is banished from this spot; instead of a palace

stands opposite the church a simple but comfortably
furnished house inhabited by the King, and which on
every side offers a view of free nature. The Grand-
Ducal pair followed the King into this retirement, and
shared with him his simple dwelling, which, like the
whole village, recalled Pawlowsk, or the camp of
Krasnoe-Selò. To the King, as well as to his daughter
Alexandra, it was most essential to pass a few hours
morning and evening alone with nature ; the soul dis-
tracted by business and pleasure is soothed by the
gracious spectacle, and feels the majesty of that creating
and preserving Power on whom we all depend. Alexandra watched the clouds in dreamy reverie, studied
the flowers of the meadow, reposed in the gloom of
the forest, envied birds and butterflies their wings, and
when the breezes played round her at sunset, they
seemed music to her ear ; she rejoiced in being able to
discard for a few moments the greatness with which
Fate had burdened her, and to inhale the pure breath of
quiet nature. In Sans Souci, as well as in Paretz and the
Peacock's Island, this enjoyment was all the greater and
more undisturbed, from the tone of the Prussian Court
being there more easy and unconstrained than that of
Russia under the eyes of the Empress-mother, and a
Court devoid of all appreciation of nature. Alexandra
here continued her morning readings, while the King
was engaged with his Ministers. The whole society assembled about eleven o'clock, and drove out of the
village in open carriages, generally to some adjacent
height, where they breakfasted, and conversed in gaiety
and playfulness. All high dignity here gave place to

nature, and when the party assembled at half-past one
o'clock for dinner at a table placed in a building partly
open, the inhabitants of the village collected together,
not only to see the royal family nearer, but often to
receive fruit, pastry, or wine from some of the most
illustrious of the group.

While the young world dispersed gaily on every side
after dinner, sometimes playing at children's games, or
jeux de société, or went boating on the water singing
German songs, the King remained alone and grave,
reflecting on impending business, or sometimes with a
book, till evening recalled the guests, and during their
simple meal each related what had occurred during the
day. Visitors or officials who meanwhile came to the
King, stayed for supper without ceremony.

The King found the Peacock Island, a mile from
Potsdam, in the circle of the Havel, an equally charming
abode, and perhaps this was even more the case with
his daughter, as it awakened a thousand memories
of her childhood and youth in the time of her beloved
mother. In former years the King and Queen had
often met strangers here, and, unrecognised, conversed
kindly with them, and invited them to breakfast or
supper, both often surprising their children, and sharing
their sports and amusements. Here the King always
cherished a rare flower under the name of his daughter
Charlotte, and cordially greeted his distant child every
morning under this type. In later years he caused a
Russian peasant's hut to be constructed, and named it
Nikolsky, after his son-in-law. To the memory of his
deeply-regretted Queen he built on the furthest point of

the island a simple temple, in which he placed her bust, and liked to visit it alone and at night by moonlight. This life restored the health of Alexandra, and enabled her to enjoy her youth free from the burden imposed on her by exalted birth and station.

Nearly eight months passed in her paternal home as quickly as a bright dream, and she must now prepare in earnest for her journey to Ems. From her childhood she had cherished the wish to see Father Rhine and his hills, and those memorable towns that have survived so many centuries of German history. A genuine German is at home in woods and hills, whereas the Slavonic races, accustomed to boundless plains, feel pent up in a mountainous district; and yet millions of Germans were obliged at that period to renounce the happiness of seeing the fairest scenes in the history of their fatherland, as travelling was rendered so difficult even to opulent people by the bad state of the roads, by oppressive tolls and custom-house dues, and discomforts of every kind. The learned man or the official seldom in that day crossed the boundaries of their province; and the University at which they had studied was the farthest limit of their journeys, while the still more insignificant *Philister* considered it a crime, after completing his year of apprentice travel, to pass a single night away from his native town. Visits to German baths, as well as the Congresses of that day, first excited a wish to travel, checked, however, by German provincialism. An Empire like Russia, the circumference of which borders on that of three-quarters of the world, where the extent of single provinces surpasses that of

our German kingdoms, whose officials are transferred
from the north to the south, from the east to the west,
witnesses a perpetual succession of travellers from the
Baltic to the Black Sea, intercourse far closer than was
to be found at that time between Bavaria and Baden.
To see Father Rhine once in a man's lifetime was and
is the first wish of all Germans, just as the Russian
longs to visit the Kremlin, the Italian St. Peter's, and the
Mussulman the tomb of the Prophet. And yet how
seldom was this desire fulfilled! Apprentices in their
year of travel often had a glimpse of this river, but more
than three-fourths of all Germans died without having
seen the district of the Rhine. The warmest wish of
Alexandra was now realized, and in after days it proved
one of the most enchanting reminiscences of her
youth. At that time she kept a journal of the impressions made on her by new objects, which, however,
she carefully concealed. Her health was quite re-established in Ems, while the presence of her husband and
the vicinity of her father, who visited with her the finest
portions of the Rhine, made her stay there quite a
Paradise on earth. At one time the King surprised
her by coming to Ems, and at another she went to join
the King at Coblenz. On one occasion Nicholas, whom
she believed to be far away attending some military manœuvres, suddenly appeared. Sometimes a
quiet circle passed the day in a forest, in a castle, or on
the banks of the mighty stream. Alexandra knew how
to enjoy life. In the middle of August she and her
husband repaired to Berlin, where they passed a happy
fortnight in their family circle, and, after an absence of

more than ten months, returned by Warsaw to Petersburg.

The Grand Duke was astonished to find himself received by his brother Constantine in a manner quite unsuitable to his rank ; for Nicholas was still only a Chief of Brigade, or, to speak more correctly, only a distinguished private individual, when compared to the Emperor Alexander or to the Generalissimo of the Polish army. A few days were most agreeably spent in Warsaw, and then Nicholas and Alexandra proceeded to their winter quarters in imperial Petersburg. During the next four years there was no essential change in the lives of our illustrious couple ; the circle of their acquaintances was enlarged, but their more intimate friendship was reserved for those whom we have already named. Alexandra presented her husband with a daughter on the 30th August 1822—Olga, now Queen of Würtemberg. Their domestic life was more retired than ever, and estranged from the vain pomps of the world. Alexandra was the mother of her children in the highest sense of the word, and Nicholas, limited to a narrow circle of official duties, found his greatest felicity, both as a husband and a father, in his own home. He never strove for the approval of society, but those who saw him in his own family discovered that the inexorably strict but conscientious military chief was a kind and benevolent man. In public, however, the pale haggard Nicholas was not beloved—indeed, not really known. Owing to the imperious character and extraordinary energy of the Empress-mother, and also to the fact of the existence of another Empress, Alexandra

could only play a subordinate part; still, those who
visited Anitschkow remarked at this little Court that
she did not sacrifice her own individuality and independence to traditional etiquette, and the prescribed
Court tone. At last people were accustomed to this,
though at first it was startling. The day of her arrival
in Pawlowsk, when she first entered the *salon*, where
the Court assembled, among the strangers who were to
be presented to her, she remarked her friend Cecilia, and
hastened at once to embrace most cordially the playmate of her childhood. This incident, however, was an
offence against the rules of Court; but it could not be
denied that a friend is dearer to the human heart than a
mere courtier, and that the noblest feelings ought not to
be stifled by high rank and birth. Just as on the day
of her marriage, when a weight of pearls and diamonds
burdened her, and she decorated herself with a white
rose that shone forth in its purity from amid the glittering gems a type of her being—simple, natural, fresh, and
charming. The crowd of courtiers delighted in the rare
splendours of imperial pomp, and overlooked the rose;
one mature eye alone observed it, and recognised its
profound meaning. Her independence of feeling was
displayed with as much modesty as that rose among the
jewels. In the society of the capital she was highly
esteemed from the frank cordial sympathy she showed
during her stay there; she was fond of dancing in all
the gaiety of youth, but it was far from having become
the passion with which the capital reproached her in
after days; her presence was everywhere enlivening,
while that of the two Empresses, probably without their

being aware of it, imposed rigid and severe restraint. Alexandra preferred the society of sprightly youth to that of the old Muscovite generals and senators; she first introduced into Anitschkow, and afterwards into the Winter Palace, the natural tone that pervaded the Court of her father; she exalted female dignity and natural charm above imperial rank. But she was dear to the whole country by having given it a son and daughter, Alexander and Constantine having no hope of heirs of their own, and imparting in this way a new charm to domestic life. She thus took deep and enduring root within the next few years in the life of the Russian Court. A grand destiny awaited her, however, in the future, sealed beforehand by a State agreement, without either her husband or herself having any true conception of the fact. The whole Russian Court had still less idea of it, because in the interior of the kingdom a widely-spread conspiracy against the throne was gradually forming, and the dagger already sharpened that was to seek the life of the noblest of all monarchs. We now turn to the idyllic family life of the Grand-Ducal pair in the last years of Alexander's life.

CHAPTER VII.

IT is a widely-spread notion that the Emperor
Alexander, by his conversations with Frau von Krüdener, and also owing to the Holy Alliance, had changed
his religious views, and since the year 1815 publicly
displayed a new gloomy mystic mood. Persons very
nearly related to the Emperor, and first of these we
name his sister-in-law, knew absolutely nothing till
the year 1819 of any mental change in this monarch.
Alexandra, in the year 1817, found him as cheerful and amiable, and his conversation as fresh and
fascinating, as in the years 1813-14. The variation of
mood therefore observed in the last years of Alexander's life in no respect proceeded from Frau von
Krüdener; the causes of this phenomenon must be sought
elsewhere. Even before his succession to the throne
Alexander was superior to the ambition that eagerly
aspires to crown and sceptre; reared in the Court of
his grandmother, married when scarcely sixteen years
of age, he witnessed the sudden and hasty successive
changes in the system of government, and learned rightly
to estimate the whole weight of an Imperial Russian
crown before it was placed on his own head. His edu-

cation taught him that man has rights, which if proclaimed and acknowledged from the throne, would win
for him, by realizing his mission, unfading laurels.   His
heart was filled with benevolence towards mankind, but
his acquaintance with the courtiers of his grandmother
and his father was not calculated to inspire him with
that high esteem for human beings that must exist if
they are to be benefited.   His modesty made him think
that he did not possess sufficient strength for the lofty
position he was to occupy, and therefore the thought
arose within his mind wholly to renounce the Crown
even before being called on to wear it.   But suddenly,
before completing his twenty-fourth year, he became
Emperor, and the new century began with a reign that
was to amend the faults of the previous one.   All Europe
greeted in him a new epoch; friend and foe equally
watched the efforts of the young Czar with curiosity.
For Alexander loudly promised that law and not arbi-
trary will should rule, that due weight should be given
to the spirit of the times and to enlightenment, and Government and the authorities armed with greater power and
dignity.   For the fulfilment of these projects Alexander
surrounded himself with men imbued with similar ideas.
We may name Count Kotschubei, with whom the reader
is already acquainted, as a man who, even in the time of
Paul, possessed and deserved Alexander's entire confidence, and likewise Count Stroganof, Nowosiltzof, and the
Polish Prince Czartoryski.   But these men, who strove to
aid Alexander in his zealous reforms, soon became objects
of calumny, envy, and suspicion.   It was indeed an admirable pretext for the secret opposition, a man being

admitted into Alexander's intimacy who, after the final partition of Poland, had come to Petersburg, and was there deemed a scourge. Alexander first lost the confidence of his capital by Prince Adam Czartoryski, who consequently soon retired from the ministry. Another far more influential man, and yet the most intimate of all counsellors, the soul of every reform to the close of the year 1811, was Michael Speransky, who excited observation and envy, and at length public enmity, by his obscure origin—he being the son of a poor village pastor—but still more by his sudden rise, and by the entire and sincere confidence that Alexander placed in him, and every year in a higher degree. The Emperor, adverse from his youth to all brilliant Court fêtes, passed most of his evenings, more especially since 1808, alone with Speransky, and imparted to him all his ideas about reform. No one could respect more than this enlightened friend the Czar's benevolent projects, or better carry them into effect. The Emperor earnestly discussed and devised with his confidant the plan of a Constitution, in which all his ideas about reform were systematically set forth. This scheme, however, appears never to have left the custody of the Emperor, as he was constantly improving it with his own hand. On one point alone the Czar and Speransky could not agree: whether the intended reforms were to take effect suddenly and at once, or to be made public singly and gradually. The Emperor, at all events, was the more prudent—Speransky perhaps not discreet enough in his sincere zeal. His amendments extended to every portion of the State —the administration of justice, lawgiving, finance,

public instruction,—and he thus made himself a legion
of secret and open enemies. All the customs, abuses,
and excited passions of five hundred years stood everywhere in the way of his well-intended projects. The
recent Council of the Empire was loudly censured as an
imitation of the French, and a limitation of the Imperial
power. The ministers who since 1802 had replaced
former presidents, treated their offices and their pro-
perties as villanages of their own. Whoever ventured
to assail such pretensions, or to improve the adminis-
trative machine, was proclaimed a traitor to his country.
As since 1808 Speransky was known to be the originator of all these revolutions, it was easy for the Opposition, by removing him personally from the Emperor,
to put a stop to all reforms. At last the Czar, besieged
on every side by attacks on Speransky, said to Parrot,
"I can no longer defend Speransky's measures against
the complaints of the public." The outbreak of the
French war was also attributed to this admirable man;
and thus, in order to pacify the public, the Emperor was
forced to sacrifice his friend and adviser to the hatred
he had incurred. With the retirement of Speransky all
reforms were at an end and forgotten, every eye being
directed towards the war, for which the monarch had
been for some years prepared by the warning of Speransky. Alexander, in taking leave of his friend, told
him that at any other less busy time he would have
passed two years, if required, in investigating such accu-
sations and justifying him. Thus the twelve years'
efforts of the Emperor to improve the condition of his
country were baffled by the force of circumstances; that

is, by obdurate selfishness, prejudice, and the ambition
of the higher class of officials; in short, by a world
incapable of comprehending the noble intentions of the
Emperor.   In the beginning of the year 1812, Alexander was depressed and disheartened.   The most vast
army that the world had seen since the days of Xerxes
and Attila had penetrated into the heart of his kingdom.   All seemed lost; according to Napoleon's own
words, "Russia is forsaken by her good star."   But
the arrogant Corsican was himself scathed by Heaven's
lightning; Russia became the grave of that invincible
army.   Alexander now took up the sword, and, after a
year of victories and losses, of hopes and doubts, after
much strife and fighting, found himself at the head
of a victorious army in Paris, and, directed by Providence, all Europe having selected him as umpire and
peace-maker. · He thus completed a greater work than
his titanic adversary in his audacity ever demanded
from Heaven.   The history of the world does not furnish a more startling change in the course of events, nor
ever witnessed greater self-control and forbearance in a
conqueror.   The man who once doubted his own strength
saw his boldest dreams and wishes—to reconcile princes
and people and to bless the world with peace—suddenly
realized, and said, "This is the work of God."   In this
elevated mood he formed the Holy Alliance, which was
henceforth to replace by precepts of justice and Christian brotherhood the maxims of modern State-wisdom.
Alexander, belonging to the orthodox Greek Church,
could proclaim these principles without reservation,
and carry them out in Russia, as well as in the rest of

Europe; for the Greek Church recognises the equality·
of mankind and brotherhood even more unreservedly
than either the Catholic or Protestant faith. The philanthropic views of the Emperor were in no degree changed
by this most wonderful succession of events. On the
contrary, his religious convictions took deeper root than
before, when he learned the heroic power of self-
sacrifice of his people in the burning of Moscow, and in
the defence of its churches. In true humility he pro-
tested against the flattering appellation of "the God-
sent," bestowed on him by the Senate of Petersburg in
1814, declaring that the peace of Europe was the work
of the Almighty. The obligations he undertook towards the Holy Alliance were only a public declaration
of the ideas that had previously occupied him, and to
which he continued faithful to his last breath. In this
spirit he repaired to Warsaw, announcing there the
restoration of the kingdom and a more liberal Constitution, and by such an act astonishing the world. When he
subsequently himself opened the Imperial Diet, he expressed the hope to be enabled to bestow free institutions on all the people whom God had intrusted to his
sceptre. In the same frame of mind, and same year, he
granted personal freedom to the Helots in the provinces
of the Baltic, with the consent of the German nobility,
who, during five hundred years, had kept the unhappy
aborigines in bondage. By the moderation of his claims
on conquered France at the Aix-la-Chapelle Congress he
amazed Europe, and by his example induced the other
Courts to be equally magnanimous. But at this same
Congress it was evident to the eager and energetic Em-

peror that he had previously taken a mistaken view of the intentions of the Holy Alliance, and at all events they were now disposed to a reaction, and that his own ideas and mode of action were in direct opposition to those of Austria, who was not disposed to grant rights or liberty to her people, and only wished to make use of Alexander's power to strengthen monarchical principles.

But the reaction of that period did not proceed from Prince Metternich and Austria alone, but from the universal longing for peace, and for an idyllic quiet life, and from the horror of nations at the bloodshed of the French Revolution, from their misery at the wounds already inflicted by war, from the universal impoverishment, and in Germany from love of old-established usages and mediæval customs, and, above all, from the political immaturity of the whole nation. Many things concurred in modifying his liberal views ; indeed, much was cunningly contrived to drive him into an opposite mode of thinking. A work "On the Spirit of German Universities" by a Moldavian, Stourdza, was written to show the dangers now brooding over German Universities. This book was justly ascribed to Austrian influence. Alexander indeed had founded a University in his Baltic provinces, and was in friendly correspondence with Parrot, one of its Professors. A manuscript that came only into the hands of the Emperor, "On Secret Associations in German Universities," written by a Courlander, excited considerable suspicion in the Emperor's mind, and with his attention exclusively fixed on European politics, he returned to Petersburg at the end of December 1818, by no means, however, in that golden

mood or with that charm that made him a demigod in
the eyes of all Europe. And such a change of mood in
the Emperor was instantly taken advantage of to win
him over to the views of the same opposition that caused
the. fall of the liberal Speransky. Prince Alexander
Nikolaewitsch Galitzin proved to the Emperor from the
Holy Scriptures that he was destined by Providence to
become the guardian angel of Europe against all revolutionary attempts ; and in the eyes of such a man all
progress and improvement were in themselves a revolu-
lution. Another event moved him deeply in the year
1819—the death of his sister, the Queen of Würtemberg, which we already mentioned. The intelligence
also of Kotzebue's assassination in March of this year,
by a Jena student, Sand, maintainèd and indeed increased his discontent. A feeling now seized him that
his magnanimous projects would be a second time, in
the face of all Europe, crushed by a reaction, which
owed its existence to his own unselfishness. Besides
having no enlightened friend, Heaven had not granted
him any family, a blessing richly bestowed on his
brother Nicholas. The misunderstanding between him
and his noble wife, created and kept alive by jealousy
and malice, was not yet adjusted. The saintly Elisabeth, living in cloister-like retirement from the Court
and the world, was in such a state of nervous excitement that she could not become the comforter of the
disturbed Emperor. In this state of dejection the Czar
often visited a private family, in order to become acquainted with men estranged from the splendour and
burden of the Crown, and in whose domestic circle

unconstrained happiness was familiar. While the renowned Emperor, the Autocrat of 50,000,000, the angel
of peace for all Europe, sought that felicity enjoyed in.
so high a degree by his ally, Frederick-William, and
that his brother Nicholas seemed to have inherited from
his father-in-law, he was himself besieged by selfish
ambition under the mask of friendship, perverting his
sincere religious feelings into gloomy mysticism, in-
venting dangers in order to alarm him, and stifling in
his heart his natural benevolence and kindly disposition towards humanity.   Under these evil influences he
removed the Professors from the Universities of Petersburg and Charkow—men in whose lectures the Emperor's mother saw so little danger that she adopted
them in her own educational institutions.   Prince A.
Galitzin, having divested himself of the epicurean
mantle of his youth, now took refuge in a nimbus of
piety, and became Minister of Public Instruction and
Culture.   Another person also enjoyed the full confidence of the Czar, Count Araktscheef, an enemy to all
enlightenment, and a terror to the whole realm.   The
opposition party, who had got rid of Speransky in 1812,
now exclusively surrounded the Emperor, and held him
entangled in their meshes.

An infirmity now assisted in aggravating the dis-
quietude of Alexander—indeed, to such a degree that
all intercourse with him was latterly a disagreeable
task. He became deaf, and, as is often the case where
this malady exists, mistrustful and suspicious — at
dinner he avoided speaking to any one seated opposite
to him whom he understood less distinctly than his

right and left hand neighbour. As he could hear
nothing of what others said farther removed from
him, and could only see the movement of their lips,
he frequently entertained the suspicion that they
were speaking of him; the motion of a hand he interpreted as a sign to call attention towards him, and
his warmest admirers in his own family could not
always escape suspicion. In this depressed state of
mind, during the Camp of Krasnoe-Selò, in the summer
of 1819, he visited his brother Nicholas there, and,
as we have already detailed, confided to him the important intelligence with regard to his future destiny.
Each word of that conversation elucidates the Emperor's
gloomy condition. This brother, hitherto little heeded
by him, being twenty years younger than himself,
suddenly attracts the Emperor's attention, who tells him
that the Europe of that day requires younger and more
energetic rulers. Alexander was at that time two-and-
forty, and his bodily strength still enabled him to under-
take the most fatiguing journeys. He did not question
either his moral or physical powers, but he much
doubted the realization of his humane projects and
schemes in Europe. It was heard with cold-blooded
indifference, that in Spain, whose people heroically
struggled against a foreign ruler, Ferdinand had commenced his reign by the dissolution of the Cortes, the
re-establishment of the Inquisition and the Jesuits,
imprisonments and executions, and instead of the
sacredly vowed happiness of the people, by systematic
oppression ensued in most States, and the private or
public denial of all those promises made in the time of

need. In such a noble heart as that of the Czar, was it not inevitable that distaste and repugnance should arise to the sceptre that he must sway, not in aid of the prosperity of nations, but for the purpose of reducing them to bondage, especially the Greeks, who were of his own faith? Austria could easily reconcile Ferdinand's conduct in Spain with her own views about the Holy Alliance; Alexander's opinion, however, was very different, and his idea of abdicating was certainly neither transient nor temporary, as the Holy Alliance rather opposed than promoted his benevolent schemes, and his influence was watched with jealous eyes. His sympathy with the Greeks had been pronounced by Metternich and the rest of Europe idle love of conquest. Alexander felt that in his realm the most severe struggles in modern history would, by the help of Providence, be successfully carried out far beyond the boldest expectations, and in contradiction to his modest doubts with regard to himself; but he also felt that many of his noblest schemes remained unfulfilled in Russia itself, contrary to the most well-founded hopes; the circumstances of Europe held him as it were imprisoned, and he beheld with sorrow the state of his own country, where the most trifling plans never succeeded, whereas elsewhere the most gigantic undertakings were accomplished. The men who called themselves his friends, hated each other, always endeavouring to disclose their mutual defects, and thus daily to undermine his confidence. The noble forbearance and humanity of the Czar, on the other hand, so superior to all ambition and selfishness, was not understood by any of his faith-

ful adherents ; he was an exotic in his native land, and
just as such a plant, without the proper soil and air and
light gradually withers, and its leaves fall and die, so it
was with Alexander since 1819, and his conversation
with Nicholas. He indeed with joy discovered that
the strength and energy of this brother, yet unknown to
the world, better fitted him for the lofty position of a
Russian Emperor than himself, the pupil of La Harpe,
the man of liberal views, that were not appreciated.
He called on him to accustom himself to the thought of
his high destiny, that it might not take him by surprise.
Yet, incredible as it may appear, he did not try to
initiate him more into State affairs, from which Nicholas
remained quite estranged till after the death of Alexander. During the six ensuing years the two brothers
never recurred to this question, and as in the conversation we have detailed no precise period nor any other
particulars were fixed as to the time when this change
was to take place, Nicholas had every right to believe
that his former refusal had released him from all obligations. When Prince William of Prussia subsequently
wished to speak to him on that subject, the Grand Duke
told him peremptorily that it was a matter long since
dead and buried, and requested him never again to
allude to it. The idea of abdication may have been
seriously entertained by the Emperor, the novel condition of Europe liberated by himself preying on his
mind ; he saw almost with certainty, and likewise with
alarm, that his living laurels were more likely to wither
than to continue fresh ; no future could offer anything
greater than he had already effected and experienced.

It was not, however, ambition that bound him to the throne, but a sense of duty, in close connection with his religious views. If he had laid down his crown to the amazement of the world, what had the world then to offer to the self-deposed monarch? Domestic and matrimonial happiness were equally unknown to him; he had met with delusions enough, both in public and in private life; in the largest and the smallest cities, at home and abroad, he had always been an object of idle curiosity, and instead of the solitude he aspired to, he had only found fatiguing and empty society. Often in the life of a prince art is a mediator, and develops sources of enjoyment. In earlier years, indeed, Alexander was not disinclined to music, but his taste for it passed away in his later days, especially since his deafness. He renounced his design of abdicating on discovering that an idle life would offer still less charm and satisfaction; but the succession of Nicholas to the Russian throne was settled since the date of their memorable interview, and subsequently confirmed by an Act of State. In the ensuing year 1820, the marriage of the Grand Duke Constantine Pawlowitsch with Anna Feodorowna, Princess of Saxe Coburg, sister of Leopold, afterwards King of the Belgians, was dissolved, and some months later, in June, Constantine entered into a second marriage with Countess Anna Grudsinskaja, who, from not belonging to any reigning family, deprived her husband, according to Russian law, of his succession to the throne. Before her marriage she was maid of honour at the Imperial Court in Warsaw, and recommended to Constantine by his own mother as a wife. As Princess Lowicz

she continued faithful to the Catholic religion, and
being, in the Polish sense, highly cultivated and amiable, she bestowed on the impetuous Constantine the
peaceful domestic happiness that Alexander, especially
in those years, sought in vain.   Although Constantine
by this union voluntarily renounced his succession, the
whole of his family were apprised of his determination, being formally expressed by the Grand Duke himself in January 1822, in the presence of the Emperor,
the two Empresses, and the Grand Duchess Maria
Pawlowna, but neither Nicholas nor his wife, nor the
youngest brother Michael, were invited to this family
conference; indeed, Nicholas had no knowledge whatever of the circumstance, although Constantine himself
imparted it afterwards to the reserved Michael.   Constantine sent his abdication in the form of a letter to
the Emperor, who shortly after confirmed it in writing.
The State Act concerning it was given a year later—in
the summer of 1823.   Though Nicholas was not yet
informed of the existence of a paper that devolved on
his future life the heaviest of all burdens, this was not
owing to any negligence on the part of the Emperor; it
was no doubt his deliberate purpose, though this can
only be guessed.   Only three persons were initiated
into this important secret: Prince Alexander Galitzin,
Count Araktscheef, and the Metropolitan of Moscow,
Philaret, who also received the commission to prepare a
manifesto, appointing Nicholas successor to the throne.
The letter of abdication, written by Constantine, and
the manifesto, were placed in a sealed cover, on which
the Emperor wrote with his own hand:—"To be kept

in the Church of the Ascension of the Virgin, with other Acts of State, until I demand it, and in the event of my death, to be transmitted to the Eparchial Bishop and Governor-General of Moscow, to be opened by them." Philaret deposited it according to his orders in a drawer of the above-named Church, in presence of several clergy of inferior rank, to whom he showed the seal, but not the superscription of the Czar. He took it for granted that the Governor-General of Moscow, at least, was informed of the existence of the paper, but did not discuss with him the commands he had received, whereas this distinguished official, expressly named on the cover, knew nothing on the subject. Yet there were three copies of this important document, one in the Senate-house in Petersburg, the other in the Holy Synod, and the third in the Imperial Council. In the latter the superscription decreed that in the event of the Emperor's death, the document should be opened at a meeting convened expressly for the purpose. Four years had passed since the conversation of Alexander and Nicholas on the subject of his succession, and nothing had since occurred to indicate any preparation on the part of the Grand Duke for his high vocation. We knew that during this period he had absented himself for ten months from Petersburg, enjoying life as a private individual with his wife. The words written on the envelope— "Till I demand it," prove that his resolution was not irrevocable, but on what grounds it was to be claimed by him can only be guessed. Possibly Alexander did not place much faith in the durable nature of his

brother Constantine's matrimonial happiness, and had
this been the case, who could have prevented the
Cesarewitsch from. rending asunder this troublesome
tie, and enforcing the claims to which his birth entitled
him? Was it not wise to observe the Cesarewitsch for
some years, to learn whether he persevered in his earlier
resolution, which was still only a family secret? Was
not Constantine the Stadtholder of Poland more prepared for ruling than the General of Division Nicholas?
The Emperor was better acquainted with his brother
Constantine than with the grave Nicholas. He knew
that the moods of the former alternated between storms
of passion and frolicsome humour; that this type of the
old Russian nature, the most striking contrast to that of
the Emperor, had something attractive to the soldiery,
who submitted willingly to his whims, both in jest and
in earnest. In comparison with his younger brother
he was idolized by the army, or else feared, but not
hated, whereas Nicholas's dignified demeanour nowhere
met with any real response. According to his own
maxim, to "deliberate ten times before acting once,"
Alexander was right to conceal from the world his
resolution, and to wait. Moreover, Nicholas had by
no means cordially met the Emperor's proposal; he had
resisted the idea, and not having the assurance of his
brother's consent, he could not consider the matter concluded.

A change at that time occurred in Alexander's private life that perhaps imperatively suggested the words,
"till I demand it." The Emperor felt himself irresis-
tibly attracted to his solitary angelic wife, Elisabeth,

who had never ceased to love him, and, as she herself said, to revere him as an angel. He now began to spend every spare moment with her, and to treat her with the most loving tenderness. He at length found the peace, rest, and happiness that he had so long sighed for. Did not this circumstance revive the idea of enjoying felicity far from the burden of a crown? But an abdication could not have taken place without very close consultation with his brothers, and under such circumstances the document must have been demanded by him to submit it to the public, changed or unchanged, in his presence, and with his own explanations. These are not groundless suppositions; those who were about the Emperor's person at that time, both from his conduct and from hints that escaped him, drew the same conclusions, that we only suggest in order to explain that important deed. Twelve years after the burning of Moscow, Alexander lived to witness the inundation of Petersburg by the floods of the Neva. He proved himself indeed a father and benefactor to the unhappy sufferers, and lavished large sums, divided among the poor and needy; but he did not succeed in conquering a prejudice of the people, who read in these devastating floods a warning from Heaven, to remind Alexander of the oppressed Greeks forsaken by him. His enjoyment of life was not heightened by this, and the health of the Empress, which began seriously to fail, affected him deeply, as he had now returned to her with his whole heart and soul. Indeed, the condition of his own health, though still in the prime of life, reminded him that he too was mortal. In the year 1823 he was prostrated by a severe illness, that threatened his life; a scarlet rash spread over the whole body to the feet, and seemed to affect the brain. This malady preyed on the imagination of Alexander still more from the fact that his sister, Queen Catherine of Würtemberg, had suddenly died of it. Thus a succession of annoyances contributed to embitter the fair and prosperous existence of the Czar; he could not but feel that the best and most renowned years of his life were passed, and that the future, judging from present prognostics, was only likely to obscure the glory he had won. The strong as well as the weak equally feel, that the greatest worldly events, as well as the lives of individuals, are in the hands of a higher power, and we submit to the will of God.

We cannot venture to guess what were the wishes and views that accompanied him on the journey to Taganrog; but his devoted tenderness and care of Elisabeth lead us to believe that after the restoration of her health he would have carried out the favourite project of his life, and devolved on his brother the thankless burden of government.

It is difficult to understand why the small town of Taganrog, by the Sea of Azof, should have been selected, and not the southern shore of the Crimea. Baden, with all its advantages, the native country of the Empress, attracted, indeed, half of Europe at that period; but Elisabeth seemed to feel the near approach of death, and declared that a Russian Empress must die in Russia. The town and situation of Taganrog was a type of her solitary existence. To the south the town looks on the dreary Azof Sea, by the ancients

justly called a marsh, and to the north, over the wildest
steppes, a striking contrast to the beautiful native country
of the Empress ; a wilderness, devoid of every charm of
nature ; the town itself, regular and new, is in these
regions (towards Odessa) the only one that bears the
appearance of being more than a village. A journey
thither from Petersburg in those days, from the Baltic
to the Sea of Azof, without regular high-roads, and without any of the comforts of a civilized country, would
have sufficed to cause illness to a person in health, yet
Elisabeth reached her distant destination in twenty days,
under the escort and protection of Prince Peter Wolkonsky. The Emperor also seemed to have a presentiment
that his own death was not distant, although he hoped
to be a stay and support to his wife. His name-day, the
30th August (September 12th, N.S.), was celebrated by
a high mass in the Alexander Newsky Cloister; he
then attended a family banquet, to inaugurate the
new Michael Palace and set out on his journey on
September 1st about four o'clock, before the dawn of day.
The profound silence of night still prevailing, he repaired
to the same cloister, without any escort, in a travelling
carriage with three horses, and found the monks, headed
by their superior, assembled in mourning robes to pray
for a blessing on their departing Czar. After listening
to these prayers beside the relics of the holy martyr, he
went to the apartment of the Metropolitan, Serafim,
who asked him if he would like to make the acquaintance of a certain Shimnik, as the cloister had recently
acquired this treasure. Monks thus designated live in
a monastery in the most entire severance from the rest,

shut up in their cell, and not unfrequently lose the use
of speech, and shrink into dry living skeletons, but are
revered as saints during their lives. The Emperor now
visited the grave-like cell of the Shimnik, humbly pros-
trating himself before the crucifix, the sole ornament on
the black wall of the little room, and looking with a
contrite heart at the coffin, in which the monk lay asleep,
under the black pall that covered his shrunken frame.
Alexander listened calmly and attentively to the bitter
discourse of the monk on the universal moral corruption
of the day, saying at its close, " It is to be regretted that
I did not know you sooner." Attended by blessings
from all the monks, he entered his travelling carriage
and left the city at the earliest dawn of day. When he
reached the nearest height of Pulkowa, he stopped the
carriage, and gazing at the city, with its golden cupolas
all glittering in the morning sun, he said, " It is in truth
a beautiful city."

The Emperor preceded the Empress ten days, and
furnished their abode plainly but with every comfort, as
he had seen the houses of German families arranged in
Petersburg, and in accordance with the simple tastes of
Elisabeth. The weather was favourable, and in the
course of a few days both began to revive. Here Alexander seemed to find the happiness that he had longed
for in his youth, and that he had never found either in
Paris, where he appeared as ruler of the world, or in
Vienna, where he was summoned as mediator, or in
Petersburg, where he reigned an autocrat. What a surprise to the poor inhabitants was their good fortune in
seeing the most beloved of all monarchs quietly walk-

ing about the streets of a town that had not yet the honour of being known in Europe.

But what a disappointment! The man who to the inhabitants of a provincial town was the impersonation of earthly omnipotence and earthly happiness, bore traces on his fine countenance of deep and heartfelt care; and this was now more strongly marked, owing to the Emperor's mind being no longer absorbed by a multitude of harassing State affairs. But though less disturbed by these for the present, the improved health of his wife and their restored happiness filling his soul with thankfulness, still, on the other hand, the question whether the hour for his abdication had not arrived tormented him more than ever. Even before this journey he discussed his intention earnestly with his brother-in-law, the Prince of Orange, who designated such a project as a very great misfortune—indeed, he set forth his views on the subject to the Emperor in writing. Although for many reasons this only strengthened him in his favourite idea, still in this very year a fact came to his knowledge that entirely banished his wish, but made life only the more hateful to him.

In June, on his way back from Poland, the first intimation of a conspiracy against the throne and the existing order of things, was given to him by a subaltern officer of the Buger Uhlan regiment; he was of English extraction, and named Sherwood. It appears that by means of this same trusty man, the complete list of the conspirators in the south was given to the Emperor in September on his journey to Taganrog, as the subsequent Emperor, Nicholas, found the list in Alexander's portfolio, which came into his hands, with other papers, on the death of Alexander. He left Petersburg in a very gloomy mood, and arrived almost heart-broken in Taganrog, and the question of his abdication now appeared to him in a different light. At this moment, surrounded by treachery, and threatened with assassination, to renounce the throne might be considered by the conspirators a cowardly means of saving his own life, —so he rejected this idea as unworthy of him. Not one of all his large retinue learned a word of what was passing in the Emperor's soul; the insignificant inhabitants of the place read in his features, better than his aides-de-camp, deep-seated sorrow and grief. His inward distress of mind drove him hither and thither; he visited Rostow, Azof, Nowo-Tscherkask, instead of enjoying repose by the side of his inimitable wife; indeed, at the suggestion of Count Woronzow he undertook a journey to the Crimea, which had been decided for the ensuing spring, no doubt in order to banish by novel impressions painful thoughts. He was not only enchanted with the picturesque scenery of the Peninsula, but also with the honest, hearty hospitality with which he was received there, both by the Russians who had settled in the Crimea, and by the native Tartars, and thus did not discern that the foreign climate and unusual food, in which fruit predominates, was preparing for him certain death. A prey to intermittent fever, he returned on 17th November to Taganrog. To the physician he declared that for a condition like his (no doubt he alluded to the secret weighing on his mind), he expected very little from medical treatment. "I place very slender faith in your draughts'; my life is in the hands of God," were his oft-repeated words; still some days afterwards he submitted to skilful medical advice.   Elisabeth, on account of whose health Alexander had undertaken the journey hither, remained by the bedside of her husband as nurse, but equally little guessed the hidden cause of his sudden failure of strength.   What Sherwood had communicated in writing to the Emperor he now during his illness heard confirmed from the lips of Count de Wette.   The chief of the conspiracy, Colonel Pestel, had been long known as such to the Czar, and watched by him; we do not know however in what manner.   It is still more striking that the Emperor was aware of the infamous plans against his life, and did nothing to render them abortive.   "Lord, thy will be done!" he was often heard to whisper to himself.

The condition of the illustrious invalid now evidently grew worse, and only in occasional moments did it admit any hope of recovery.   On the 27th November the father confessor was summoned, with whom he conversed for some time alone, and perfectly conscious, but he partook of the holy sacrament in the presence of Elisabeth.   At her request he submitted willingly to all the necessary treatment, but soon no longer recognised his oldest acquaintances.   A delusive hope, however, cheered the Empress once more on the 28th November, but by the 1st December all the energies of life seemed to give way, and raising his hand with difficulty Alexander made a sign to his wife, bidding her an eternal farewell, and kissing her hand, his sublime spirit breathed its last on the same day at 10.50 A.M.   Thus

died the most beloved and revered of all Russian and
European rulers—not from poison, according to the
report universally spread in credulous Germany, nor by
the dagger of the conspirator, which, indeed, had been
very near him. He died a quiet natural death, lamented
with bitter tears by his loving wife, who gently closed
his eyes, and after making the sign of the cross over
his remains, embraced his still warm body with the most
passionate tenderness. Then, turning her eyes, full of
piety, grief, and humility to a picture of our blessed
Saviour, she said meekly, " Almighty God ! it has pleased
thee to deprive me of my husband. Thy will be done !"

We leave the unhappy widow alone in her sacred
sorrow, on the confines of Europe, and shall now endeavour to make the reader acquainted with the conspiracy,
which, indeed, could no longer affect the Emperor, but
threatened to obstruct the path to the throne for his
successor.

CHAPTER VIII.

THE CONSPIRACY.

THE change in the Emperor Alexander's disposition during the last seven years had not been unobserved by the public at large. The old Opposition party, who formerly frustrated all his intended reforms, might possibly declare that they understood it, but this was only a small fragment of the whole. While all Europe, after the campaigns, allies as well as conquered foes, admired and revered him, many secret and murmuring voices in his own country blamed him for his long absence, his unselfishness, and his sacrifices to foreign interests. The opening of the Polish Diet excited almost universal discontent in Russia, for it was considered an indication that a conquered kingdom was preferred to their own country. The army had returned inspired with a different spirit from that in which it had gone forth. Those men who had followed the steps of the youthful monarch in the first twelve years of his reign with satisfaction, nay, with enthusiasm, were disgusted to see by the side of the noble monarch, as his friend and most intimate adviser and executor of his commands, a man universally detested—indeed, entirely excluded from the society of the higher classes—who was leading a solitary old Russian life in a wooden house, his whole nature forming the most offensive contrast to Alexander's noble character. That man was Count Araktscheef. His loyalty and. unbounded admiration for Alexander, as formerly for Paul, his pedantic love of order, and his stern discipline in military commands, had acquired for him the Imperial confidence; but his own contemporaries in Petersburg judged him differently. They called his sternness hateful bloodthirsty revenge, his veneration for the Emperor slavish obsequious servility to all his opinions, or even suspicions; and his incorruptibility was doubted by many, as he had amassed a large fortune, and his zeal was by some considered only hypocrisy. There was in his person something mysterious, enigmatical, and repulsive; his face was coarse, his expression cold, ignoble, and unfeeling; his cunning eyes observed sharply, and his appearance in society made every one silent. In the absence of the Emperor he was accounted a narrow-hearted, secret Minister of Police, who watched with eyes of suspicion even the most cheerful and unconcerned demeanour. This man stifled the love of the people for the Emperor, his power and efficiency eclipsing all other ministers and high dignitaries. His official position alone by no means entitled him to such great power; he was Inspector-General of the whole infantry and artillery, and also Commissary-General of stores and provisions, and a member of the Military Council. The hatred and abhorrence of Araktscheef increased, owing to the repeated absences of Alexander at that time, when the unlimited authority of the dreaded man seemed incalculable and unbounded.

No one had the courage to accuse this minister (as Speransky had once been accused)—indeed, no one of opposite opinions had the opportunity of representing to Alexander the odious impression made on the country by Araktscheef's doings. Alexander, indeed, in all his plans and projects, was now entirely severed from others, and only heard through Galitzin and Araktscheef what it suited them to tell him. Since 1819 several public newspapers had been suppressed, while others, threatened and watched by the censorship, were silent, so that not the smallest hint of the universal discontent reached the ears of the Emperor. No single careless word spoken at a banquet in Petersburg escaped these despots, and from this petty persecution arose a great and terrible enterprise—a conspiracy which aimed a dagger at Alexander's life.

Its character was very widely different from those palace revolutions of which Petersburg, in the eighteenth century, had often been the theatre. It is amazing that a secret society, consisting of so many branches, and entertaining such criminal ideas, should remain for years unknown to Government, and take root also in so many parts of the kingdom. Subsequently the origin of this revolt, and the spirit that actuated it, were attributed to foreign influences and foreign culture, and particularly to the acquaintance made by the Russian army, in those glorious years, with Germany and France. One of the heads of this conspiracy in Petersburg once said, " A comparison between cities like Dresden, Leipzig, and Frankfort, with our Tschernigof or Kaluga and others, makes me blush. Saxon peasants, in the

vicinity of Dresden, live in better houses than our
governors and generals in the interior of the country."
Certainly such a comparison could not be to the advantage of the latter. The returned army, however,
went further in their opinions and conversations, often
discussing the conduct of Clitus at the table of Alexander of Macedon.

When the names of all who shared in this conspiracy
are collected, not only those who were seized as guilty,
but also those who had withdrawn before the outbreak,
we find many great families involved, especially some
nearly connected with the Court. The Trubetzkoi
family, descended from the Lithuanian Grand Duke
Ghedimin, was particularly distinguished in 1612, when
Moscow shook off the yoke of Poland. In our time the
Trubetzkois were among the intimate friends of the Imperial family, yet one of their cousins stood at the head
of this odious enterprise in Petersburg. The name of
Wolkonsky, especially in later years, seems almost inseparable from that of Alexander the First, and Princess
Alexandra Nikolaewna Wolkonsky we have already
named as Mistress of the Robes to the young Grand
Duchess; but one of her sons was engaged in the conspiracy. Prince Odojewsky, both by his descent and the
valiant deeds of his family, is one of the most eminent
names in the kingdom of the Czar. Of equal importance was the princely family of Odolensky, who
trace their origin to the Princes of Tschernigow. Here
were also the families of Schtschepin-Rostowsky and
Schachawskoy. We have already alluded to the estimation in which the Narischkins are held in Russia.

When to these we add the names of Orlof, Turgenief, Mussin-Puschkin, Murawief, and Bestuschef, it would appear at first sight as if all the highest nobility of the Imperial realm were here comprehended. However, such is not the case. Among those whom we have not mentioned are few known names, but many, on the contrary, who had joined the plot from disappointed ambition, dismissal from office, or a personal feeling of revenge; and even in the greatest families we find only individual members, and chiefly young people. Though the threads of the conspiracy extended from the north to the south, still they included a very small portion of the society,—young excitable spirits, who mistook a *mirage* for reality. It was unjust to attribute the source of this mischief to foreign culture or education, or to acquaintance with foreign countries. In Petersburg the sole civilisation was foreign. The levity with which the Russian undertakes almost every project, without reflecting on the difficulties of carrying it through, the indifference, indeed the undaunted courage, which never deserts him even on the failure of his plans, the self-confidence, generally grounded on his ignorance of circumstances, the belief that he must succeed : these are traits of character with which all may be charged. Many speeches taken from antiquity were heard in the assemblies of the conspirators, such as " to pass the Rubicon," " Brutus knows how to die," and yet from such lips these were phrases not understood. Many entertained the belief that the development of political freedom in the kingdom of Russia would be as easy and rapid as the manner in which Petersburg had become one of the capitals of the world, out of nothing. Vanity and ambition played a greater part in this undertaking than either patriotism or sacrifice for the common weal.

It is not necessary for our purpose to enter into further details ; only, thoroughly to comprehend the events of 14th December it is essential to know that in Russia two seats of rebellion existed, one in the south, under Colonel Paul Pestel, the other in Petersburg itself, established by Alexis Murawief. These two men had become acquainted with Germany and France in the campaigns of 1813 and 1814, and the effect on both was precisely similar to that exercised by the spirit of antiquity on Cola di Rienzi. Both thought they must and could introduce another form of government, another spirit into the administration, and into official life, without knowing exactly what was to be done, or how it was to be done; thus it was only in the fact of a change of some kind that the ambition of Pestel harmonized with the enthusiasm of Murawief. It seems incredible that these two societies, whose heads we have named, could, during nine years, in spite of their internal variances and anomalies, gradually diffuse their influence over a great part of the kingdom, without either the secret or public police receiving the most remote hint of the plot. The perpetual absences of Alexander explain indeed sufficiently the indolence of the police, and likewise the remissness of the Government, and the discontent, that furnished the conspirators with a plausible pretext for their enterprise. The spirit of the society in Petersburg, who delighted in criticising everything and sparing no one, yet without themselves

doing anything, formed no.obstacle to the conspiracy.
While the mass of the Russian people, the peasants, the
inhabitants of small towns, had scarcely made any progress since the days of Peter in any one respect, Petersburg, on the other hand, offered the spectacle of a hot-
house with many French and German exotics, whose
existence was utterly artificial, and entirely deprived of
their native soil. But we must not forget that Petersburg also produced men who took root in the soil of
their fatherland, and did not sacrifice one iota of their
national peculiarities to the cultivation acquired in
Western Europe. These were devoted faithfully to the
power of the Imperial House, submissive to the strict
discipline of their Church, combining with those qualities
European polish. Murawief appears to have approxi-
mated most to this class; he aspired to do good to his
country, as did its ruler, without violent measures, and
by gradual improvement. He however overlooked the
fact that in Russia the weal and the woe of the whole
kingdom is placed exclusively in the hands of the Czar,
that hitherto nothing whatever had been developed without the knowledge and consent of the Emperor, and that
this powerful monarch knew better than those young
people imagined the obstacles interposed to his noblest
views. Had Russia been only the size of a German
dukedom, and the magnanimous Alexander at its head
—a man among men—a portion at least of these plans
might have been realized. We entertain no doubt of the
justice of Murawief's projects to bestow on the Russian
kingdom more benevolent institutions and a better provi-
sion for the poor, universal diffusion of enlightenment

by education and instruction, and a fairer administration of the public revenues; but we are convinced that such a work requires for its execution several centuries, and likewise the co-operation of vigorous governments and rulers.

Murawief is described by his contemporaries and fellow-workers as handsome and highly cultivated, full of benevolence, true piety, and enthusiasm for all that is noble, grand, and good. The sincere wish might arise in his heart for changes and reforms, and continue a fair dream, but the execution was impossible, and the very effort to accomplish these was a crime. Pestel, on the other, hand, tormented by ambition and the love of notoriety, and instigated by his qualifications as a commander, not only formed the society, but urged on its members to action.

The tumults in Naples, Piedmont, and Spain, quickly inspired the conspirators with the wish to proceed to deeds. In the summer of the year 1823, the Emperor Alexander and his brother Nicholas were expected in the government of Minsk, at a grand review of the troops. Such an opportunity seemed very favourable to seize both Alexander and Nicholas; but no one could be found bold enough for the traitorous deed. In the summer of 1825, dark rumours of a conspiracy reached the ears of Alexander, which that noble-minded monarch neither could nor would believe. Ten regiments in the south were at that period all at the certain disposal of the secret society; but since Alexander's absence from Petersburg the conspirators believed themselves betrayed, and wished to commence the terrible spectacle by the murder of the Emperor, when he was suddenly seized with illness at Taganrog.—Colonel Artamon Murawief, brother-in-law of Count Kancrin, who had been loaded with benefits by Alexander, exclaimed, " He shall die by my hand!" In fact, several of these bloodthirsty heroes were found. A captain in Pestel's regiment, Maiboroda, at length disclosed the whole conspiracy to General Roth, who instantly despatched a courier to Taganrog, with written documents, but the Emperor was dead before they arrived. Diebitsch opened the papers containing these melancholy revelations, and, in order to guard against an outbreak of rebellion, sent off General Tschernichof to the spot where the conspirators were assembled. By the 14th December Pestel was arrested, and the whole of the southern society left without a leader; they could exercise no influence on the order of events in Petersburg; we therefore leave them scattered and helpless, to turn our eyes to the capital, where the unexpected tidings of Alexander's death called forth terror, confusion, and at length open rebellion, on the part of the conspirators.

There had been very little essential change in the position of Nicholas and Alexandra since we accompanied them back to Russia in 1822; the family was increased, and now numbered, in addition to the first son, three daughters, the last of whom was born in 1825. The health of Alexandra had rendered it necessary for her to take a second journey to Germany; they went by sea to Mecklenburg, and had to struggle against wind and weather during the last few days of their voyage; their stay had been chiefly in Silesia, where the same family circle assembled as in 1821. In the beginning of February 1825 they returned to the Anitschkow Palace. It was thought that the Czar would now make known to his brother his future destiny, as from the beginning of this year a journey had been projected for the Empress Élisabeth on account of her health, and Alexander was himself to accompany her, and remain with her. When Prince A. N. Galitzin was arranging the Emperor's papers before the journey, he asked Alexander whether these important documents ought not to be communicated to Nicholas and to the public. Alexander refused. On his name-day, during the procession to the Newsky Cloister, the Emperor seemed even more depressed than usual; Nicholas was by his side during their progress there and back; with his usual kindness of heart, he mentioned to his younger brother that he had purchased some land for him in Peterhof, near the Imperial Gardens. In the evening the brothers took leave of each other, while Nicholas, without the most distant presentiment of the truth, was approaching a great future and a gigantic struggle. The Grand Duke Michael left for Warsaw, and a few days later the Empress Elisabeth started on her journey, so thus the Empress-mother and Nicholas and Alexandra were the only members of the Imperial family remaining in Petersburg. A practised and observant eye can ascertain at once in the capital whether the Emperor is absent or not; there is less, but freer, movement in the principal streets in the absence of the monarch. When he is in the capital couriers, estafettes, and the highest military and civil authorities, all crowd from early morning to the Winter Palace to the Emperor, and the entrance is as thronged by handsome carriages-and-four as by common kibitkas. Now as many, and even more, couriers were daily despatched to the Czar, and the Winter Palace stood desolate.

Towards the end of September the city is filled with its most aristocratic inhabitants, who, scared away from the country by the first snow and frost, hasten to regain their palaces. The Grand-Ducal couple, scarcely even now known to the public at large, had withdrawn into quiet domestic life. During the day, Nicholas, like every other general, was on duty; Alexandra, with her youngest child in her arms, instructed her little six-years-old daughter, Marie, and played with Olga, only three years of age. Her young son, Alexander, now seven years of age, took daily walks with his tutor, Colonel Mörder, his good looks making him an object of admiration to the kindly-natured people. Alexandra, even in this retirement, found time for her favourite pursuits, music and literature, and during that autumn she showed a particular preference for Hummel's charming pianoforte music. She wrote with her own hand in her album the first movement of his concerto in A Minor. The inundation of the previous year caused thankfulness to God for this harvest, and such prosperity seemed doubly welcome. In no autumn had there been so much music as in this during Alexander's absence. Prince Nicholas Galitzin, a personal friend and warm admirer of Beethoven, endeavoured, in conjunction with professional pianists, to introduce at that period the pianoforte and orchestral works of that king of musicians into the capital. Orchestral and quartet amateur unions were formed, and a numerous society of the most genuinely aristocratic nature assembled, in order to arrange a grand musical performance during the Lent of the ensuing year.

Like a flash of lightning, on the 25th November the news flew through the city that the much-loved and idolized Czar was dying in Taganrog. The most terrible consternation now prevailed, not only in the Winter Palace and the town, but in the wooden huts of the most distant suburbs. But when, two days later, Elisabeth wrote with her own hand to the Empress-mother these memorable words, " Our angel is in heaven, and I am still on earth," silence fell on the whole city, and those who chanced to meet had tears in their eyes when they greeted each other. The governor-general of the capital, the grey-haired Count Miloradowitsch, on the 25th November conveyed the intelligence to Nicholas that the Emperor Alexander was at the point of death in Taganrog. At that moment ended the happy period of Nicholas's private life; a new epoch was now inaugurated; three weeks scarcely remained for him to be still called Grand Duke; but he did not himself know the momentous hour that had struck. Indeed, he did not even remember the conversation that had taken place about his future destiny, being entirely absorbed in the death of his brother; but the thought never occurred to him that the burden of the crown was now to rest on his own head. He hurried to the Empress-mother in the Winter Palace, and re-

mained all night beside her; but even she, who was
perfectly acquainted with the great mystery, did not
prepare her son by a single word for his approaching duties. Her anguish in knowing that her eldest
son was dying, at an unattainable distance, by the Sea
of Azof, paralysed her presence of mind; and when, two
days later, on the 27th of November, she read the fatal
news in the face of her son Nicholas during mass,
she fell to the ground senseless. A terrible moment, a
fearful blow indeed! Five-and-twenty years before, she
had lost her husband and three daughters in the course
of a few years, and now death deprived her of her eldest
and most beloved son, who had been her comfort and
her pride during quarter of a century. No wonder that
such a storm of grief robbed her of her recollection, and
that she did not inform the son beside her that Alexander's duties had devolved on him. While the swoon-
ing mother, accompanied by her daughter-in-law, was
carried into her apartments, Nicholas announced the
death of the Czar to the palace guard, commanding them
at once to take the oath of allegiance to the Emperor
Constantine Pawlowitsch. He himself, with several
generals, set the example, by taking the oath and sub-
scribing it in the Hof Kirche; a well-meant, but rash
step, which he also enjoined at once on various other
authorities. Not till this the most sacred duty of his
first subject to Constantine was fulfilled, did he apprise
the Empress-mother of it, who, restored to consciousness, was in fresh consternation at this over-hasty pro-
ceeding. "What have you done, my son!" exclaimed
the terror-struck woman; "do you not know that an act

of State long ago named you successor to the throne ?"
"Neither I nor others know anything of the kind,"
answered Nicholas calmly, "but every one does know
that after the Emperor Alexander, my brother Constantine is the rightful ruler of this country, and to him,
therefore, I have sworn allegiance." Immediately after,
but unhappily too late, arrived Prince A. N. Galitzin,
who, with the Empress-mother, was the sole official
depositary of the secret in Petersburg, severely re-
proaching Nicholas for what had occurred, whereas
this censure was more deserved by himself, having
allowed a whole day to pass without imparting the
secret to his future sovereign.

At two o'clock in the afternoon the Council of the
Empire assembled, and Galitzin informed them of the
existence of the important document regarding the
succession, which was produced, opened, and read.
Many members at once acknowledged Nicholas Pawlowitsch as their Emperor, others maintained that he
had renounced the throne, by having taken the oath
of allegiance to Constantine. The Council in a body
repaired to Nicholas, and learned from his own lips
that he had taken the oath of fidelity to his brother,
and in spite of his cognisance of the paper now
opened, he, as his brother's first subject, proclaimed him
Emperor. He exhorted the Council to imitate his
example, and to take the oath in the Hof Kirche, which
was done in his presence. On the same day the troops
and the civil officials did the same, and an aide-de-
camp carried the tidings of Nicholas's act of renunciation, in presence of the Senate, to Warsaw. Nicholas

despatched an aide-de-camp with a letter of the same purport to his brother Constantine and the Senate, announcing to the whole kingdom by printed ukases, where the oath of allegiance was shortly to be taken.

In Moscow, much nearer the death-bed of Alexander, the sad news did not arrive till after Constantine had been proclaimed Emperor in Petersburg. Here the presence of the Archbishop Philaret, and his knowledge of the existence of the secret document, called forth doubt and indecision, but only for a short space, as the ukase of the Senate of 27th November put an end to all differences of opinion. Constantine, however, had received intelligence of his brother's death two days earlier in Warsaw than it reached Petersburg; for as not one person in the whole court and retinue of the Emperor, not even the Empress Elisabeth, knew anything about the succession to the throne, the Imperial adjutant-generals, Wolkonsky and Diebitsch, considered it their duty at once to send off to Warsaw a report of Alexander's death to the Cesarewitsch, who was in fact now Emperor. Constantine at once announced his irrevocable resolution to the first of his suite who approached him with the title of " Your Majesty," and despatched his younger brother, Michael, to his mother and brother at Petersburg, confirming his abdication.

Thus occurred an incident, unparalleled in history, of two brothers at the same time renouncing the throne, and each devolving the crown on the other. The messengers that conveyed these strange tidings must have met between Warsaw and Petersburg. An interregnum of course occurred in the Government, which Nicholas,

as the only Imperial Prince present, could alone fill.
The Grand Duke Michael, in spite of the dreadful state
of the roads, reached Petersburg on the 3d December,
and went direct with the papers intrusted to him, to the
Empress-mother, who at once summoned Nicholas into
her presence and received him with these words, " My
son, do homage to the honourable conduct of your
brother Constantine; his renunciation was no mere
idle words : he· gives up the throne to you." " Well !
mother," answered Nicholas, "I almost believe it is
easier to renounce than to accept."

.Nicholas was at last convinced that the Cesarewitsch [1] had long since renounced his rights, and now
only strongly confirmed his determination; he must therefore decide on accepting the government, although aware
that he had not been educated for such a mission, and was
quite unprepared for it. But another difficulty, indeed
danger, now opposed and obstructed his decision. How
could the whole realm be convinced of Constantine's abdication, after Nicholas himself had done homage to him,
.and Petersburg and Moscow followed his example ?   It
was thought that the presence of the Cesarewitsch in
Petersburg could alone prevent inevitable confusion;
for a verbal declaration on his part, of his intentions, in
presence of the highest dignitaries must naturally call
forth a different conviction in the public mind, from
that of an Act hitherto kept secret, and letters from the
Cesarewitsch in Warsaw to Petersburg.   Mother and
son instantly urged Constantine, by letters despatched

---

[1] Constantine enjoyed this title from 1799 as a reward for his sympathy
in the Italian campaign.

the same day, to come himself to Petersburg. In the
city all was quiet; the oath had been taken, and to the
millions in the kingdom it was probably indifferent
whether the succeeding Emperor was called Constantine
or Nicholas, the one having been absent for years, and
the other seldom seen in the city. One fact, however,
puzzled not only the busy town, but the curious gossip-
ing salons, which was, that the second brother, Michael,
just arrived from Warsaw, had not sworn allegiance to
Constantine, whereas the elder one had fulfilled that
duty at once. The causes of this discrepancy were discussed, and the right conclusion arrived at, that Constantine refused to accept the throne, and that within a
short time a new oath would be administered. With
the unquestioning submissiveness peculiar to Russians,
at that time at least, one ukase would have been as
quickly and readily obeyed as another; they would have
shown no resistance, far less any inclination to rebel.
As the Grand Duke Michael was the object of much
idle talk in society, the Empress-mother determined to
send him back to Warsaw, to try to prevail on Constantine to come to Petersburg; she empowered him, however, to stop all couriers whom he might meet coming
from Warsaw to Petersburg, to open their despatches,
and to act according to circumstances. And in effect,
Michael, at 260 versts from Petersburg, met a courier
with a letter from Constantine to Nicholas, in which he
repeated in the most decisive terms his renunciation of
the crown. From that moment there was no longer
a prospect of Nicholas being able to return to private
life; he must soon perceive that not only the will of

both his elder brothers called him to the throne, but
still more the pressure of circumstances, and the welfare
of the kingdom demanded that he should take up the
sceptre.   And when he did so, he would wield it with
that energy of which he gave so many proofs in his
subsequent reign.

Three important pieces of intelligence in one day,
(12th December) exacted an intrepid, manly courage.
On that morning, so early as six o'clock, a communication was made to the Grand Duke from Taganrog by
General Diebitsch, of a widely spread conspiracy through
the whole kingdom, not only purposing to change the
present constitution, but even the present dynasty.
Fourteen days had elapsed in harassing doubts and just
grief, and now a storm approached heavy with dark
thunder clouds; and yet it was uncertain whence the
lightning was first to descend, and who it was to destroy.
The most distressing part of the intelligence was, that
Nicholas was obliged to keep it secret from the Empress-mother and his wife, and in fact make no one
acquainted with it.   Alexandra was accustomed to
see him always grave during the day, and since
Alexander's death their countenances bore marked
traces of grief and anxious care and tribulation;
Nicholas therefore succeeded in keeping his wife in
ignorance of this burden.   She had scarcely quitted the
palace during the last fortnight, four children being intrusted solely to her motherly care, while her husband
passed every spare moment with his mother, in the
Winter Palace.   They sat down to dinner alone and in
silence at four o'clock, while the thoughts of Alex-

andra strayed occasionally to Berlin, where the Holy Christmas Eve, 24th December, calls forth a lively but peaceful excitement through the whole city. Then arrived a courier from Warsaw with a letter to Nicholas, calling on him at once and without further delay to take possession of the throne. Both remained speechless, and while Alexandra mentally bade farewell to her calm domestic happiness, her husband saw before him a perilous future, and felt that his first step must be a struggle with a secret lurking power, which possibly had already invaded his palace.

CHAPTER IX.

THE 14TH DECEMBER 1825.

In the lives of the most commonplace men, there are days more fruitful in events than perhaps whole years, when fate sometimes capriciously pours forth either the whole vials of her wrath or her favour; indeed, occasionally both at once. Alexandra was at that period seven-and-twenty, mother of one son and three daughters, and in all the bloom of female loveliness. During the ten years since she had attained the age of entering into society, she had known only the gifts of fortune in and beyond her home, in foreign lands, as well as in her native country; she was beloved and esteemed by all, but chiefly by the man to whom she had given her heart and her hand, and whom she idolized. Destiny now seemed to have determined to add a crown to all this felicity, for since the arrival of the Cesarewitsch's last letter she had become Empress of Russia. Good fortune, as an ancient Greek sage declares, is more difficult to bear than misfortune, for it leads to the display of qualities that the world at large do not possess; above all, it demands equanimity of mind, never too much uplifted, wisdom in the enjoyment of prosperity, and prudence in preserving it. And

thus no one was more fitted for the peculiar bounties of
fate than Alexandra Feodorowna, whose sole anxiety
was whether she could continue to make the Emperor
as happy by her love as when he was Grand Duke.
She wished quite as little as Nicholas to ascend the
highest pinnacle of human greatness; on the evening
when Alexander had spoken to them both on the subject of the future, she had been rather troubled than
delighted, and the obstinate refusal of the throne by
Nicholas, even after being apprised of the secret document, was sufficient proof to the world that he was
devoid of ambition, and only sought to continue his
quiet domestic life.   At the moment when the curtain
of their future fate was unrolled they were alone, and
could without witnesses exchange their feelings, and
anxieties, presentiments, and hopes, before leaving the
scene of their youthful unclouded happiness; they were
snatched away from it against their will, and left a
thousand dumb witnesses in the deserted palace of the
good old times.   In the boudoir of Alexandra stood the
bust of her mother, Queen Louisa, the lofty ideal of a
German woman; both knelt before it in silence, and
then embracing each other they looked forward to the
future with composure.   But that same evening on
which Heaven had conferred on them the greatest and
most responsible of all earthly gifts, brought yet a third
report, which was to be kept secret from Alexandra.
Information was conveyed to Nicholas on the morning
of this day, from Taganrog, of the existence of a conspiracy, and confirmed on the same evening by an
eye-witness in Petersburg; at nine o'clock in the even-

ing a letter was given to Nicholas, which contained a warning not to accept the crown, as the army swarmed with his secret and open enemies; his ascension of the throne would probably be the beginning of a terrible civil war. As we have already said, Nicholas was far from being beloved; he was gloomy, strict in discipline, reserved, abrupt, and the many admirable qualities of his heart were reserved for his family alone, and a select circle of friends, such as Adlerberg, Perowsky, and some others; reserve was with him a principle; to strive to gain the favour of the people was opposed to his whole character, but the consequences of such a demeanour seem never to have been apprehended by him. After reading the letter Nicholas gave orders to conduct the bearer into his cabinet—a sub-lieutenant of the Jäger regiment of Guards, Jacob Rostowzow, whose demeanour inspired confidence, but his speech was difficult to understand, as he stammered. That same day he had heard in a society of officers the most daring speeches uttered against Nicholas Pawlowitsch; this alone, however, would scarcely have induced him to take so bold a step, for in Petersburg violent outbreaks from malcontents against the Government and Court are not unfrequent when distant from the powers that be, while in their vicinity the most extravagant praise is alone uttered. The young man in question had evidently heard more revolutionary speeches than in this last assemblage. *Tête-à-tête* with Nicholas, he enforced the absolute necessity of the Cesarewitsch himself coming to Petersburg, and, in presence of the people, proclaiming his brother Emperor; for the recent oath of allegiance had been made use of by the conspirators in aid of their plans. Nicholas dismissed the young man as a friend, but saw more clearly than ever the terrific storm that was gathering over his head. " In two days Emperor —or dead," said he.

The news of Alexander's death caused great consternation and perplexity to the conspirators in Petersburg; a peaceful death had rescued the well-beloved Emperor from the dagger that was to have struck him in the ensuing year. The course of events in the history of the world takes a very different direction from what the most acute human intellect can foresee. The invalid Empress, weary of life, survived her husband, who had undertaken the journey solely on her account. Fate seemed almost to favour the republican plans of the conspirators, especially as both Grand Dukes at the same moment refused the crown. Constantine was acknowledged by Nicholas's oath of allegiance, and also by the Council at Petersburg, and he was now, at all events, too distant for the dagger of the northern conspiracy to reach him, and as, shortly after Constantine's renunciation, Nicholas proved his legal rights, the conspirators were as much dismayed by this step as by Alexander's death; it was as if the irony of fate were smiling at them in mockery and warning. A captain Jakubowitsch had come in summer from Georgia to Petersburg, to offer his services as an assassin to the confederates, but shortly after his arrival Alexander set off for Taganrog. Instead of seeing in this a providential warning; the man, at the news of Alexander's death, gave way to the most furious words and gestures at the disappointment of his bloodthirsty designs, which, however, too soon acquired a fresh object. A report was circulated in the city that, as Constantine stedfastly persevered in his refusal of the throne, a new oath of allegiance must be taken. The conspirators considered this a favourable moment for more wide-spread and effectual changes, so they held frequent meetings, and at last agreed to dispute Nicholas's claim to the Crown as a usurper, and when he had been got rid of, to proclaim a republic. About twenty young men met to deliberate together; at their head was Rilejef, formerly a lieutenant, and now an employé in the Russian-American-trading company. His name has been quoted as one of the best Russian poets, but he placed most value on being called a citizen of the State, and in promoting the interests of the despised burghers of Russia. All the others were members of the military profession, several of high and princely descent, others of obscure origin. To the former belonged Prince Trubetzkoi, son-in-law of Count Laval, and, by his marriage with the daughter of this French émigré, not without means; he was highly cultivated and refined, but devoid both of courage and prudence. Prince Eugene Obolensky, an officer of the Imperial Guard, aide-de-camp of the excellent General Bistram, was, like the former, entirely French in education, and cherished an especial hatred against Nicholas. Ensign Prince Odojewsky and Prince Schtschepin-Rostowsky were the most prominent names. Various plans were brought forward, but on December 12th, Rilejef's views were adopted by the whole assembly. On the day of the new oath of allegiance being tendered, the Guards were to refuse it, on the pretext of this being an affront to those who, only a few weeks previously, had sworn fidelity to the Cesarewitsch; the pretended refusal of the Crown on his part being false, and a silly invention of Petersburg. These disaffected regiments were to be stationed in the Senate square, and Prince Trubetzkoi as leader of the rebels, to act according to circumstances; Colonel Bulatof and Jakubowitsch were to be under his orders. It was hoped that the new Emperor, alarmed by such demonstrations, would give up the throne, while, during this interregnum, the Senate would accept a Constitution from the hands of the conspirators, and proclaim it to the country. This secret society was minutely informed of all that was thought and spoken in the city; they knew, through spies, every word exchanged between the Empress-mother and Nicholas in the Winter Palace; they were apprised of every approaching step of his, though the Grand Duke himself had no suspicion of the abyss that threatened to engulf him. But danger and destruction not only menaced him and his family, the whole kingdom was at stake as well as the Royal House. For more than two hundred years they had been the rock and refuge, the spirit and the will, of the nation; the stroke of a dagger, a pistol-shot, could shatter this colossus into impotent fragments. But though a legion thus stood against one individual, the whole enterprise was more the effect of levity, grounded on no moral courage, and simply on sanguine hopes, without confidence in the justice of the cause, and without any religious convictions; the first abortive step must inevitably discover the folly and criminal credulity of their undertaking. Very differently was the man constituted who was imperatively called to the throne by the right of birth and the laws of his country, and for the benefit and preservation of the kingdom. In spite of the thousand cares with which he was burdened, Nicholas late in the evening sketched the following plan. The change in the succession must be made known to the people by a special manifesto, and Speransky, who had been recalled to the capital in 1819, was commissioned, at a late hour at night, to draw it up. The new Emperor decided, however, on announcing his accession to the throne in full assembly of the Council of the Empire, and in the presence of his brother, Michael, and this was to be done on the very next day, December 13—a Sunday. On Monday, December 14, the manifesto was to be publicly distributed, and succeeded by the new oath of allegiance.

Next morning, December 13, the Emperor subscribed the manifesto drawn up by Speransky, and told his son, seven years of age, the great event. At eight o'clock in the evening an extraordinary meeting of the Imperial Council took place, in which Nicholas did not appear till very late, and without his brother Michael. There he read aloud the manifesto proclaiming his accession to the throne, and quitted the assembly at two o'clock in the morning. Thus the 14th December had already dawned—Monday, a day well known to be of evil omen in Russia; the Empress-

mother and the young Empress went to rest with no
feeling but that of a great and burdensome change,
for they knew that next morning they would wake
to tedious ceremonies. With Nicholas it was very
different. The spectre of a conspiracy haunted his
brief slumbers of a few hours, and diminished the
vigour which he required in full measure on the ensuing day.

Before day dawned he received the commander of
the Guards, and read to him the manifesto, ordering
him to administer the oath to the military staff, and to
the various regiments : "You must answer with your
head for the tranquillity of the city ; and if I am only
to be Emperor for one hour, I shall be so with dignity."
He then summoned all those who had the privilege of
attending Court to appear at a solemn mass in the
church of the Winter Palace, at ten o'clock in the forenoon. Nicholas, on the previous day, had informed
the Governor-General, Count Miloradowitsch, of his
uneasiness about the outbreak of the conspiracy on this
day, immediately after receiving Diebitsch's letter ; so
he now appeared to inform him that the city was
perfectly quiet, and not a trace of any conspiracy
visible, but that, in any event, all precautions were
taken. The ringleaders had carefully avoided making
an accomplice of the grey-haired old soldier, and
yet their plans had been by no means veiled in im-
penetrable darkness, for many families were aware of
them, but either could find no proper way of denounc-
ing their treason, or did not strive to find it. Nicholas
was called to the throne by his birth, but on this day

he was first to conquer it by the qualities he displayed as a ruler. Thus passèd the morning hours, in arrangements and fears, the realization of which quickly followed.

Alexandra, after a short morning's rest, was already occupied in preparing an imperial toilette for the day; such ceremonies are even more fatiguing to empresses than to monarchs, for thousands throng to kiss hands, and each expects not only a gracious look, but a gracious word. During this feminine employment, the Emperor entered, evident uneasiness portrayed on his grave countenance, and said, "The artillery refuse to take the oath of allegiance;" and immediately after the Emperor, the Empress-mother arrived in consternation, exclaiming, "No toilette, my child—tumults, insurrection!"

The tenderness of her husband usually spared Alexandra every disagreeable intelligence, but this was no longer possible, for his presence on the spot where the threatening storm seemed likely to burst was indispensable. The first report about the artillery had been followed by a second, to say that not only did the Muscovite regiments refuse to be sworn, but were in full rebellion; two distinguished generals and a colonel dangerously wounded, and a portion of the troops, stationed in the Senate Square, their banners flying, were shouting, " Long live Constantine and the Constitution !" In the course of fifty years the Empress-mother had suffered many very severe strokes from fate, and outlived many sudden and terrible changes, but an open revolt on the part of the Guards, at such a moment, was equally novel and extraordinary to all. Alexandra was more collected than her mother-in-law, because she knew her husband's heroism, whose courage would even rise with danger. Nicholas had only intimated in general terms what he had heard, but Alexandra had fortitude enough to hear the details her husband could only hurriedly relate. In fact, most regiments had taken the oath, and the great distance from the Winter Palace was considered an excuse for those of whom as yet no tidings had been received. Nicholas passed more than an hour in expectation, and the Palace already began to fill with those invited to attend high mass, when General Suchosanet appeared with the intelligence that the horse artillery at first hesitated about taking the oath, but their officers had succeeded in restoring them to order and obedience. Happily at this moment arrived the long-looked-for Grand Duke Michael, whom Nicholas at once despatched to the troops suspected of disaffection. Very different, however, were the next tidings, brought by General Neidhardt, of the Moscow regiment. Four companies of these, won over by Prince S. Rostowsky, and Michael, and Alexander Bestuschef, were in open revolt, having been persuaded that the new oath was a cunning deception. The soldiers shouted, " Give us cartridges and muskets !" and when they were again ranged fully armed, and an order reached them from Major-General Baron Frederik, Prince S. Rostowsky exclaimed, " I no longer acknowledge any general." General Frederik himself now appeared, when the Prince struck at him with his sabre, while Alexander Bestuschef aimed a

pistol at his head. Frederik fell senseless to the ground ;
then came galloping Brigadier-General Schenschin, but
Prince Rostowsky cut him down also, seized the flag
of his regiment, and led two companies away into the
court-yard. The others were held back by Colonel
Adlerberg and Prince Lieven. With flying banners, and
loud shouts and hurrahs, the rebels approached the
Senate square, sweeping with them on the way many
other soldiers and officers, but also numbers of the
lowest mob, and took up their places beside the equestrian statue of Peter the Great.

After this report, even Alexandra's courage began
to falter, for she saw that she could not appear on
her husband's arm at high mass till the revolt was
quelled, which could only be effected by his personal
appearance on the place of danger. Nicholas, with
his usual imperative brevity, commanded the Semenow
regiment to march against the rebels, and the Dragoon
Guards to hold themselves in readiness, and a battalion of the Preobraschky regiments to advance and
fetch his three daughters from the Anitschkow Palace,
and a charger to be saddled for himself. Nicholas and
Alexandra felt that not a moment was to be lost, and,
after a prayer in the little oratory, they bade each
other farewell, embracing in silence, with too well-
founded doubts whether they should ever meet again.
Nicholas commended his family to the protection of
the Almighty, and, leading his little son, seven years
old, now heir-apparent to the throne, to the Sapper
Guard on duty in the Palace, he placed him under
their care, saying, " It is your duty to guard the

heir-apparent." The Jägers swore to defend him with
their blood if the palace were attacked, while pride
and pleasure beamed in their faithful faces. And now
the Emperor, in the uniform of the Ismail regiment,
and no decoration but his blue ribbon, repaired to the
scene of danger, of victory, or of death.

The back of the Winter Palace, which forms a long
quadrangle, lies to the north side of the Neva; the front,
opposite the War Office, forms a long square, that
stretches away far beyond the Admiralty (adjoining
the Winter Palace), for where a fourth side is expected the cavalry boulevârds begin, which carry on the
square almost to the mouth of the Neva. The site of
the War Office is traversed by three great streets, that
run in the same direction as the three streets of Rome
from the Piazza del Popolo. The line of the Winter
Palace is interrupted by two adjacent squares, the first
between the Winter Palace and the Admiralty, the
second between the Admiralty and the Senate-house.
In the latter stands the colossal equestrian statue of
Peter the Great, on a granite block. There the mutineers
had ranged themselves. When Nicholas quitted the
Winter Palace and appeared in the square opposite the
War Office, he seemed a verst removed from where the
rebels had taken up their position. Here stood thousands
of carriages and sledges belonging to those invited to
attend high mass in the Winter Palace at eleven o'clock;
but a still more vast throng of curious people of every
class, and in every kind of costume, crowded every inch
of space. Nicholas appeared alone, and on foot on
this spot, facing the multitude. Here he learned that

no one knew anything of the great change, but that the news of the revolt of the Muscovite regiment had spread through the whole town. Nicholas himself now read aloud the manifesto, which was received with universal hurrahs, and he displayed on this first public occasion that air of sovereignty which knows how to control a tumultuous crowd, both by look and word. " Give way!" exclaimed he, " go home!" and in a few minutes the multitude dispersed, and the battalion took possession of the square; three companies of another regiment shortly appeared, who were employed in the protection of the Palace. The address of Nicholas to the battalion was responded to with thundering hurrahs, by which the soldiers expressed their profound devotion. Count Miloradowitsch presently came up in considerable embarrassment, and in direct contradiction to the assurances he had given an hour before, informed the Emperor that the rebels had already surrounded the monument of Peter the Great. " Go to them, Count; you have long been commander of the Guards; they will listen to you better than to any one else." The Emperor himself led the 1st and 2d Preobraschky battalion across the square, so that they stood between the Admiralty Square and the War Office.

What a frightful moment for the two Empresses, who had taken refuge in the corner wing of the Winter Palace, whence they could overlook the greater part of the spacious square! The mother saw her son, the wife her husband, proceed at the head of his regiment to encounter imminent danger, and a few minutes after he mounted his horse, they lost sight of him. What deadly terror seized them both, when immediately after several shots were heard, and no one knew who the victim was that they had reached. Not till a quarter of an hour of fearful anguish had elapsed did they learn that these bullets had wounded Count Miloradowitsch. By command of Nicholas, this officer, by a wide *détour*, and at last in a borrowed sledge and horses, contrived to press forward into the centre of the rebels, although admonished by Count Orlof not to proceed nearer. Shortly before, the aide-de-camp of the Emperor, Perowsky, succeeded in crossing the square, and making his way into the cavalry barracks with an order to Count Orlof to hold his regiment in readiness ; his usual lucky star did not hover over this honoured hero of battles innumerable. At ten paces from the first column he halted, and told the soldiery that Constantine had renounced the throne ; as a proof of his friendship with the Cesarewitsch he drew a dagger from its sheath, a present from Constantine, with the inscription, " To my friend Miloradowitsch." His speech, his eyes, his noble appearance, the ribbon of the Order of St. Andrew, always so significant in Russia, and other decorations on his breast, a number of stars, proofs of his valour, strongly moved the soldiery, and he would probably have succeeded in bringing them back to obedience, when a shot struck him under the St. Andrew star, and the hero sank from his horse into the arms of his aide-de-camp. It was not the mutineers who fired the fatal shot, but a cowardly Lieut. Kachowsky, who had been dismissed from the service, and who shot from the

side ; at the same moment, however, the bayonet of
Prince Obolensky cut him down. The shots that followed could never be quite accounted for. The mortally
wounded grey-haired man was carried into the adjoining
barracks, out of which the Guards had just marched.
The deadly fear of the Empresses was calmed on hearing
from afar the thousand bold hurrahs of an advancing
regiment; a proof that Nicholas was still alive. But
this shouting alternated constantly with the sounds of
firing, and thus the two ladies passed the next few hours
in mortal terror. Nicholas now found himself in the
long square between the Admiralty and the Senate,
in the centre of which stands Peter's monument.
The dragoons joined the troops led by Nicholas, but
in still greater numbers the populace crowded round
him, not from curiosity alone, but also to protect him
by their faithful loyalty. But by so doing they block-
ed up the space for any movement, and exposed themselves defenceless to all kinds of dangers. Here also
Nicholas commanded them to go home, and they would
learn on the morrow how the affair had ended. "They
will fire at me and hit you; go, put on your hats,
and pray to God;" and in a few minutes the crowd
dispersed. The rebels also, who, half-intoxicated, but
hungry and shivering from the frost, stood there in
wild disorder, filling the air with their savage howls,
were reinforced by the first company of the Grenadier
Guards and the Marines, and were in connection through
the Isaac Bridge, with Wasiliostrow, one of the largest
islands on which Petersburg is situated. The Emperor
ordered the bridge to be occupied, and rode forward

with General Benkendorf to have a better view of the position of the enemy. Here bullets showered round him, and it would have been foolhardy to have pressed onwards. But astonishment seized the returning Emperor when he saw the other half of the revolted Moscow regiment advance to meet him with their officers, imploring his permission to shed their blood on the spot for him, against their comrades. What could have brought about this miracle? The courage of his brother Michael, who, when the horse artillery were pacified, repaired to the quarters of the Moscow regiment, the chief centre of the rebellion. In order to convince the soldiery that they were deceived, he took the oath of allegiance to Nicholas along with them, in the open air, placed himself at their head, and led them to the square where the Emperor was. The Grand Duke Michael wished to renew the attempt Nicholas had made to advance towards the mutineers, but the latter prohibited it in the most determined manner. Meanwhile every access to the Senate square was filled on all sides by fresh loyal troops ; but the construction of the square and its adjoining streets hindered their being deployed, while the rebels, favoured by a larger space, could move freely in every direction. A charge of cavalry was tried in vain, the unshod horses being prevented from galloping boldly forward by the slippery ice, while the balls of the rebels hit but too surely. Colonel Sass alone, and his well-shod cavalry, cut their way through, and joined the troops stationed on the bridge. Nicholas sent for the artillery, and being convinced

that nothing could be undertaken without their aid, he
returned to the Winter Palace.

The interior of the palace offered a singular spectacle
on this day. An immense assemblage of those who enjoyed Court privileges had collected there since the
forenoon in State uniforms, and ladies in their richest
gala dresses, for the purpose of hearing high mass, but
instead of a solemn religious service they shared the
cruel anxiety and alarm of both the Empresses. As mass
could not be held without the Emperor, every window
and every corner was crowded, whence the eye could
reach the scene of tumult. Every one who entered was
besieged with questions, in the hope of learning something tranquillizing about the progress of events ; but
no certain tidings relieved the increasing dismay and
excitement. No one was admitted into the apartments
of the two Empresses ; Karamsin alone, the historian,
who was well versed in the joys and sorrows of the
annals of the world, witnessed the tears shed by the
mother, and the fortitude of the young wife. Fortu-
nately, they had no presentiment that danger threatened
them more closely than even Nicholas. A company despatched by the conspirators, had made their way into
the court-yard of the palace, in order to seize the persons
of the whole Imperial family. They were admitted,
under the belief that they were ordered there by Nicholas
himself. Happily their purpose was discovered by Lieutenant Baron Salza, and the audacious leader of the
company instantly quitted the palace with them. This
troop met Nicholas on his way back to the palace, who
asked them to whom they had sworn allegiance. " To

Constantine," was the reply. "Then your way lies in that direction," answered Nicholas, himself pointing out the way to the rebels. The commander of this company, Colonel Stürler, hurried after them, hoping still to prevent them joining the disaffected troops, but the same hand that murdered Miloradowitsch fired a pistol at Stürler, and with the same result. The danger that the Empresses and his children had been exposed to in the palace had not escaped Nicholas; it was often subsequently related that the plans of the conspirators, after obtaining possession of the Imperial family, were to keep up a fire from the tower of the palace; for this building, with a hundred cannons bristling on its walls, lies in an oblique direction, nearly opposite the palace on the other side of the Neva. Nicholas therefore desired carriages to be secretly prepared, that if any emergency occurred, he might convey his family to Zarskoe - Selò. Adlerberg, an Imperial aide-de-camp, at length presented himself before the anxious ladies, and assured them that all was likely to end well, and immediately after came Karamsin, who of his own accord had ventured to go to the square, where he met Nicholas. He also declared that the bold and intrepid demeanour of the Czar, and the devotion of his people, were the best pledges of a happy issue. Then the first ray of hope beamed on the terror-struck ladies, although the decisive moment was not yet past, and the rebels had even been reinforced.

The artillery made their appearance without cartouches, and began by firing several salvos without ball; the rebels responded by an irregular fire, and the

bullets again whistled round the head of Nicholas, whose
horse shied, and carried him into the thick of a crowd
of ruffians of the lowest class, who, with their dirty
hats on their heads, did not attempt to conceal their
sneers at this occurrence. The Emperor quickly perceived the disrespect on these insolent faces, and called
out in a loud imperious tone, "Hats off!" Startled
and terrified by his flashing eyes, the crowd scattered
in a moment like dust; though many of these went to
join the enemy's camp. When all the expected regiments were assembled, and the decisive moment
approached, Nicholas sanctioned his brother Michael
making a last effort to parley with the enemy. Accompanied by Adjutant-General Lewaschof, he therefore presented himself before the Marines, receiving
and returning their salute. They demanded, in the
most composed and deliberate way, that Constantine
Pawlowitsch, to whom they had vowed allegiance only
fourteen days previously, should appear himself to confirm his renunciation of the throne. Michael could
not force any other conviction on them, so he was
obliged to return without having attained his object.
At that moment an official, Küchelbecker, in the most
cowardly and crafty manner, aimed a pistol at the
august messenger close beside him; three sailors in the
ranks of the insurgents snatched it from him, and thus
saved Michael's life. All three were subsequently
handsomely rewarded by Nicholas. Even still the
patience of the Emperor was as little exhausted as his
courage shaken. The last means of a peaceful solution
were now resorted to; the two Metropolitans, who, as

well as the whole Court, had since morning been awaiting the Emperor in the palace, to perform high mass,
were summoned; Nicholas expected as great, or perhaps a greater effect from their words than from his
cannons, for the Russian people are in deep humility
devoted to their Church. They both appeared; Serafim,
the Metropolitan of Petersburg, went forward courage-
ously, an uplifted cross in his hand, to meet the motley
crowd. The people fell on their knees and crossed
themselves, the soldiers did the same, and laid down
their arms. The ranks in the various companies
listened to him quietly, indeed with entire confidence,
but the ringleaders gave the guileless troops a different
example : they mocked the man of the Church and
his gorgeous robes, called him a Pope, intended for an
insulting epithet, and at length, amid shouts of laughter,
they made the drums beat, and seized their arms in
order to respond to his remonstrances by cowardly
murder. Undaunted, but unsuccessful, Serafim returned to the palace with his companions. General
Toll then addressed the Emperor in his usual straightforward manner, saying, "Your Majesty, our last resource
now is our cartridges!" "How can I," replied Nicholas,
"mark the beginning of my reign with blood?" "If
you have the welfare of the empire at heart," interrupted Wasiltschikof, "you must put a stop to this
rebellion." Everything contributed to confirm this;
the approaching night, the insolence of the mutineers,
as well as the impatience of the loyal troops that had
been summoned to the town, and at whom the enemy
had repeatedly fired with impunity, and unpunished.

Nicholas thought of the alarm the salvos of
artillery would cause his venerable mother and his
delicate wife, and sent an aide-de-camp to tell them
what was about to take place—but before he could
reach the palace, a bright flash lit up the whole length
of the square, followed by a thunder of cannon, that
caused the Empress-mother to sink on the ground,
and terrified the more self-controlled Alexandra to
such an extent, that subsequently a nervous spasm in
her face continued through life—a memento of this
terrible hour. Speechless, but with a resigned mien,
she remained praying for her husband, kneeling beside
his insensible mother; flashes, and the crash of cannon
went on, and seemed to paralyse the last energies of life ;
a mysterious and terrific gloomy pause ensued ; thoughts
of the iron will of fate bowed down both mother and
daughter; suddenly the door was thrown open, arousing
them from their anguish and terror. "The Emperor
comes !" they heard General Toll exclaim, and these
words made them both spring from the ground with
electric strength; Alexandra, borne on the wings of
love and excitement, rushed to her husband, and in
speechless emotion, but with the impulse of a loving
woman's heart, filled with gratitude to God, she embraced a hero—an Emperor.

CHAPTER X.

SUCH is a picture of the most eventful day ever known in Russian history. It began with gloomy fears, it passed on in heroic struggles, and it closed with the victory of a hero. Now at length came high mass, inspiring the exhausted combatants with fresh strength. When the Emperor entered the church with his wife, and leading his young heir-apparent by the hand, the Metropolitan advanced to meet him with these words, " Blessed art thou, Nicholas Pawlowitsch, for thou comest in the name of the Lord!" After the celebration of high mass, the Emperor entered on his new position with fresh vigour. A band of traitors and reckless people in their train had obstructed the steps of his throne, and these he had defeated with manly intrepidity. He was now seated on the throne that he had won for himself. The first step was to see that the city was properly protected during the night; the second, to punish the ringleaders; the third, to reward courage and loyalty. The guards in the Winter Palace were reinforced, the troops remained all night besides watch-fires on the deserted snow-covered square, and cannons were placed at the entrances to all the principal streets; the faithful Wasiltschikof watched over the security of the actual city; the protection of the Wasiliostrow was confided to General Benkendorf, and patrols of Cossacks galloped through the streets in all directions. The conspirators had distinguished themselves only by base crime, but not at all by Republican courage. At the beginning of the tumult Prince Trubetzkoi did not appear in the square, but in a cowardly and sneaking manner hurried to the War Office, in the hope of clearing himself by tendering the oath in favour of Nicholas. But the terrific spectacle of the day, and his evil conscience, drove him from one place to another; and at last, when those first tempted, and then forsaken by him were lying bleeding, he took refuge under the protection of the Austrian Ambassador, Count Lebzeltern, his brother-in-law. His name must, however, have been mentioned to the Emperor by Rostowzow, for the same evening his papers and the plan of the whole conspiracy were in the hands of Nicholas. The fugitive, with a total want of head, had left them all lying open in his house. He was safe from the police in Count Lebzeltern's abode, but the Austrian Ambassador was requested, in diplomatic form, by Count Nesselrode, to surrender his brother-in-law. The noble Lebzeltern did not agree with England in the principle of sheltering political criminals; at ten o'clock the same evening the Prince stood before his Emperor, but after the first few words he cast himself slavishly at the feet of his sovereign, and —begged for his life. The Emperor answered sternly, " If you have courage to endure a dishonoured existence, it shall be granted you." Prince Odojeffsky, more cowardly than Trubetzkoi, fled to his relations during the battle, but was delivered up by them to the authorities. Rilejef found himself on the same evening in his own house, with almost all his confederates, feeling despair and remorse that so much blood should have been shed in vain, but the very next day they were seized by the police and placed in safe keeping.

During the torturing suspense of that day of terror, the young Empress had been unable to measure the whole extent of the danger she had escaped, as she now did, when, separated in the evening from her husband, she was seated alone in her boudoir, and could recall all the various events. "What a commencement of a reign!" had they both said—all the fear, horror, terror, and anxiety, that she had endured twenty years before, when accompanying her mother at the time of her flight, fate had now accumulated on her head within the space of a few hours; but she had been saved from destruction, under Providence, by the courage of her husband; feelings of gratitude filled her heart, and wholly absorbed her, to the exclusion of all else. The same evening she began a letter to her father in Berlin, but her trembling hand could not hold the pen for more than a few lines; a feeling of faintness, bordering on a swoon, made her drop her head partly unconscious, and she had nearly dropped asleep beside the lamp, when her equally exhausted husband, after his interview with Trubetzkoi, entered, to tell her that he had seen far into the abyss of the conspiracy, but hoped, within the next few days, to be master of the

whole net. " I knew yesterday, from an early hour,"
said he, "what a terrible day awaited us, but I hoped
to be able to spare you such tidings, indeed, perhaps to
disperse the storm that did eventually break on us; but
we are not overthrown." This night also Nicholas
scarcely closed his eyes, for the state of his wife added
fresh anxieties to the thousand perils that already
threatened him.

Next morning the Emperor appeared in the square,
and rewarded the loyalty of those attached to his
person, and the regiments also, with promotion, orders,
and other tokens of favour. On the previous evening,
in sincere sorrow, he wrote to Count Miloradowitsch, a
chevalier sans peur et sans reproche, who died in the
course of the night, and the Emperor paid him the last
honour by assisting in carrying his coffin, and placing
it on the hearse. The Winter Palace was in the greatest
confusion, the whole of the Imperial family, with their
numerous retinue, having come there on the 13th December, and being as yet only temporarily provided for, as if
arriving at a camp. Hitherto no reigning Sovereign had
inhabited the rooms of his predecessor, for in the Czar's
palaces the apartments are innumerable; now, in addition to the Emperor, it was to receive three Empresses,
the heir-apparent, and his three sisters, the youngest of
whom was only six months old, and under the care of
English nurses.

All these children, meanwhile, were in rooms of
which the windows overlooked the inner court of
the palace. The little Marie alone guessed by the
unusual commotion in the palace, and by the anxiety

and alarm of her mother and grandmother, that her
absent father was in danger. The two Englishwomen
would not allow them to leave this remote room, and
tried to amuse them by games and stories, but the
thunder of the cannon terrified them, and they clasped
their hands in prayer, childish uneasiness visible on
their faces.   The first care of the Empress was to
regulate a new household, and to establish a home like
that in the Anitschkow Palace, where it had never been
seen in greater perfection; it was indeed a difficult task
to maintain the splendour of majesty in the kingdom
and the city, and yet to remain the loving wife of
her harassed husband, and the careful mother of
four children.   As, however, her goodness of heart
was known in the city, many of the conspirators,
through their relations, appealed to her, hoping
by her interposition to mollify their stern judge
Nicholas, he being only known to the public as yet
by his severity towards military offenders.   It was
feared that he would wield the sword of Ivan, "the
Terrible," who, however, on his death, was lamented
by the people more than any other Sovereign.   The
Emperor and his Council required time to disentangle
thoroughly the whole of the vast web, and to gain a
clear insight into the affair, so that they might distinctly distinguish between what really was high
treason and State treason, or only imprudence and
reckless imitation of foreign countries.   All danger
seemed at an end in the capital; astonishment and
admiration filled every heart, and gratitude to Providence for granting them such a hero for their ruler,

curiosity also to see face to face the man whose
sudden greatness had taken them by surprise. Nicholas
was at that time admired in every country, but in
Russia he was soon idolized. After Alexandra had
in some degree recovered, she and Nicholas, wrapt in
warm cloaks, drove through the town in a one-horse
sledge. Thousands, in spite of the bitter cold of December, besieged the steps to see them enter the
carriage; many at sight of the Emperor fell on their
knees, but all took courage, while confidence and joy
beamed from every eye, when they saw their sovereign
in nowise different from other generals, and the arm that
had quelled a rebellion tenderly supporting his wife,
and lifting her into a simple sledge, drawn by one horse,
whereas the higher officials never stirred without four.
Since the days of Sophia and Peter, many old Russian
customs had vanished, but not the veneration of the
people for their Czar; and although the conspirators
had been disloyal, still they scarcely formed a millionth
part of the realm. Even the misled and deluded
soldiery, when they were told of a republic, asked who
was to rule over it. Another time, when the conspirators disclosed to the troops their foolish plans,
they begged to know whether the Emperor had
sanctioned these, and on being told that he had not,
they agreed it was better to put an end to the project.
The peasant and the soldier equally regard the Czar as
their natural protector against noble proprietors, sor-
did officials, and a corrupt police. The spirit of the
government may be severe or mild, but the people are
unaffected by it, for a stern or gracious sway of the

sceptre affects only the Czar's immediate *entourage* and the higher classes of society. The stronger and more despotic the will of the monarch, the better does the peasant find himself protected. The people therefore hailed with delight the dawn of so absolute a reign, expecting severity towards the criminals, while the guilty alone trembled, and sought refuge with the Empress against their threatened punishment.

The public learned by degrees that Petersburg was not the chief seat of the revolt, but that it had spread far more widely in the south, where men of greater energy had placed themselves at its head. We know that Pestel was imprisoned on December 14th—perhaps the only man who could have succeeded in carrying out the detestable enterprise—with him the head of the conspiracy was cut off, and the remaining members in dismay met their fate with feeble resistance. General Tschernischef arrested twelve colonels besides Pestel, and a number of other officers, and took possession of their papers. This occurred in the second *corps d'armée*, who were under the orders of the admirable Prince Wittgenstein, and where the roots of the conspiracy had spread the most. But in the first *corps d'armée*, under General Count Osten-Sacken, conspiracy was also rife, its head being Sergius Murawief-Apostol, the scion of a Russian family with many branches, of glorious memories and names, perhaps the most enlightened and honoured of all others. Murawief-Apostol, educated in Paris, and devoted to classical studies, lived more in the spirit of Horace and Virgil than in that of Lomonossow and Dershawin, and on his return found all the crimes of the

Roman Empire in Russia, but none of its virtues. He
and his younger brother were more at home in the society
of the disaffected than in that of the Semenow Regiment.
Another glorious name had joined the brothers, Bestuschef-Rumin, descended from Elisabeth's renowned
Chancellor.   They learned the disaster of their confederates in Petersburg, but found time and opportunity
to escape imprisonment.   Colonel Hebel, intrusted with
the charge of the Murawiefs, took the affair too lightly,
and continued on the most friendly terms with the
criminals.   One evening he was sitting at tea with the
two imprisoned brothers and a good many young officers,
when they suddenly seized him and made him their
prisoner. Hebel fell a victim to his foolish good-nature,
and Sergius-Murawief placed himself at the head
of the fallen colonel's regiment. This regiment, the
Tschernigof, had been long since won over by the conspirators, but, being suspected by General Roth, he purposely dispersed the companies into various places far
distant from each other.   Sergius, and those who were
still loyal, collected the rest, and arrived with them at
Wasilkof, after a resistance soon overcome.   Here he
took possession of the entire regiment, their cash, flags,
and supplies of powder, and reinforced the troops by
criminals whom he found in the prisons.   Before he
marched from here he caused a religious service to be
performed in the marketplace, and the soldiers received
from a priest a catechism of the new Constitution, which
was greeted with great rejoicing by the officers, but
listened to by the soldiers with stony indifference—in
fact, with total want of comprehension.   They were

ready to take the oath of allegiance to the Cesarewitsch
Constantine, as they had heard his name oftener than
that of Nicholas, and to kiss the picture of a saint; everything else was to them a mere empty sound. Sergius,
with six companies, and accompanied by Bestuschef-
Rumin and two of his brothers, marched toward Kiew.
Half-way he found himself surrounded by overpowering
numbers. A fight, however, ensued, and Sergius was
twice wounded; the troops deserted him, as indeed they
did not know why they were opposed to their brethren,
and thus the two Murawiefs (the third was killed on the
field) and Bestuschef-Rumin fell into the hands of
General Geismar, who had been despatched against them.
The southern conspiracy was in this manner also happily
disarmed on the 4th January 1826. Many of its members had relatives in Petersburg, where the criminals
shortly arrived, but this fact was kept secret and remained unknown to the greater part of the populace in
the town. The personal courage of the Emperor, the
severity experienced by Prince Trubetzkoi, made it
appear hopeless to all the connexions of the participators
in the revolt to risk a petition to the Autocrat. They
turned, however, with the greater confidence to the young
Empress, whose kindness of heart seemed a pledge that
if she had been sole judge she would have granted a
pardon to all, or at least mitigated their punishment.

When all the threads of the conspiracy were in the
hands of the new government, the Emperor, from a sense
of justice, appointed a committee to investigate the
whole affair in its most minute details, to ascertain the
guilty heads of the projects of assassination, to distin-

guish the share each had taken and their degree of
criminality, and not till then to surrender them to a
court of justice. Alexandra could only influence her husband by gentle compassion, of which he was himself far
from being devoid. Nicholas seldom was known to
make use of his regal prerogatives, though his views,
often heard from his own lips, were, " We all hope for
mercy from God, but from me, its ruler, my country
must only expect justice and rigour of the law." The
last days of December passed rapidly in the grateful
conviction of having happily escaped a great danger, but
also with the consciousness of having been suddenly and
quite unexpectedly precipitated into another course of
life, which required at every fresh step giant power.
About eight days after the 14th December Alexandra
awaited her husband in vain at ten o'clock in her
boudoir. She thought he was detained by business with
his ministers and generals, but was told that he was
seated alone at his table, so she surprised him, contrary to her usual custom, by a visit. Nicholas was
sitting, his head leaning on his hands, so buried in
thought that he scarcely observed the entrance of his
wife. To her question as to what was occupying
his thoughts, and making him look so sad, he answered,
after a pause, " If God does not aid me, I shall sink
under the burden of the Crown, even in these early
days; how little did we a few weeks since, in the enjoyment of our quiet domestic happiness, anticipate that I
should be seated in this place in the Winter Palace?
Have I ever been brought up with the idea that I was
one day to sway the sceptre over fifty millions? Do not

be surprised that these new duties are more strange to
me than to my ministers; and this does distress me, for
I am not disposed to be dependent on others, and yet for
the moment I must allow myself to be led by them in
order to learn my duties." In the presence of his
wife, however, lay a magic feminine charm, that like a
warm sunny ray cheered the spirit of her dejected
husband, and inspired him with fresh courage. She
understood what her first duties were in her new position; she only needed to appear to restore Nicholas's
cheerfulness. But it was not the brow of the Emperor
alone that was gloomy; all in the Winter Palace and the
whole city bore outward signs of mourning, and in too
many families internal peace had fled. The sympathy
for the death of Alexander was universal and sincere.
The words of the Empress Elisabeth, " Our angel is in
Heaven," were repeated in every house, for all knew
what they had lost in him, and still secretly dreaded a
new outbreak of rebellion. Sledges, carriages, coach-
men, and footmen were placed in mourning; the ladies
wore crape, and in many houses the rooms were
draped with black, and even the reckless indifference of
the lower classes had given place to gravity. The
splendour and cheerfulness that usually prevail in
December, January, and February, up to Lent, were no
longer to be seen, and in many *salons*, where gay music
had formerly been heard, tears were now shed for the
far-away dead. Very soon Alexander's bust, with Elisabeth's words inscribed on it, was to be seen in every
house, and people gazed at it as at the image of a
saint.

The transference of the beloved remains from Tagan-rog to Petersburg, from the Sea of Azof to the Gulf of Finland, occupied the whole country in the first months of the new year. The Christian world had never witnessed so long a funeral procession, antiquity alone possibly, might have done so at the burial of Alexander of Macedon, whose body was conveyed an almost equal distance, from Babylon to Alexandria. Who could describe the agony of grief which the Empress Elisabeth suffered in seeing the mortal remains of her idolized husband carried away ! In the desert and arid steppes of Taganrog, close beside the gloomy Sea of Azof, she was forced to remain desolate, alone, and deprived of hope. The slow and solemn procession moved along the endless surface of snow, prayers were offered up beside the coffin in the various dialects of the Nogaisch Tartars, the Kirghisses, and Baschkirs, and also the Kariate Jews, who had all hurried hither from their distant homes to weep for the deceased Emperor, whom they had honoured and appreciated during his life, but had never seen. But louder than all these thousands of voices howled a terrific hurricane, which came rushing from the sea, tearing along the wastes of snow, and whirling in gusts round the coffin. Far from her German home, far from the capital of which she had been the ornament for a quarter of a century, the unhappy Elisabeth remained, dead to life and to the world, her sole hope that of rejoining ere long her departed husband. The city in which she was left was scarcely known in Russia, far less in Europe. And now the news spread through the world that there Alexander had

died, and Elisabeth was alone and dying.   The corpse of
this Christian Emperor was drawn by eight horses, hung
with black, like the carriage ; the Macedonian conqueror
was drawn by sixty-four mules, and bells everywhere
announced the arrival of the deceased hero, whereas the
pealing of Christian bells summoned all hearts to show
the last marks of respect to the Russian Czar.   Torches
lighted up the gloomy road, and the severe frost did not
prevent the loyal and devoted people thronging from
many miles distant to meet the coffin, which rested at
night in village churches, resounding with solemn hymns,
and happy those who were permitted in the morning
to assist in lifting the precious burden on the carriage.
When at length the procession drew near the ancient
seat of the Czars—Moscow—the whole populace
streamed out to meet it; the great imperial bell
lamented his death in loud peals, echoed by a thousand
others, and the wind conveyed the sounds towards the
bier; it was like the lamentation of an entire country.
The people on their knees formed a long line, through
which the procession moved forwards; the crowns of
Russia and Poland, etc., decorated the coffin, which was
deposited in the Cathedral of the Kremlin, where all
Czars lay before the time of Peter the Great.   During
three days the people were allowed to approach and
kiss the mourning drapery.   From the Twersch to the
Petrofsky gate the carriages were surrounded by the
population of the country, and before they reached retired Zarskoe-Selò, Alexander's beloved abode, the
Emperor and the Empress-mother joined them in the
village of Tosna.   The coffin was opened, but the face

that six months before smiled so lovingly on his mother,
and so graciously on every one, remained veiled.   The
young Emperor stood before the corpse of his brother,
and a quarter of a century's glorious career spoke to him
even out of decay and corruption.   But in the heart of
his venerable mother were revived the memories of half-
a-century of intense happiness and also of deepest
sorrow, and the latter chilled her heart.

In Zarskoe-Selò, where the corpse lay in state for several days, the steps of the catafalque were encompassed
by the whole Imperial family, and bedewed with bitter
tears.   From here the body was transferred to Tschesme,
about twelve versts from Petersburg, where it remained
till March 12, when a new state-carriage was employed
to convey it to the city gates of Moscow.   Sixty pages
carrying burning torches opened the procession, followed
by the assembled priesthood of the capital in mourning robes, and also the Court singers and those of the
Newsky Cloister bearing pictures of saints; and beside the
carriages walked the Adjutant-Generals of the deceased.
When the procession approached the city, the Holy
Synod and the Governor-General came to meet it; the
reports of cannon and the chiming of innumerable bells
announced its arrival.   The Emperor, in deep mourning, and all the members of his family and foreign
princes, joined the mournful train on foot.   The Empress, and all her children, followed in a carriage, and
behind them came an interminable train of dignitaries
and Court officials and authorities.

Similar to the hour of departure from Taganrog, on
this day also nature was in a state of stormy tumult.

Not till two hours had elapsed did the procession reach
the Cathedral of Kasan, in the centre of the city, where
it was received and conducted by the Metropolitan, Serafim, into the interior of the church, hung with black. The
coffin was deposited on a catafalque lit up with thousands of wax-candles, where it remained, free access
being granted to the people, for eight days and nights.
The highest dignitaries kept watch on the steps, the
priests read prayers day and night, and the whole Imperial family attended divine service three times a day ;
from hence the last progress was to the fortress, in the
church of which their remains repose.   This building,
on the Petersburg Island, on the right bank of the Neva,
includes within its walls the circumference of a city.
In its centre stands the Peter and Paul Church, with a
lofty, slender-pointed gilt tower, a *point de mire* for
the whole city. Here rest the remains of Emperors
and Empresses, but in other parts of the church State
criminals were once buried alive. A hundred cannon
planted on the walls defend the entrance. This building lies in profound solitude, rather shunned than frequented, and in winter alone a solitary foot-passenger
can traverse the frozen Neva to reach it. In the nave of
this church a catafalque was erected, that by its height
and size, by the pomp of its candelabra, trophies and
figures of angels, far surpassed that in the Kasan Church.
Admission to high mass was only granted to those of the
highest class—indeed, chiefly persons who stood in near
connection with the lamented Czar. In the Kasan Cathedral the loss of the ruler of sixty millions was deplored,
but within the fortress, the head of the Imperial family.

During high mass every heart was melted; but when
the coffin was borne to the grave, the two Empresses
sank to the ground, and the old grenadiers of Austerlitz, Borodino, and Leipzig, were overcome with sorrow,
and their steps. faltered.   The late Emperor's body-
coachman, Ilia, seemed turned into stone.   He had
driven his deceased master during his life, and after his
death to this spot, and his tears flowed with those of so
many illustrious mourners over the grave of Alexander.
The Emperor's charger, too, escorted the coffin to the
fortress, and was taken back thence to the retired pleasure-grounds of Zarskoe-Selò, where he was to remain,
and, like Ilia, never to serve another master.   The close
of the mournful ceremonies was announced to the city
by a salvo of three hundred cannon, and the running
fire of every regiment.   Many houses, however, continued hung with black, and the first official prescribed
mourning lasted forty days more, because our Lord,
after his resurrection, passed that number of days on
earth.   On the 9th, 20th, and 40th day, reckoned from
that of the interment, special prayers in memory of the
dead were said by the family of the deceased beside the
grave.

What strength, what courage and endurance, did these
winter months demand from the young Emperor and Empress ! If kind Providence has armed men with strength
and courage to fight, so has He also bestowed on woman
patience and fortitude.   At the termination of the forty
days of mourning, all eyes were turned to Moscow,
where the coronation, with its solemn splendour, was
intended to efface the last traces of mourning ; and the

Emperor's magnanimity and mercy healed many wounds and revived many shattered hopes. Then came the news of Elisabeth's death. She had left Taganrog in May, and journeyed to the north along the same desolate road on which her deceased husband had preceded her. She wished once more to embrace the mother of her beloved Alexander, and the Empress-mother went to meet her, according to her wish, but found she had died only two hours previously. She had reached a small rural village, Below, but already so weak that she felt the absolute necessity of rest, and her sole wish now was to see once more her mother-in-law next day. But even this last cherished hope was denied to Elisabeth, for the morning sun rose on a corpse. A blissful dream seemed to light up her dead face, and her ladies did not for some time discover that hours before the angel of death had pressed his last kiss on her cold lips. The last struggle had passed calmly and quietly, like her whole life. Her name descended to the second daughter of the Grand Duchess Helene, born a few days afterwards in Moscow; but this child too was not favoured by fate, as she did not survive her twelfth year. We shall refer to her hereafter.

The whole period of mourning was renewed at Elisabeth's death, just as we have already described—the same procession, the same ceremonies at the interment. The strength of Alexandra was so exhausted by the terrors of the 14th December, that during the performance of the last rites at Elisabeth's funeral, she swooned several times, and was obliged at last to be carried out ; and yet the approaching coronation required at least as much power of endurance as all that preceded it. The Empress Elisabeth, owing to the restless energy of her mother-in-law, her independence and vigour of mind, and the respect due to age, had been always cast into the shade. The people only heard of her, but seldom saw her. During the whole of Alexander's reign, Maria Feodorowna appeared in her place on public occasions. Her interment, therefore, did not meet with the sympathy she merited from the populace; but those noble persons who, by their cultivated minds and position, enjoyed her intimacy, never named her otherwise than as a saint. It is difficult to understand why the Empress Catherine should have caused her eldest grandson, Alexander, when scarcely sixteen, to marry Elisabeth, only fourteen years old; but it is evident that so early a marriage could in no respect have the happy results expected from this connection. The immature age of both gave rise to misunderstandings which even after days failed in entirely smoothing over, and which the frequent absence of the Emperor only assisted in maintaining. Their last journey, however, at last reconciled two souls, among the noblest of their century, and, though late, convinced them of their mutual worth.

But the same month of July that witnessed their obsequies and the holy peace in which both how rested, was destined also to behold a spectacle that, since the days of Elisabeth Petrowna, the autocrat Empress, seemed to have been banished from the city, indeed from the history of the country. The Tribunal of Justice pronounced sentence on the criminals of December 14th, and laid it before his Imperial Majesty for ratification.   Both they and the Sacred Synod considered the crime of so aggravated a nature, that they not only dissuaded the young Emperor from mercy, but earnestly recommended the most severe measures. Nicholas's heart, on the day of the revolt, long resisted having recourse to extreme measures; but on that occasion his own life alone was endangered, whereas now the welfare of his kingdom influenced his resolution. Seven months had elapsed, and the people were accustomed to see an Emperor who, in addition to heroism, had shown much benevolence, and whose own wife urged him to a degree of clemency that the Court of Justice prohibited.   But mercy on the part of an autocrat is limited by no law.   The Roman Nero hesitated to sign the first death-warrant offered to him.   A hundred and twenty-one persons were accused, tried, and condemned to death.   Nicholas, however, found that all were not equally criminal, and not only his clemency, but also his sense of justice, made him oppose such a verdict.   The Tribunal of Justice, informed of the Emperor's sentiments, restricted sentence of death to thirty-one persons, the penalties of the rest being mitigated to political death, banishment, *travaux forcés*, and other punishments.   But even this verdict was moderated by the Emperor.   The number of the hundred and thirty condemned to death was reduced to five, who were, however, to suffer immediate execution. These five unhappy men were, Paul Pestel, Conrad Rilejef, Sergius Murawief-Apostol, Michael Bestuschef-Rumin, and Peter Kachowsky.   Although all in the army they were condemned to the gallows.   After the

announcement of their sentence they were granted
only one day to prepare for death, but permitted to
enjoy the consolations of religion in the last moments
of life.   Rilejef bade farewell, in writing, to his lovely
young wife; he seemed the most gentle and penitent
of all; but Paul Pestel was as intrepid as ever, and
equally devoted to his own views.   The Emperor
comprehended that executions of so deplorable a nature
must not be degraded into a show for the populace,
as, alas! was too much the case half a century ago
in our petty German States, where curiosity rejoiced
beforehand over the expected spectacle; the compassion
of women melting them into tears, and sympathy with
misfortune insensibly inspiring the wish to imitate the
criminal, or furnishing an occasion for the most base
malice to display itself.   The hour appointed for these
executions was one in which most people are usually
asleep, and the spot, a wall of the fortress, on the other
side of the Neva, and by no means easy of access.   On
July 25th, 1826, at two o'clock in the morning, in a
northern twilight, the hour of their approaching death
was announced to the unhappy culprits by the sound
of muffled drums and wailing trumpets.   Amid these
melancholy sounds the companies of the different regiments from every part of the town assembled, to take
leave of their deluded comrades, in silence and military
discipline, and also to witness a solemn warning spectacle that had never occurred during the latter reigns.
The ghastly gallows had been hastily constructed, perhaps not with the necessary skill, and at all events
without those numerous appliances formerly connected

with its erection in Germany. First appeared those who were to undergo the apprehension of death, but eventually to be pardoned. Their uniforms and decorations were cast into a fire of blazing fagots. They were dressed in grey blouses, and after being led past the gallows, were taken back to the fortress. Then followed the five chief criminals, in grey, their faces covered. The executioner alone could distinguish between them, and he placed Pestel on the extreme right, Kachowsky on the extreme left. All five had already the death-noose round their necks, and the executioner only awaited the close of the prayers to come down from the scaffold, when the spectacle became even more horrible than had been anticipated: as the executioner was descending, after performing his duty, the scaffold broke, and only Pestel and Kachowsky were found to be dead, the others, during the crash, having escaped the noose and rolled down from the walls alive. One of them implored his life from General Benkendorf, Heaven having so mercifully preserved him; while another, Rilejef, exclaimed, "I cannot succeed even in dying!" No one ventured to grant a reprieve on his own responsibility, for the Emperor was far away from the city, in Zarskoe-Selò. Bestuchef-Rumin was so injured by the fall that he was obliged to be carried to execution. In the course of a few minutes the scaffold was again erected, and the three last culprits rejoined their deceased comrades in death. Princes Trubetskoi, Obolensky, Schtschepin-Rostowsky, and also Captain Jakubowitsch, were sent to Siberia for life, deprived of their rank and their dignities. Princess Trubetskoi implored permission to follow her husband. Matthäus, Murawief-Apostol, Küchelbecher, Alexander Bestuschef, Nicholas Murawief, Jakuschkin, were sent into less severe and shorter exile, as well as Prince Sergius Wolkonsky, whose wife left her parents in order to share the sorrows and privations of her husband. The wives of the two Murawiefs also sacrificed their luxurious lives in the capital, in the hope of alleviating the misery of their husbands. Every trace of the crime now disappeared. The Church deemed it necessary that, after the just punishment of the guilty, and the fortunate preservation of the kingdom and the Imperial family, public thanksgivings should be offered up to God, and, moreover, on the same spot in the town where, on the 14th December, rebellion planted its standard. Next morning, on a platform, an altar was erected between the Isaac Church and the monument of Peter the Great, surrounded by all the regiments of Guards in the capital. The people thronged thither from every street; the Emperor and the Metropolitan came on foot; the Empress, with her brother, Prince Carl, in a gilt State-carriage, and a solemn religious service began; hymns of thanksgiving and praise resounded, for the preservation of the Imperial family, imploring a length of happy days for them, and rest for the souls of those who shed their blood for the throne on the 14th. After high mass, the priests sprinkled the troops and the square with holy water, and thus the crime was obliterated and the expiation completed.

The eyes of the sovereign and his people might now turn in security and peace to another spectacle, that of the

Coronation, which the ancient city of the Czar looked upon as the most enviable privilege that she possessed over her younger sister—Petersburg.   The Russians approach this holy city with something of the reverence a child feels for its mother, and the Kremlin, rearing its head in the centre of this motley scene, is the heart of its historical existence.   Here are cherished the fairest memories of the people; here repose their Czars, their Patriarchs, their Grand Duchesses, and many of their heroes and saints.   The Kremlin tells a tale equally of the barbarism of a Tochtamisch, and the Church desecration of a Napoleon.   Here the weapons were blessed with which Dmitri Donskoi and Peter the Great armed themselves in setting out against the Tartars and Sweden. Here are the holy pictures of various provinces, whose inhabitants, both by Church and Monarchy, are bound to this capital.   Here also is the wonder-working picture of the Virgin Mary, attributed by tradition to the apostle St. Luke.   Among other relics this Church possesses a nail of the true cross.   From here the golden tower, Iwan Weliki, commands a view over the whole city, and its massive church-bell proclaims the death of Emperors, and also their coronation.   Here the Czars once lived simply in the Terema, surrounded by all the ecclesiastical pomp of the kingdom, as did the Patriarchs, who with the Czar held the reins of the nation in their hands.   We find ourselves in a historical sanctuary, which no western European nation can boast of, not even those of Asiatic origin, in so vast an extent, and likewise so concentrated.   In the Seraglio of Constantinople alone can it find a rival.   A glance over the town from

the Kremlin shows how far Church-life in Russia predominates over every other ; the numerous churches
quite throw into the shade the many institutions and
private houses. Most of these sacred edifices, in spite
of the ruthless blows of fate from which the city has
suffered in all centuries through fire, are in good preservation. Tochtamisch burnt Moscow to ashes in 1382,
leaving 24,000 unburied corpses. Before the days of
Tamerlane the picture of the Holy Virgin protected the
city ; but in the sixteenth century it was three times
burnt to the ground, and in 1612 the retreating Poles
left it a heap of ruins and rubbish, just as the French
did in 1812. In all these calamities the Kremlin has
been little, or in fact not at all injured. The Cloister
of Tschudow served the French as a refuge for their
staff, the largest and most sacred of the cathedrals for
a slaughter-house, and the holy pictures for kitchen-
tables. The gate of St. Nicholas, and a part of the walls
of the Kremlin, were blown up by the French when
they left Moscow ; otherwise the greater part was left
untouched, and speedily purified from Gallic filth. The
gate called the Holy Gate, through which no one passes
except bare-headed, was also unmolested.

Among the many churches of the Kremlin, three
cathedrals are appointed for the highest and last solemnities of the Emperors. In the Church of the Annunciation they were formerly betrothed and married, and
in former days, as well as now, crowned in the Church
of the Ascension, and in the Church of the Archangel
Michael, the Czars all found their last resting-place, till
Peter the Great, who was the first monarch interred in
the Fortress Church.

The grandest preparations were therefore made in the Church of the Annunciation for the Coronation. After the conflagration of the city, it had been rapidly rebuilt in a more solid manner than before. The 14,000 wooden houses at that time consumed by the flames had been replaced by many new private palaces; the interior of the city had acquired more of a European appearance, but the exterior aspect was unaltered, owing to the numerous churches. The higher classes of society were all initiated into the ideas of the Petersburg school. Among the people, however, the old reverence for their rulers still existed, and the hope of so soon seeing their new and still-distant Czar enlivened their usually stolid faces. For weeks previously deputies and others, attracted by curiosity, flocked to Moscow from all the provinces of the realm, both European and Asiatic, and in the usually deserted streets the most quaint physiognomies and the most singular costumes attracted the eye. There were to be seen, wandering about, the natives of Georgia, Mingrelians, Grusinians, followers of Islam and the Cross, and the races of the endless steppes, all in the brightest dresses; some wore arms and diamonds, some caftans and fur caps, while others exhibited their turbans to the inquisitive people. Many boasted of the proud names of Sultan or Khan, and within their own domains wielded the lash of Tamerlane, whose descendants they were, and yet acknowledged the still greater power of Russia. The Russian nobility do not permit themselves to be excelled in anything, so many of the Boyars of the present day appeared with royal retinues. The nine-

teenth century could show, in Moscow, families, who in
pomp and wealth, and in lavish generosity also, might
vie with the Czars of the sixteenth century.   Added to
all these strange sights were the representatives of
European powers, and if the eyes of the people gazed
with delight at the foreign costumes, the interest of the
more cultivated classes was keenly excited by the
illustrious names borne by many of the latter.   But all
who had been despatched to Moscow from Europe and
Asia sunk into insignificance before the rejoicings caused
by the arrival of the Imperial family, every member of
which appeared, from the Empress-mother down to the
nine years old heir-apparent.

The Emperor and Empress first rested at the country
palace of Petrofsky, three versts from Moscow.   From
here to the Kremlin a line was formed of 50,000
soldiers, chiefly the Guards, and between them the
Imperial procession slowly and solemnly advanced.
Nicholas on horseback, accompanied by his brother
Michael, and Prince Charles of Prussia, opened the brilliant spectacle; close behind them followed the gold
State-carriage, drawn by eight horses, containing the
Empress and the heir-apparent.   Many thousand bells,
and among others the Iwan Weliki, strove to drown the
tumultuous hurrahs of the soldiers and the rejoicing
multitude, but even the thunder of cannon was not
audible in the streets through which the procession
passed, owing to the uproarious greeting of the populace.
The majestic appearance of the Emperor, and the feminine charm and dignity of the Empress, attracted all
eyes, causing admiration and reverence in the hearts of

the people.   The Emperor rode bareheaded through the
" Holy Gate of the Redeemer," into the Kremlin, and in
accordance with ancient custom proceeded straight to
the Ascension Church.   Here the body of priests of
the metropolis met their Majesties and offered them
the Holy Cross to kiss.   They then entered the church,
kneeling before the sacred pictures, and uttering a short
but fervent prayer for the protection and blessing of
Heaven.   When they returned, the body of merchants
welcomed them with bread and salt on gold dishes,
after which they all disappeared from the gaze of the
thronging people, the Imperial family retiring into the
little Tschudof Palace (a few hundred steps from the
Ascension Church), that had only space to receive one
happy family divested of all Imperial splendour.   They
quitted a great stage for the privacy of home, and knew
how to enjoy that felicity so often crushed by mere
pomp.

Next morning, to the joyful surprise both of the
family and the city, appeared the Grand Duke Constantine Pawlowitsch, from Warsaw.   He presented
himself before the astonished Nicholas in Polish uniform, as his first subject, a written document in his hand.
The Czar welcomed and embraced him as a brother,
while their tears mingled.   Constantine testified that his
abandonment of the throne was voluntary, and his recognition of his brother cordial, and wherever he appeared
in Moscow, the people paid the tribute of admiration of
his magnanimity.   Such traits were not unknown in the
Romanow family.   ' Ivan once gave up the crown to his
younger brother Peter, and only consented to share the

throne when urged to do so by his sister Sophia. The
three brothers now showed themselves together in public,
and the city understood the inference intended to be
drawn from this.

The great Coronation-day was initiated on the previous evening by a mass, attended by the Imperial family,
in the Church of the Czar, behind a golden grating,
before which the pious crowd stood bareheaded. In spite
of its enormous circumference, the Kremlin could only
receive a small portion of the pageant-loving people.
Elevated amphitheatres were erected for about 5000
invited guests; through these the grand' procession proceeded from the Tschudof Palace to the Ascension
Church. The distance is only some hundred paces from
this Palace to the Church. All the bells from the dawn
of day summoned the people from the most distant
quarters of the city, but they were obliged to remain
outside the walls, or take advantage of the adjacent
roofs to look down on the pageant from a distance.
The high dignitaries, the provincial deputies, and the
diplomatic corps invited to attend the ceremony, filled
the interior of the church from an early hour of the
morning. The first procession appeared at ten o'clock
—that of the venerable Empress-mother, who traversed
this path for the third time: thirty years ago, in order
to be herself crowned with her husband; then rather
more than twenty-five years previously, to attend the
coronation of her eldest son; and now that of her third
son. Under a canopy, in a purple mantle, a crown on her
head, this Empress of sixty-seven moved on in majesty
and vigour and dignity, and the respect she inspired caused

many to fall on their knees. By her side was the Grand
Duchess Helène and Prince Charles of Prussia, who led
the young heir-apparent by the hand. An hour afterwards the chief procession appeared. The two crowns,
the sceptre, the imperial ball, and the imperial mantle
were borne first. The Emperor walked bareheaded in
front of a canopy, carried by sixteen adjutant-generals.
Beside him were his two brothers, and a number of
generals, while Count Orlof bore the unsheathed sword
of the Empire. Under the canopy walked the Empress
in a silver gauze dress, with no ornament save her own
beauty. Then followed the Council of the Empire,
about thirty in number, the Senate, the chief burghers of
the various towns and guilds, the Hetman of the Cossacks, and a number of officers. The priesthood, the
venerable Serafim at their head, in robes sparkling with
jewels, advanced to meet the Imperial couple, extending
the life-giving cross for them to kiss, and sprinkling
them with holy water; the ground, too, which they
traversed to the Ikonostas was also sprinkled. Arrived
at the steps leading to the throne, they bowed three
times and ascended, still under the canopy, to the spot
where two thrones awaited them. On the one destined
for the Emperor, the first Romanow had formerly been
crowned; the second, appropriated to the Empress, had
been sent by Schach Abbas to Boris Godunow, and
glittered with 1500 rubies, and turquoises innumerable.
All the costly treasures contained in the Kremlin, only
brought to light on festive occasions, had been sent at
the approach of the French to Nischnei-Novgorod for
safety. The church service began with singing of

psalms, followed by the benediction of the superior clergy on the Czar, and by reading of the Gospel. After this three priests, in the name of the Trinity, delivered to the Emperor the insignia of the realm; he assumed the purple mantle, bent his head before the Metropolitan, who touched it with the cross, and laying hands on him, supported by the choir, he offered up a prayer for the salvation of the Emperor, who received from his priestly hands the crown, which he placed on his head, and while this was being blessed, the sceptre and the imperial ball were presented to him. Thus adorned with the attributes of the highest power, he once more seated himself on the throne. The Empress now rose, and bowed before the newly crowned Czar, on which he took off his crown, touched with it the forehead of his consort, placing another crown prepared for her on her head, and at the same moment she was invested with the ribbon of St. Andrew and a purple mantle.

After the Emperor and Empress, thus crowned and decorated, resumed their seats on their thrones, a priest proclaimed all the Imperial titles, and the choir sang, "Domine fac salvam Imperatorem," which, with a slight change in the words, was repeated for the Empress. The coronation was completed, the great bell of Iwan Weliki announcing this to the city by its loud and solemn tolling; the thousand bells of the other churches began to peal, a hundred and one cannons were fired, and the hundreds of thousands who swarmed round the Kremlin shouted hurrahs as if from one throat.

During this universal intoxication of joy out of doors, the Empress-mother went up to her newly crowned son,

and taking him in her arms she pressed him fondly to
her heart.   Like this mother and son, once on a
time, the first Romanow, with the crown on his head,
bowed down before his father the Metropolitan, who
acknowledged in him his son and Czar.   On this occasion, the elder brother, Constantine, bent low before
his younger brother, who embraced him with tears,
while their revered mother rose once more in order
to bless the harmony between her sons, and the thousands from the Caspian to the Tajo looked on in emotion
and surprise at this unprecedented spectacle, never
before seen in any country, or even read of in any history.
The other members of the Imperial family followed, the
foreign Princes, and the assembled priesthood, who all
bowed thrice.   The Emperor was crowned, and now
came the anointing.   This is the most essential distinction between the Russian and other European corona-
tions : here the coronation takes precedence of the
anointing, whereas in Germany, France, and England,
the monarchs are first anointed and then crowned.
After the Emperor had placed on one side the sceptre
and imperial ball, he received from the priest's hands a
mass-book, and kneeling down, prayed to God for success on all his undertakings, and taking the crown from
his head, he and the Empress kissed the holy book.
From the steps of the throne to the doors of the sanctuary, a splendid carpet was spread, and the Imperial
couple descending the steps, placed themselves before
the open doors.   The Metropolitan of Novgorod immersed a golden branch into the vessel containing the
chrism, and with it he anointed the Emperor's forehead,

eyelids, nostrils, ears, and lips, and the backs and palms of his hands, saying, "This is the token of the gift of the Holy Ghost."

The high priest proceeded to lead the monarch within the holy sanctuary, and while two Metropolitans held up his purple mantle, he bowed three times before the altar, receiving the sacrament in both kinds, and returned to his throne. The Empress received the unction outside the doors of the sanctuary, and only on the forehead, and likewise the sacrament, when she also returned to her throne. During the ensuing hymn, "Many years of happy life," the whole body of the priesthood and the dignitaries of the realm passed before the Imperial pair, bending in homage before them. After they had once more kissed the Holy Cross, the procession proceeded in the same order out of this cathedral to two others, that of the Archangel, where the newly crowned sovereigns inclined themselves before the graves of their forefathers and the sacred relics, and thence to the Cathedral of the Annunciation, and so back to their apartments in the palace.

In accordance with the usages of Czars of the olden day, the banquet was held in *Granowitaia Palata*, a building of the fifteenth century, in the purest Byzantine style. The hall is not so spacious as that in the Winter Palace, but the largest in the Kremlin, and remarkable from its singular old-fashioned aspect; it seems as if it belonged to another century. The vaulted roof rests on columns round which was placed the magnificent silver plate. Beside the Emperor's throne were two arm-chairs for the two Empresses, whereas in

former days, during the Czar's banquets, the Princesses
were only allowed to look on through a secret window.
An orchestra, unknown in days of old, to the delight of
all assembled, played, out of compliment to Alexandra,
all her favourite pieces, and among others the overture
to the "Freischütz." Before the banquet Nicholas received in the hall the congratulations of the priesthood,
the dignitaries and the *corps diplomatique.* The Metropolitan said grace. The Imperial family were waited on
by the highest Court officials, and the dishes offered kneeling. After the Emperor had drunk, all seated themselves
at the different tables. Towards the end of the banquet
night set in, disclosing the same fiery spectacle that
illuminated the city in Napoleon's day; but on this
occasion it was joy that displayed itself in fiery wreaths,
crowns, names, and fountains, and from the loftiest
pinnacle of the Iwan Weliki to the most insignificant
wooden house in the suburbs, all were illuminated. The
city revelled in rejoicings. The inoffensive lower classes
delighted in the spectacle of the illumination, the middle
classes were proud to feel that the Imperial family were
within their walls, and the most aristocratic could boast
of the richest proofs of favour. Many who yesterday
were only colonels, were now generals; many were
decked with ribbons of different orders, others showed
rings and snuff-boxes adorned with brilliants, while
some found their yearly salaries augmented and their
income improved. Imperial favour was even extended
to political criminals, and lastly on the greatest scale
of all to the "black people," as they are called. In
the largest of the squares was hastily erected a whole

town of booths, *carrousels, montagnes Russes*, tents,
swings, etc., and in the centre 240 long tables, covered
with the favourite national dishes.   Close to these
spouted forth sixteen fountains of wine, beer, meth,
quass, and brandy.   At the appointed hour the whole
Court appeared ; the Czar left his carriage, and gave
the signal for the onslaught on the provisions to the
hundreds of thousands awaiting his pleasure bareheaded, while he and his retinue walked down the entire
length of the tables ; in a few minutes the food quickly
disappeared, and he was encompassed by happy shouting crowds of his subjects.

The Emperor of 1826 was still for his people the
same omnipotent, gracious, and inexhaustibly wealthy
father as in the sixteenth century.   His presence in
Moscow always constitutes the greatest festival of the
year ; the indifference of the lower orders is quickly
transformed into cheerfulness, nay into delight, curbed
indeed by respect, as soon as even a glimpse is seen of
the Czar in the distance.   In Petersburg they are
more overawed by his presence, and the Russian proverb, "The nearer the Czar the nearer death," is less
appropriate in Moscow, where it originated, than by the
Neva.   The people actually besiege the Kremlin and
the Emperor's abode, and receive and follow him
with hurrahs, while in Petersburg he drives through a
silent population.   According to Russian tradition, the
Emperor in Moscow is more fully recognised by the
lower orders as "Father Czar ;" in Petersburg such
traditions do not exist : he is simply their master and
ruler.   Boris Godunow, during a famine, caused 30,000

dollars to be daily distributed among the hungry, dressing those in white linen whom he found dead in the
streets and burying them; when, however, after the
lapse of some months the resources of the Czar were
exhausted, he commanded all princes, clergy of degree,
cloisters, and landed proprietors, to sell their stores of
grain to the city magistrates at half price, which were
immediately distributed among the poor.

Even the lavish munificence of the Roman Cæsars
did not equal the truly paternal care of the Russian
Autocrat; these traits live in the grateful memory of
the people, and will be transmitted to succeeding
races; the Czar therefore, even to the people who have
never seen him, appears as the all-potent father of the
country.   Government has conferred on the country
and on Petersburg a hundredfold greater benefits than
that of feeding the starving by Godunow; but the very
lowest classes have not been so closely affected by them,
and therefore consider themselves slighted by their
sovereign so seldom dwelling amidst them.

CHAPTER XI.

THE IMPERIAL FAMILY.

THOSE who have attentively read our previous chapter cannot fail to perceive that since their ascension of the throne the Emperor and Empress had renounced all the enjoyments of family life, not having a moment they could call their own, but obliged to sacrifice their entire existence to the kingdom, and even then not enjoying the satisfaction and pleasure of knowing that they had satisfied all claims. No one knew better than Nicholas the burden and the emptiness of external splendours and fictitious grandeur; he therefore wished to avoid the throne, and would not have exchanged the happiness that brightened his domestic life through his wife, for anything else in the world. Their return to jubilant Moscow entailed a new life full of cares and burdens, under which every trace of domestic felicity seemed to vanish. There are natures to whom display and formal etiquette are a necessity, and who without it find no pleasure in the interior of their own family, and their domestic hearth. Neither Nicholas nor Alexandra belonged to this class. The Emperor Francis once told the King of Bavaria, his father-in-law, that his first three wives were genuine Empresses, but the fourth was

the true wife of his heart.   The Emperor Nicholas had
the good fortune to find in his Alexandra what Francis
sought in vain in his three wives, and besides being
the best wife, she was the most majestic Empress that
ever lived. She was the daughter of that royal pair who
first in Germany set the example from the throne of
happy family life.   But in addition to her Court and
family duties, Alexandra had other claims on her time.
By the death of the Empress Elisabeth, two of the institutions she had so lovingly fostered in her seclusion
from the world now devolved on Alexandra. The reader
is aware that female education in Russia was the peculiar object and the care of each Empress since the days of
Catherine the Second, who during her reign founded at
Smolna an establishment for upwards of 2000 pupils.
As the capital increased with the kingdom, this institution, even in Paul's time, no longer sufficed for the demands made on it, so that Paul founded a second precisely the same, the "Catherine School," appointing
his wife, Maria Feodorowna, directress-in-chief of both,
and of all other female schools in the kingdom.   Two
were added by Alexander, the Patriotic Institute and
the "Elisabeth School," both situated in Wasiliostrow,
about a mile from Smolna—the "Catherine School"
being in the centre of the town, close to Anitschkow. In
these four establishments upwards of a thousand young
ladies were educated at the expense of the Government.
   Smolna, the oldest, is also the most richly endowed,
and there the daughters of those state officials are educated, who in the course of their service have risen to
the highest rank. The extent of the building is equal

to that of a small town, with one of the most beautiful churches in the kingdom, a garden, and a spacious square, several adjacent buildings being devoted to the reception of widows, besides large halls and rooms to welcome friends—bearing more resemblance to an imperial palace than a place of education. The Empress Elisabeth Petrowna, the foundress, changed it into a convent, where she herself would have taken refuge if her father's throne had not been securely her own. The situation is close to the Neva, removed from the tumult of the city, with a fine view of the majestic stream and its green banks opposite. The training of these young ladies is intended for the great world, and by the various branches of instruction not to be equalled in similar circles in Europe. The pupils learn modern languages in the greatest perfection, music, dancing, drawing—and even science, in many of its branches, is taught. The young ladies in this school later in life were distinguished from others by their graceful exterior and deportment, by their elevation of mind, and the charm of manner which animated the *salons* they frequented. The six best pupils when they leave school are decorated with the cypher of the Empress, and such a distinction obtains for them an easier access to Court.

It is evident that such an institution must have worked a very great change since the days of Catherine in the spirit of the higher circles in Petersburg; the Western European is amazed, and often declares publicly, that on his entrance into society in the capital, the refinement and polish of the ladies there attract him far more than that of the gentlemen, whose unbounded ambition keeps them in a state of constant restlessness. The Catherine School has kept pace with its original model, only the number of pupils is less than in Smolna, and the building smaller, although more in the centre of the town, beside the Fontanka.

While the aim of these two schools is to educate, in accordance with their rank, the daughters of poor though well-born parents, the two latter foundations are on a different footing. The " Patriotic Institute " is specially appropriated to the daughters of those officers who distinguished themselves in the wars with France. In 1826 there were only 100 pupils, whose education chiefly tended to make them good managers of families ; but here also their future position in society is by no means forgotten, the subjects of instruction being nearly the same, and this institution has produced many distinguished women, both in a *salon* and in domestic life. In the fourth school, Elisabeth's plan was to educate the daughters of civil officials for a retired and quiet home life, with instruction to enable them to become governesses in the Russian kingdom, especially in the interior. Both these latter establishments were confided to the young Empress Alexandra after Elisabeth's death, and as neither of their Majesties were at all acquainted with these schools, they now visited them in order to ascertain their wants. Nicholas determined to double the number of pupils, to rebuild and enlarge the house, and, in order that Alexandra might superintend the progress of the Institute, and learn the duties connected with it, he resolved to transfer the pupils of the Patriotic School for two summers to his own abode,

the new palace at Zarskoe-Seló. The Imperial family
were contented to inhabit one side wing, and to give up
the other for the use of this youthful flock of girls in
their uniform dresses, with their governesses, and the
ladies who acted as superintendents. A large hall
was cleared out for their games and recreations, and
another served as a chapel. Thus throne and school
were under one roof, and the young girls, as well as their
governesses, enjoyed the enviable advantage of seeing
daily in the Empress the fairest type of female excellence. Alexandra made acquaintance with the staff of
teachers as well as with all the pupils, attended their
lessons, opened her garden for their games and amusements, and awoke their emulation by prizes, inviting
the best pupils to the table of her eldest daughter, Maria.
The old Empress-mother and the Emperor often appeared
in the garden, and refreshed their eyes by watching the
gay swarm, without by their presence in the smallest
degree causing any constraint, while their young daughter Maria wore the uniform of the school, and shared in
the games of the other young girls. The chief super-
intendence, however, of all these establishments, remained in the hands of the Empress-mother until her
death in 1828, Alexandra having previously come to the
conclusion that she would not have to alter anything
when her turn came to superintend the Institute.
Strangely enough each of the three Empresses conducted
these schools for thirty-two years !—the Empress Catherine from 1764 to 1796 ; the Empress Maria Feodorowna
till 1828, and Alexandra Feodorowna till 1860.

These four schools were not the only ones subsequently

intrusted to the Empress ; several more existed in Petersburg alone, and among these the great House of Education for Orphans, the numbers being raised by the Emperor from 300 to 1000. In the latter the practical duties of life were chiefly attended to, although talent was sought out and cultivated; the original purpose of this house being the reception of foundlings as well as orphans and the poor. It was on the same plan as the great Foundling Hospital in Moscow, erected by Catherine immediately after ascending the throne. Although that in Petersburg also owes its existence to Catherine, still its foundling hospital may be considered rather a creation of Maria Feodorowna, as by the fostering care of that illustrious superintendent-in-chief, it became an almost unparalleled institution. Many princely German capitals do not embrace such an extent as this gigantic structure, with its church, courts, and gardens. The Emperor Paul purchased for the purpose two of the most splendid palaces in his capital, and all the adjacent houses. It has been correctly estimated that from 1822 to 1831 about 40,000 foundlings and orphans were received there, and on leaving were provided for by Government. Under the Empress Alexandra the orphan school was entirely separated from that of the foundlings, and similar institutions were founded by her through the whole kingdom, even so far as Tobolsk, and Irkutsk in Siberia. These schools, with their multitude of directresses, governesses, class teachers, physicians, house-stewards, and others, formed a most extended sphere of activity—the sovereign head of them all being Alexandra. Each school sent a weekly report to the Empress of their progress and occupations, and soon female energies did not suffice to overlook and to conduct the whole. On that account, and to relieve his consort of part of this burden, Nicholas appointed a council of twelve persons of talent, and named Prince Herr of Oldenburg their president. Secretaries of State brought the resolutions of this council to the Empress for ratification. The slightest changes in the schools, the appointment or dismissal of a directress, of a teacher or physician, an official or a pupil, required the Imperial assent, and the selection of the directresses was attended with peculiar difficulty. When the Empress in 1830 was for the first time obliged to name a directress for the Elisabethan School, she with her usual prudence for some time deliberated, although only two ladies presented themselves for her choice., At length she said, " I have known both ladies for three years, and I give the preference to modest merit," and thus Baroness Amalie von Bistram was selected, under whose guidance the school flourished exceedingly. The Directress of Smolna was the first in rank and dignity ; she drove with six horses, enjoyed the title of " Your Excellency," and her social position was considered one of the highest in the realm. This important post was at that time in the hands of Frau von Adlerberg, who had been known to Nicholas from his childhood, having watched over the first years of his life with motherly care. Next to Princess Lieven, who died shortly after Nicholas ascended the throne, scarcely any other lady in the city was held in such high estimation as this Frau von Ådlerberg, whom even the

Emperor received with reverence, invariably kissing her hand, and always addressing her as " Mamma ;" more than any other directress she had at all times free access to the Empress, not only in business matters, but as a visitor. Like all superiors of these schools, she was chosen by the Empress-mother, and held her high position more than twenty-five years.

The subject of the education of their children now began to occupy the thoughts of the Emperor and the Empress. When Grand Duke, Nicholas had already appointed a military tutor for his son, Captain Mörder of the cadet corps, and for his secular studies the Russian poet, W. A. Joukowsky. In the first years of his reign Nicholas felt more than ever that the education of an heir-apparent must be differently conducted from his own. Above all, he desired to have one responsible person as superintendent, and not several, as in his own case, whose eye alone was to watch over the boy, and if his powers did not suffice, an assistant was appointed to replace him when requisite, but under the same conditions. The beginning of his own reign had forced on him the conviction that in the various studies of an Emperor, military qualities should be one of his first acquirements. The young heir to the throne was therefore to be initiated into all the hardships and privations of war and of the camp ; his bed was to be hard, his food simple, his recreations to consist in military games, and his body strengthened by all sorts of gymnastics. He was to show military obedience to those set over him, and the Emperor himself interposed and punished him if this discipline was

infringed. While Nicholas thus strove to form the
future military commander, Alexandra's endeavour was
to ennoble her son's heart, and to cultivate in his spirit
a genuine love of humanity, and for such a purpose the
whole kingdom could not offer another man of a more
profound and childlike nature than Joukowsky. She
comprehended that all moral development lies in the
nobility of sentiment that we show towards the world,
and that so far from interfering with those other qualifications exacted by the prospects of her son, it would
only tend to ennoble them. The life of even the happiest
monarch entails a succession of dry avocations, which
rather oppress than elevate the mind. It is therefore a
happy thing when young princes are endowed with a
taste for higher and more intellectual attractions, and
learn in early life to rise above a matter-of-fact existence;
for their own position is too apt to make them rather
sink beneath it, and to be absorbed in details, instead of
embracing the world with a comprehensive eye. Joukowsky was no scientific professor; he could not have
given lectures on any erudite subject; he was a poet,
and still more, he was the most noble and pure-
minded of men, whose whole being breathed the most
genuine love of humanity, free from the petty ambition that, more particularly in Courts, is apt to stifle all
intrinsic good feeling. He adapted himself with effort
and difficulty to his new calling, and to the various
modes of teaching of the instructors placed under him—
indeed, his interference with their systems was often
more a hindrance than a furtherance of progress, and
his views sometimes fantastic, but his personal influence

over his young pupil was of the most beneficial kind,
and both powerful and striking; he was the interpreter
of the great and profound mind of the Empress and of
her noble thoughts.   Joukowsky was the first who recognised the superior character of Alexandra, and he
appreciated her as the *beau-idéal* of woman.   He had
been destined for his present vocation ever since the
birth of the heir-apparent, and had prepared himself for
it for some years, by foreign travel, as well as by close
observation of his future pupil.   He selected the various
teachers from an educational institute that flourished at
that time in Petersburg, under the reformed preacher,
Johann von Muralt, the pupil and friend of Pestalozzi, and Alexandra, remembering his name, having
often heard it from her mother's lips, fully approved
of the choice.   The boy's education, however, was not
carried on away from the Imperial House, which had
been the case with Paul's two younger sons; the young
Prince grew up under the eyes of his father and mother.
Two companions had been given him, who shared his
life, having been purposely selected of different nation-
alities and abilities.   The people saw with curiosity
and satisfaction the heir-apparent and his companions,
accompanied by Colonel v. Mörder, walking about the
city in every different direction, as if making topo-
graphical studies.   No rain, no cold detained them at
home, but no balls, no society interrupted the routine
of their day.   The sons and daughters of the Emperor
Paul had been kept strictly apart.   The Empress Alexandra, accustomed in her childhood and youth to the
most intimate family life, sought to unite all her chil-

dren in one spirit, in her motherly heart, and, prior to
all her duties to society, she devoted an hour every
evening to her young people, when all royal pomp was
banished, and the mother lived happily with her children. A picture from a masterly hand in the Romanof
Gallery shows us Alexandra playing with her two eldest
children. Among all the Empresses she is the only one
represented as a mother, and in that quality her influence and efforts have been the most efficacious. On
Sundays and festivals a large number of young persons
were invited to be the guests of the heir-apparent, who
had thus an opportunity of seeing various families in
the town, and learning the spirit in which they were
educated. Both their Majesties took lively interest in
the sports of the gay little flock, and though warlike
games took the lead in these, yet the Imperial mother
strove to introduce equally into her family the more
peaceful arts, and banished on those evenings everything that could recall etiquette. A German musician
was invariably present on such occasions, and by his
pianoforte-playing, not only endeavoured to amuse the
young people and awaken in them a taste for music,
but often incited them to dance. The Emperor and
Empress amused themselves by conversing with the
boys invited, and also with their tutors; and Nicholas,
while engaged in talking to Joukowsky, recalled Henry
the Eighth of England, and the talented Holbein. In
the higher society of Petersburg French was universal,
and the sound of a Russian word was scarcely ever
heard, so the young Grand Duke might have thought
himself in France with his companions, as most of them

were educated at home by French tutors. A French
teacher had been purposely selected for the heir-apparent, Florand Gilles, who, knowing no other European
language, thus constrained his pupil to address him
in the language of Voltaire. Nicholas soon suspected,
with regard to his boy, so carefully educated, that his
native tongue had been almost purposely neglected, and
on investigation this proved to be the case. Trifling
as this circumstance may appear, yet the measures
Nicholas adopted to remedy this oversight had eventually the most beneficial results for his whole kingdom.

The youth, besides his scientific studies, was trained
also to military service, and initiated into the higher
branches of the art of war; he was made acquainted,
too, with all kinds of crafts, and visited manufac-
tories and other workshops of burgher industry, and
thus brought into contact with the various interests
of life.

In the country, and in Zarskoe-Selò in particular, the
hours of recreation were differently spent. An island
on one of the little lakes was given up to the three
pupils; this they planted, with their own hands, with
trees and flowers, building a little cottage with trowels
and bricks in the middle of the island, and making all
the furniture themselves. In later years, the Imperial
youth caused the bust of his instructor, Joukowsky, to
be placed there, in grateful remembrance of his happy
boyhood. In another spot, in the same garden, those
lads erected a fortress, dividing a number of youths into
besiegers and defenders; a separate portion was likewise
allotted to them, where only bodily exercises were

practised, such as running, jumping, climbing, and wrestling. All the members of the Imperial family had a peculiar talent for painting, and love of sketching. The latter was cultivated in the heir-apparent, under the guidance of a man who had long been counted among Nicholas's home friends, the celebrated battle-painter Sauerweid, as remarkable for his talent as for his eccentricity. Simple in manner and pretensions, a stoic in equanimity, free and unbiassed in his opinions, he had always maintained the independence of a philosopher towards the Imperial family. There was so much humour and irony in his mode of expressing himself, that even the all-potent Emperor's indignation, though sometimes roused, was quickly appeased. Nicholas, when Grand Duke, became acquainted with Sauerweid in England, in the happy days of his youth, and it seems as if this gay period of both their lives revived whenever they met. But even without this circumstance, Sauerweid was quite the man for the Emperor. No one had so narrowly studied the Russian soldiery, and no one could equal him in rendering with brush and pencil all their peculiarities; unluckily, his talent was confined to this sphere, and he never attained to a higher style of painting.

The heir-apparent showed, however, fully as much inclination for music as for painting, though the Petersburg of that day and its denizens were not calculated to promote this taste, or to cultivate it; but his mother took care that it should not entirely die out, by causing operas to be performed from time to time, suitable to the youthful mind; thus the boy, only eleven years

of age, and his companions, were sent to see Mehul's
"Joseph in Egypt." Russian history was read to him
by Arsenief, a man who, even in the time of Alexander,
had distinguished himself at the University by his
uprightness. He was instructed in universal history
by a foreigner, Liepmann, whose historical lectures
were seasoned with Attic salt. Such studies and
literature were preferred by the youth to mathematics, and thus interest in the welfare of mankind
was developed to the uttermost. Count Joseph Wielhorsky, the companion and fellow-student of the heir-
apparent, his dearest friend from the days of his
childhood, was full of good sense and deep feeling, and
endowed with his father's talent for music. He was a
stay and support to his young companion during their
studies, and every one rejoiced to see him subsequently
placed near his person. His appearance was naturally
noble, and cultivated by education; he sacrificed his youth
to his future ruler, for he had scarcely a moment that he
could call his own; he was quite estranged from his
family, and his mother, one of the most admirable
women of our century, only saw her eldest son when
she went to Court. Independent of the studies he
shared with the heir-apparent, he pursued on his own
account other branches of education, such as the classics
and music, for which he could only find time at night.
The influence of this young man over his companion
was not inferior to that of his teachers and governors.

The Empress bestowed the same care on Maria, her
eldest daughter, whose education was intrusted to
Frau v. Baranof, daughter of Frau v. Adlerberg. This

lady far surpassed the teachers of the heir to the throne
in refined manners and the tone of good society, and it
seemed as if her express vocation was to educate princesses : she was a model of dignity, animated in conversation, of enlightened understanding, devoted to the
Imperial family and to her duties, a benefactress to the
poor, the mediator in all petty misunderstandings, and
her heart truly benevolent; thus she could not but
acquire good influence over her young pupil.   She was
one of the most intimate friends of the Empress, not
only by her position, but the amiability of her character,
and very useful likewise in managing the schools.   The
education of the younger children, Olga and Alexandra,
was also under her charge, though they had each a
separate governess.   The arts of painting and music
played a greater part here than with the heir-apparent.
Sauerweid was the instructor of all the Imperial children in drawing, and at the age of twelve and thirteen
their daughters presented their parents with sketches
—indeed, with small pictures of their own composition.
Music was even more popular with these young girls,
especially pianoforte - playing.   Maria, subsequently
Duchess of Leuchtenberg, and also Olga, now Queen of
Würtemberg, studied profoundly the masterly instru-
mental works of German composers.   The three sisters
surpassed, both in beauty and charm, all their contemporaries, and yet their exterior, as well as their
accomplishments, were very different.   The Grand
Duchess Maria was extremely lively, of quick percep-
tions, condescending, winning all by her goodness of
heart, full of life and energy, and free from all petty

forms and prejudices. Her presence never checked the
most easy or unreserved conversation; she was cour-
teous to those whom she liked, and loving to her friends;
her father's dignity was reflected in her regular features,
while the heart and freshness and energy of her mother
invested her whole being with a singular charm. The
majestic mien of the Grand Duchess Olga evinced more
calm repose; hers was a finished beauty, more remarkable for stateliness, never in intercourse with others for
a moment forgetting that she was of regal birth, and con-
cealing her real goodness of heart by a certain degree
of reserve. Her perceptive faculties were not so quick
as those of her elder sister, but her studies more profound; her disposition led her thoroughly to investigate
every subject and every question, and to persevere with
industry and patience in all that she undertook. During
the latter years of her education she often gladly gave
up evening parties, seeking and finding compensation
in reading history. She was in the habit of playing
to her family and their suites Beethoven's trios and
sonatas with accompaniment, aided by Count Mathieu
Wielhorsky. When the three sisters were together,
Raphael's ideal seemed to be realized; and it is a source
of regret that this great artist no longer existed to per-
petuate their charms of youth and loveliness in all their
perfection. The Russian painter Brülow has attempted
portraits of the three sisters, but neither in drawing nor
in colour have they attained their object, and the whole
conception only shows the failure of this unusually gifted
man in representing the highest class of female loveliness. Olga was indebted to Fraülein Dunker for

finishing her education, having been under her care for nearly seven years. This lady had a masculine understanding and a profound intellect, and her intercourse with her youthful pupils could not fail to leave its marked impress on the character of each. Unhappily, owing to some misunderstanding, she was suddenly dismissed from her situation, and was long lamented and her return wished for by her young pupils; her great qualities not being replaced by any of her successors.

The two eldest daughters most resembled their father, but the youngest, Alexandrina, bore a greater likeness to her mother, and indeed to Queen Louise also. She was born shortly before Nicholas came to the throne, and in her early infancy his time was so engrossed by cares and anxieties that he could not show as much tenderness towards this child as to the three elder ones. In her eighth year, however, she excited her father's attention by a remarkable speech. The Greek Church admits children of that age for the first time to confession and communion, and the childish mind of this youngest girl was so agitated by the prospect, that, for several days, so great a change was visible in her countenance, that the mother inquired the cause. "I have prayed and confessed day and night," answered the child, "but shall I ever become as pious and blameless as God requires?" Her mother could scarcely succeed in pacifying her excited feelings. When the Emperor was told of this, from that moment he looked with peculiar affection on his youngest daughter, who had also the misfortune to be obliged to change her governess in her tenth

year, although the loss was not so great to her as
to her elder sister. Till the age of thirteen, she gave
no promise of equalling her sisters either in beauty or
talent; she showed very little inclination for serious
matters, and cared more for childish games; but suddenly a change took place that astonished her mother,
and a few months seemed to have done the work of
years. Such changes are caused not only by girlish
nature, but often produced by circumstances. A
pedantic teacher often crushes all interest in a subject
instead of increasing it, another imparts a free and
natural impulse to the thoughts; nature compensates
for what she has hitherto withheld, and surprises the
observer. This change occurred in Alexandrina in her
thirteenth year; her charming figure was developed,
her pretty features refined, an eager interest in her
studies ensued, and unexpected talents were displayed.
From this time she showed a love of music, and for
singing in particular; and occupied herself much with
nature. She rambled perpetually in the parks of Zarskoe-
Selò and Petershof in every direction, observing closely
trees and wild-flowers, and carrying to her mother the
treasures she discovered. She gave no signs of wishing
to remind others of her high rank when in society, but
her amiability made the greater impression on all who
saw her, as every word she uttered was accompanied
by the most unaffected cordiality. The young sisters
had not, like the brother, any companions in their education, but their governesses were their friends, and the
tie between the parents and children was so close that
no one could interpose between them. Their apartments

were simple, devoid of all imperial luxury, which indeed
they never enjoyed in after life, having married in
Germany. Like their brother, they were to be seen
enjoying the fresh air at all seasons, and their table,
like that of all the Imperial children, was submitted to
the strict directions of physicians. As their occupations
began at eight o'clock in the morning, the whole family,
the Emperor included, assembled for breakfast at ten
o'clock in the boudoir of the Empress. Sometimes
affairs of State deprived Nicholas of this family hour,
and then the children went to see him in his cabinet.
"What a different man the Emperor is at his writing-
table from papa beside our mother," said the young
Alexandrina. "There he sits buried in papers, with
a gloomy face, the Ministers standing beside him in
anxious expectation; he often does not for some time
observe our entrance; we scarcely dare go near him to
interrupt his meditations by our greeting." This grave
Emperor certainly was never seen when the tender
husband and happy father entered his family circle.
He kissed his wife's lips, hands, and forehead, in token
at once of his love, reverence, and homage; he was
in the habit of lifting up the youngest children in his
arms, and sharing in the merriment of a happy youth,
that he never himself had known; in this circle all
gloomy care disappeared, and he forgot for the moment the burdens that oppressed him, and quitted the
scene of his paternal happiness with knitted brows,
when a minister or an adjutant-general was announced,
—for his maxim was never to keep any one waiting,
though he allowed seven minutes to the person ex-

pected. Besides these morning hours, the children visited their parents again after dinner, but not so regularly, because they only did so when it was a strictly family party. Nicholas and Alexandra always dined without attendance; neither marshals nor an equerry stood during dinner; the number of those invited during the whole year did not exceed, on week-days, from fifteen to twenty; in this list were included different ministers, the aide-de-camp of the day, or persons with whom the Emperor had affairs to discuss. In the latter case, the children did not appear, as they would only have disturbed business matters. Even the evening hours, that belonged exclusively to the mother and children, Nicholas was sometimes obliged to give up from the pressure of affairs, and yet this family circle formed the chief charm of his existence. He had no enjoyment in dinners or in wine, in balls or play; he did not even permit himself the minor luxuries of smoking or taking snuff. Lord of himself, like the ancient Stoics, he lived only for his high calling and for his family; and, like Cato of Utica, he was happy and content when the day's business was accomplished to his satisfaction.

The Empress also had not as much leisure at her disposal as might at first sight appear. Her secretary devoted much time to the petitions of the poor and needy; he furnished her with the entire list of those who must be wholly provided for, and even the resources of her privy purse could not always suffice for the claims made on it; for she was the refuge of all the persecuted, the neglected, the calumniated, and, above all, of the wretched, who daily attempted at every hour to knock at her door; indeed, in the course of the week, she saw more persons than even the Emperor himself, as State affairs necessarily absorbed so much of his day. She received regularly twice every week Secretaries of State with school reports, and their consultations and transactions often lasted till her strength was fairly exhausted. Her early morning hours were devoted to this kind of correspondence; so voluminous, that besides her secretary, she was often obliged to have recourse to the aid of her maids of honour and state-ladies, and yet in addition to her family correspondence she wrote a vast number of letters with her own hand. The time between twelve and two o'clock was reserved for the reception of different persons. Her ante-chamber was during these hours filled with an expectant throng; military men who had received promotion, and civil officials in the same way, were all presented to her. Among these were many who on such occasions entered the Winter Palace both for the first and last time, and never saw the Empress in all their lives but that once, and seldom left her presence without a kind word from her. In the lives of princes they have often no second opportunity thus equally to display dignity and goodness, and at a casual presentation of this sort, to leave for life the impression of these qualities by a few kind words. Sometimes from two to four o'clock the Emperor and Empress drove out together in the most opposite quarters of the city, to show themselves to all classes of the population; but this did not often occur: Alexandra frequently occupied these hours with her schools, while Nicholas drove like the wind through the town in every direction, often appearing where he was least expected. At one moment he was to be seen in a Court of Justice, at another in a school; if he was expected in military barracks he yet found time to take a look at some adjacent manufactory in his way. When he was believed to be at the other end of the town, he would appear suddenly on foot in that most crowded street, the Perspective, greeting people in his dignified yet kind manner. In barracks and in those schools supported by the Crown, he often tasted the food, and when in a cheerful mood tried feats of strength with the young men there. Nothing distinguished him in the street from other superior officers, except his all-comprehensive eye; he drove in a one-horse droschky or sledge, and was usually recognised too late by the crowd. The Empress, on the other hand, drove about the town in a carriage with four horses, the sole difference between her and the many other ladies who did the same, being two Cossacks on the footboard of the carriage. The stranger who visited the capital in the early years of Nicholas's reign heard for months the perpetual question, " Have you yet seen the Imperial family ?" and the inhabitants used to relate with pride and complacency the fact of having met the Imperial couple, and having received a gracious salutation from them. Neither of their Majesties disdained to court popularity, and they gained it almost unconsciously. As the Imperial family never visit Petersburg in summer, during the first days of their reign they passed the early fine days of the northern spring in a small palace on the island of Jelagin, as much part of the town as the

Thiergarten in Berlin.   The public resort there in
countless throngs in the evenings, to take leave of it,
as it were, for six months, so Alexandra thought it
advisable to station several military bands round the
Palace to play for the amusement of the spectators.
At the beginning the Russian band of horns played,
but these did not attract at that time ; they were replaced by the Corps des Gardes, who were obliged to
overstep their usual confined repertoire of marches ; at
first they played dances, but subsequently introduced
overtures and other grand orchestral pieces, the practice
of which improved their playing and raised the taste
of the public.   In these islands both natives and
foreigners had the most favourable opportunity of seeing
the Emperor and Empress, and not only in the many
avenues of trees, but also in the gardens of the palace,
where Nicholas often played with his children in the
evening, and on the terrace, where they drank tea like
plain citizens.   No one could be in Petersburg at that
time without a near sight of the Imperial couple.

Did this charming family union continue quietly
without any disturbing forces from without ?   The year
1827, when the Grand Duke Constantine was born, the
first son of Nicholas after he became Emperor, was
the ·only cloudless one ; the following one summoned
their Majesties to the seat of war, leaving the city,
as the Governor-General truly said, orphaned.   When
the Imperial pair returned in autumn, a melancholy
duty was next to be fulfilled—to escort the venerable
Empress-mother to her last resting-place.   She was born
in 1759, a period that had been anything but fortunate

for little Würtemberg. Her education began at a time
of the most reckless expenditure on the part of the
Duke, and the utmost discontent of the country, who
appealed to the Prussian Court to mediate between
Prince and people. She was scarcely seventeen when
she married the Grand Duke Paul, by whom she had four
sons and six daughters. Her memory is cherished as one
of the most admirable women in Russia, and her active
energies were à model for all in her elevated position.

Her son Constantine appeared at her interment for
the last time in Petersburg, to show the last marks
of respect by following her remains on foot with his
brother Nicholas. The bitter cold of a late November
day, the insecure state of the coating of ice on the
Neva, the gloom of the northern sky, rendered the
progress of the mourning procession very irksome.
During the whole ensuing winter not only was every
one clad in black, but profound sympathy prevailed ;
not only the Imperial couple, but the whole kingdom
knew what they had lost.

But even in the first disturbed years of Nicholas's
reign the fact of his domestic life had a visible effect on
the spirit and tone of the city. The melancholy that
engrossed Alexander the First in his latter years resulted
more from the want of a family than from an inclination
for solitude, as much in accordance however with his
nature as his detestation of all tumultuous Court gaieties.
He was only once seen in the theatre. By the sympathy
that Alexandra Feodorowna testified towards these
temples of art, every space was filled in order to see
the Czar and Czarina, and by the suggestions of the

young Empress a higher and better taste gradually
prevailed both on the stage and in the parterre.   While
during Alexander's time the deserted Court only attracted a few persons, and was entirely avoided by the
public, to be received there was now eagerly sought, and
the object of universal ambition.   The care devoted to
the education of the royal children extended to all great
private families.   Alexander sometimes took by surprise
some private family in the evening for an hour, but the
present Emperor and Empress regularly accepted invita-
tions from the greatest houses, where they appeared in
all their Imperial splendour, but also with the most
amiable condescension, taking sincere delight in those
gay evenings, and thus endearing themselves more and
more to the public.   In those first years it was the eager
anxiety of all families of distinction to be remarked
by their Imperial rulers, and more especially to share
with the Empress her tastes, ideas, or amusements.
Alexander used to disappear regularly once a week, to
pass some days at Zarskoe-Selò, even in the most severe
winter, whereas all through these cold months the
society of the city was enlivened by the social warmth
caused by the presence of the Imperial family.   The
summer of 1829 found the Emperor in Warsaw for the
Coronation, and the over-worked Empress in Germany
for the restoration of her health.

CHAPTER XII.

FOR a distant person it must have, no doubt, a peculiar charm to hear of a Coronation, and all the splendours and festivities connected with it; but any one closely observing those engaged in it, must confess that they submit to an oppressive burden in order to furnish a pageant for the people. The Empress at that time was in very delicate health, and the physicians properly insisted on entire rest for some months, in a milder climate. She could not, however, evade the Coronation, and yet in those days a journey from Petersburg to Warsaw was a severe undertaking for a person in her weak condition. The sincere enthusiasm with which the Coronation had been hailed in Moscow was not to be expected in Warsaw; mutual suspicion pervading all hearts in Poland and Russia. Since the restoration of the kingdom to the Russian sceptre, many cherished the idea of reviving once more, in all portions of their ancient Polish fatherland, its former grandeur and independence. A spectator devoid of party spirit asks himself in what then did Polish greatness and splendour really consist during the last two centuries? Although that country could proudly boast that a Polish prince had once been crowned Czar in Moscow, still in all succeeding times they had only to deplore the loss of the finest provinces, while the rights and power of their kings became every day more feeble. The liberty of the nobles had been transformed into the most unbounded license, and no progress made by the nation, either in prosperity or in social development. The gradual decay of the State began with the year 1652, when it was the privilege of a provincial deputy, by his own dissentient vote, to over-throw all decrees, however carefully discussed. The country and the Government were split into hostile confederacies, while the boasted patriotism of the Poles yielded to petty and personal vanity, indeed to folly. A law was made that no king could abdicate after Johann Kasimir had renounced his tottering throne and his royal impotency. His chosen successor long resisted the felicity of being called a king, and at length, when forced to accept the crown, he did so with tears in his eyes. The Primas, on the first day of the Imperial Diet, boldly prophesied the downfall of the kingdom; thus a century before the first parti-tion of their fatherland, those arrogant men were fairly warned; in spite of the renown Johann Sobiesky won as a military commander, against the Turks, he never succeeded in gaining any reverence for the Crown, and he died hated and despised. For the space of sixty years the country was under Saxon princes, and the unnatural union of two such very different crowns on one head was equally pernicious to both countries. While Prussia elevated her dismembered territories

into a kingdom, and Russia raised herself to the rank
of a European power, Poland in every branch of culture
failed in meeting the demands of political life and of
the day. The King did not win the confidence of the
nation, and the lavish monarch cared as little for his
people. Under its second Saxon ruler, Poland took no
part in any of the wars of that period, and this was no
proof of prosperous peace, but of inward weakness, that
bore within itself the seeds of speedy ruin and destruction. Thus the country disappeared from the political
map of Europe under a native ruler, who, after the
downfall of his kingdom, died in a private station.
When the Emperor Alexander, twenty years later, re-
established the kingdom under the Russian sceptre, he
certainly had no intention, as their monarch, to be
tossed about like a ball by the supercilious nobles;
and though the idea of restoring the ancient power
again haunted the thoughts of both young and more
mature patriots, this was in fact pitiable and childish
self-deception.

The rulers of Russia in their old country never
favoured the claims and peculiar privileges of the
nobility, whereas in Poland it was a class now especially regarded. Dissatisfaction with a government
that took the same paternal care of every class in the
land, but in no respect peculiarly favoured the nobles,
was soon displayed in secret societies, which, in turn,
gave birth to conspiracies, quickly discovered, however,
and rendered harmless, but the Russian Government
now exercised more strict surveillance than ever over
the enterprises of the nobility, but did not withdraw

their attention from the progress of prosperity in the country. Their ruler, Constantine, happily married to a Polish lady, seems to have felt a peculiar affection for this people, and both Alexander and Nicholas honoured this national feeling. The name, arms, and colours of the kingdom were re-established, the ashes of Poniatowsky solemnly deposited in Warsaw, a mass held in honour of the manes of Kosciuszko, and his bones conveyed from a foreign country to his native land. Alexander wore the Polish uniform in Warsaw; Constantine appeared in it at the Coronation in Moscow; Nicholas sent Turkish cannon from Varna, as a monument to Wladislaw, who fell in that city in 1444; the Russian heir-apparent learned the Polish language with one of his tutors, named Jourjewitsch, and in Petersburg Polish dances were preferred at balls. But there was considerable fermentation in the core of society, and such discontent was soon no longer concealed from the public. Every step of the Russian Government was wrongly interpreted, and such never-ending misconceptions at length demanded strong measures. When the Emperor, the Empress, and the heir-apparent quitted Zarskoe-Selò to repair to Warsaw for the Coronation, projects for their assassination were openly discussed by young men and by the army, but afterwards renounced. The indignation increased when the Russian Crown and all the Imperial jewels were sent to Warsaw for the Coronation, and intrusted to the watchfulness of Russians, and not of Poles. The actual people, however, received the Imperial family with hearty rejoicings, for they enjoyed a better fate under the new government, acknowledging with gratitude that heavily-laden waggons now rolled along with ease and security on newly-paved streets, whereas, under the Polish sceptre, they sunk into bogs. The real privileges of a civilized nation, utterly ignored by the insolent nobles, were hailed with thankful hearts by the burghers and peasants. The entrance of the Imperial family into Warsaw was both peaceful and brilliant; the Emperor and the Grand Dukes were on horseback, the Empress in a State carriage, drawn by eight horses, escorted by a Russian equerry at her right hand, and by a Polish one on her left. She was first greeted in Prague by the municipality of Warsaw, at the nearest church by the Catholic priesthood, at the palace by the members of the Polish Court, and within the palace walls by the highest civil and military authorities. From thence the Imperial family proceeded to the Greek Chapel, and then retired to their apartments. Within the next few days appeared the Provincial deputies and the delegates of the Woiwode Palatinate, to offer their felicitations, and to perform the act of homage.

The coronation of an orthodox Greek Prince could not, of course, be completed in a Catholic church, a circumstance that only augmented the coldness of the nobility. A throne-room was therefore arranged in the palace, and another for the coronation itself. In the hall where the Senate holds its sittings, a throne was erected on an elevated platform, covered with crimson velvet, surmounted by ostrich feathers, and on it were inscribed the name and titles of the Emperor,

and the national arms. The Coronation Hall was
adjoining. Three days previous to this festive occasion,
three mounted heralds proclaimed the happy event to
all subjects, recommending that on this festive day they
should pray with increased zeal to the King of kings.
On the evening before the ceremony a *Te Deum* was
sung in all the churches. On the Coronation day the
crown, with its various appendages, was borne first to
the Church of St. John, where it was consecrated by
the holy mass, amid chanting, and when brought back
to the Coronation Hall, the Emperor and Empress
appeared, wearing the order of the White Eagle, the
latter with the crown on her head ; the Russian military
authorities, the ministers and aides-de-camp formed her
suite; but all the requisite insignia were carried exclusively by Poles. Thence they repaired to the adjoining
hall, where the priesthood received them with holy
water. The Emperor made a sign to the Primas, who,
after a short prayer, gave him his cloak, which the
two Grand Dukes, his Majesty's brothers, placed on
his shoulders. He demanded the crown, which the
Primas gave him, with these words, " In the name of
the Father, and the Son, and the Holy Ghost," on
which the Emperor himself placed it on his head. He
then presented the Empress with the chain of the
White Eagle, and she received all the other decorations
from the hands of the Primas, who, after the investi-
ture, said in a loud voice, " Vivat rex in æternum."
In accordance with ancient custom, the Provincial
Deputies must assent to this proclamation, and repeat
it audibly. But they were dumb, and a painful, gloomy

silence ensued that discomposed the whole assemblage. They subsequently excused themselves by saying that in the programme of the ceremony nothing was said on the subject, but it was well known to be done on purpose. After this, the Emperor knelt down and repeated a prayer from a book in French. Oppressed by the weight of the crown and its jewels, and also the tight-fitting uniform worn at that time, Nicholas twice paused in exhaustion to draw breath, which was interpreted as a token of his aversion to the Constitution, and a. proof of his secret intention not to keep faith with it. After this prayer the Primas went to the St. John's Church, close to the palace. The Emperor followed, took his place in the centre, and heard the *Te Deum* sung. After this the procession returned to the palace, and the coronation was completed. The rooms in the palace, however, scarcely sufficed for the guests invited. The people too had no entertainment provided for them, and only during the transit of the procession to the church and back, was its love of a spectacle gratified. Seats had been placed in the form of an amphitheatre, chiefly occupied by ladies. Military bands played the well-known air, " God save the King," but its notes were as little familiar to those present as the substance of the words. Within the next eight days the same grand fêtes given in Moscow three years before were repeated, and foreign countries contributed their most admired artists on this occasion. Paganini enchanted the cultivated world by his violin, and the athlete Rappo delighted the people by his Herculean feats. Nicholas's stern countenance everywhere inspired fear and respect, but the charms of Alexandra won all hearts. Both appeared in an open calèche without any escort or retinue before the public during the day, and also at the illuminations at night, and finally at the dinner given to the people in a tent. And yet little incidents were not wanting to cause discontent. Directly after the coronation, a Pole demanded from the Emperor, in the most unseemly manner, to enlighten him as to his brother's fate. Such things caused Nicholas to lose more than his favour could win from the people; violent toothache prevented him being present at the brilliant ball, which was interpreted as reluctance to appear; and at length a sudden storm interrupted the popular fête, in which they read an evil omen for the whole reign. Polish nationality, however, thought it had obtained a triumph in the theatres, only giving operas with Polish music, and in the Polish language, which foreigners did not care to hear. These were wearisome, exhausting days for Alexandra, although her chivalrous husband had spared her all knowledge of the fact that they were both on the edge of a volcano, for the last ten years constantly threatening to burst into an eruption. Happier days awaited her in the family circle of her former home, which she had not yet visited as Empress. Oppressive duty had called her to Warsaw, but her heart led her to Berlin.

Berlin in the latter years, 1820 to 1829, had made wonderful progress in the path pointed out by Frederick William the Third; it was enlarged, embellished and adorned with every species of works of art. The University was the most brilliant in Europe, uniting all the

heights and depths of German learning; the lecture-
rooms were crowded, not only with young men anxious
to learn, but also with grey-headed warriors, while the
exhausted statesman attended the lectures of the philosopher Hegel and others, in which he found instruction
and refreshment. Many philosophical questions were
topics of social discussion, and the theatre and opera-
house created a more lively interest at the domestic
hearth, from the fact of politics being then excluded
from the reasoning powers of Prussian subjects. An
inoffensive spirit at that time pervaded Berlin, a romantic
love of *belles-lettres*, the centre of which was to be
found in Rahel's and Varnhagen's house, where diplo-
matists and military men were as often to be seen as
artists and literati. But now the petty citizen, the true
German *Philister*, visited the newly opened German
Museum, and over a pipe of tobacco and a glass of white
beer talked in booths of the wonderful works he had seen,
not forgetting to dilate with satisfaction on the *Coryphées*
of the theatre, and Clauren's tales. Provincials, even
from a great distance, paid an occasional visit to the
handsome capital, and thus brought back subjects of
conversation to their homes. Besides the Museum, in
this same year the Academy for Singing was opened, as
the noble-hearted King had provided a new building for
the purpose. The exertions of that society were everywhere proudly extolled, and the vocal performances
were considered as perfect as those of the Paris Con-
servatorium. The memory of the great military hero
was publicly honoured in bronze and marble.

Devoid of all external decoration, plain and simple,

like the King himself, was the palace of the monarch,
in the midst of those stately buildings that form Berlin's
greatest ornament. But strangers lingered there for
hours to see the father of the country at his window, or, enveloped in a simple soldier's cloak, driving
through the streets. And yet it was the burgher simplicity of his house, and his whole mode of life, on
which the splendour of his capital was founded. The
royal revenues had erected all these new monuments.
Strict order and economy enabled the King not only to
build art institutions, but the same source supplied the
means of erecting churches, to which he devoted great
attention. This father of his people contrived to attract,
and to retain in his immediate circle, some unusually
celebrated men. Duke Carl of Mecklenburg, his brother-
in-law, equally skilled in using the pen and the sword,
wise and prudent in State councils, intellectual and
witty in society, was the very soul of the Court. Prince
Anton Radziwill is already known to the reader as a
Mæcenas and composer, an ornament to the Court and
to the city. Wilhelm von Humboldt, for years a fruitful
source of intellectual interest to the King, and Alexander von Humboldt, who, at the close of his travels,
settled in Berlin, were included from that moment
among the King's intimate friends. The world has
never seen probably two brothers of equally high distinction, and certainly not at the same Court. The
King, without either knowing or intending it, gained the
renown of the Medici or of Pericles—a fame that other
princes so jealously strove to appropriate. The men,
too, of his Court, Prince Wittgenstein, Baron Schilden,

and the minister Ancillon, understood the art of animating society, and Count Brühl was highly esteemed throughout Germany as an enlightened connoisseur of the fine arts. It was the last year of that tranquil romantic period that began after Waterloo, and cradled the world for a short time in the sweet slumber of refreshing repose, in which past centuries only appeared in dreams, when the melodies of the "Freischütz" and the "Barber of Seville" were to be heard both in palaces and cottages, and the "Muette de Portici" appeared on the distant horizon like a light passing cloud.

The King's abode had long since been deprived of the happy circle of his children, almost all having their own domestic hearth; his eldest daughter, the Empress of Russia, had fulfilled the prophetic words of her mother, the second was Hereditary Grand Duchess of Mecklenburg-Schwerin, the third Princess of the Netherlands; but these connections with different countries enlivened the city from time to time. No year passed without some princely visitor claiming the hospitality of the King, and when he received them with royal splendour, strangers saw his Court as brilliant and magnificent as that of Saxony in the days of Augustus the Strong, but so moral and dignified that Frederick William the First's pure feelings would not have been revolted, as formerly in Dresden.

The Princesses of the royal house were severed from their home, and two of the Princes had brought daughters-in-law to their father, the Crown Prince having married, in 1823, Princess Elizabeth of Bavaria, and Prince Charles, Princess Mary of Saxe Weimar, and

in this year Prince William was to bring as his bride to
Berlin the sister of the latter Princess.

The King anticipated this summer the happiest
family delights that a father can enjoy : he was to
welcome his eldest daughter as Empress of Russia,
not having seen her for five years, and embrace his
new daughter-in-law, Princess Augusta of Saxe Weimar.
The former indeed arrived with an imperial crown, but
not without visible and lasting traces of that day of
terror—December 14th.   It was not the desire alone to
embrace her father that led her hither, but also her
invalid state, that required German baths.   That no
leaf might fail in the family wreath of the venerable
monarch, the Prince and Princess of the Netherlands,
and the Hereditary Grand Duke and Duchess of Saxe
Weimar, had already arrived in Berlin in May.   The
King's failing health, however, prevented his being able
to meet his daughter in Silesia, and therefore she resolved
to go to Berlin.   Her brothers were at Frankfort on the
Oder to receive her, the King and the Princesses at
Friedrichsfeld.   At such a meeting crowns and all outward considerations are lost sight of; man feels that
his greatest treasure, his truest happiness, is to be found
in the heart ; it was not a king and an empress who
met—it was a father and daughter, linked together by
the enduring ties of nature, who now embraced in
silence more eloquent than words.   In such moments
our throbbing pulses revive whole years in our lives.

After five momentous years, and a hundred events of
magnitude, Alexandra once more saw her father, her
brothers and sisters, and her German home, but the

King had a further pleasure in store for him. Nicholas, · to his surprise, accompanied his wife, bringing with him the King's first grandchild, the heir-apparent, now eleven years old. The Emperor had added a new crown ·to his own in Warsaw, and came from there straight to Berlin, where they all arrived on June 6th, and on the ·9th went to Potsdam. On the same day arrived Prince William's fair bride-elect, Princess Augusta of Saxe Weimar, welcomed by all the customary festivities. The marriage took place on June 11th. The Emperor and his young son attended these fêtes, and on the night of the 12th returned to Warsaw. The Berlin public felt as warm an interest in all these family occurrences as if their own, always speaking of the Emperor of Russia as "our son-in-law," and of the Empress as "our daughter." When the populace heard of the arrival of that illustrious lady, they thronged to Friedrichsfeld, and filled the streets with shouts of joy. The King with his three daughters occupied the first carriage, and flowers and wreaths were showered on them from every window. In the second sat the Emperor, the Crown Princess, Princess Charles, and the Crown Prince; Prince Charles and the Russian heir-apparent in the third. When the procession approached the long bridge, and Alexandra caught sight of the distant palace, she was overcome with emotion, and the public were for a few moments deprived of her friendly greetings. Scarcely had they arrived in the palace when the Empress appeared first on the balcony with her son, then the whole of the family followed, the venerable King pressing his grandson fondly to his

heart. All the regimental bands the same evening
played the most exhilarating strains. It was not however the populace alone, or the higher classes of society,
who expressed their homage; the honoured corporation
of the University offered their welcome in antique form,
and in the language of Pindar. A Greek ode sung the
victory of the Emperor over the Turks for the freedom
of Greece, and also the attractions of the Empress, and,
what was still more rare, the virtues of an Imperial
couple so closely united by domestic felicity. A Greek
poem, in spite of its admirable translation into German,
can however inspire little real interest. In these days
of active life, with its stirring claims, such displays
vanish like stars of the seventh magnitude in the
heavens, and the tap of the drum at the right moment
is more appreciated than a creation of the brain that has
cost so much toil and effort. Many hearts and eyes in
that century felt revived interest in the chivalrous
splendours of the mediæval age, and on this account a
fête was prepared for the Empress in Potsdam, which
deserves to be minutely recorded. Not only in the
annals of Berlin Court life is it the last and most
brilliant of the kind, but in all European Courts also
for it was a year before the revolution of July, which
erected other standards than those of the middle ages,
and it occurred to no one that it took place about the
time that the "Muette de Portici" was given. Duke
Charles of Mecklenburg and Count Redern were
intrusted with the arrangement of the fête.

On July 13th the Empress celebrated her thirty-first
birthday; the second half of her reign then began,

though she had no presentiment of the fact, while the close of this period of her youth, and the commencement of a new one, was one of the brightest days of her life. No one had known greater happiness and unhappiness, splendour and honour, terror and sorrow. She knew how a mourner weeps, she had learned to pray in the hour of need, but she had also breathed the sunny atmosphere of human happiness. She now rested in Sans Souci, beside her father and her brothers and sisters, an object of love and honour to all who knew her or even saw her, and the wish to do her homage was displayed by fêtes, from which sprung the most beautiful of all —" The magic White Rose." It was beyond all others her favourite flower. When encompassed by every pomp the world could bestow, adorned with the most costly gems, and two crowns on her head, she added a white rose, and under all circumstances continued a lover of flowers, and delighted in showing to her guests in her boudoir, both in summer and in winter, flowers that had grown under her own eyes. But from her youth upwards the white rose had always been to her the fairest symbol, and in her own familiar circle she was called Blanchefleur.

The new palace in Potsdam was chosen for the fête, the first portion of which was open to the public, so that a large number of the inhabitants of Berlin came to Potsdam. The front court of the palace was arranged as the site of a tournament, separated by balustrades from the tribune and the spectators, and ornamented with crimson and gold-embroidered draperies, and hundreds of tall flagstaffs, on the pennons of which

every variety of colour, and embroidered with white
roses, waved in the breeze.   In the centre, under a
green canopy, was erected the dais for the queen of the
fête.   Thousands of invited guests were on the tribune,
but beyond the lists, crowds of Berliners were assembled,
although rain threatened all day.   At last, towards six
o'clock, the sky cleared up, and, led by her father, and
accompanied by the other princesses, the Empress
appeared. Her dress was cut in the fashion of a previous
century, embroidered with pearls and diamonds, and
dazzling as light, while she was herself as pure as the
rose they were about to celebrate, and all the ladies
wore wreaths of white roses.   After she had taken her
place, a king-at-arms, with two heralds, rode into the
course up to the centre tribune, and asked the Empress's
permission to admit a number of knights, who wished
to distinguish themselves by feats of arms.   Having
received her sanction, the company of knights advanced
towards the colonnade of the palace to the inner court-
yard, preceded by a corps of trumpeters in orange and red.
The procession consisted of ten quadrilles, including
a standard-bearer, two pages, who bore shield and
lance, four knights and three squires, each preceding
his princely leader.   The royal princes were : Prince
Frederick of the Netherlands, Duke Charles of Mecklenburg, Duke William of Brunswick-Oels, and the
Hereditary Grand Duke of Mecklenburg.   The spectacle of the different banners and colours, the arms, the
brilliant richness of the costumes of a long-vanished
time, gave the procession the aspect of having been con-
jured up from a dead century into the present one, as

if the past were striving to displace the present. The procession first moved round the lists twice, and then, pausing before the tribune, Duke Charles of Mecklenburg recited some verses of homage addressed to the Empress, and asked her consent to their jousting in chivalrous strife, in honour of the white rose. To this request she acceded, and appointed two umpires, Prince Charles of Mecklenburg and Prince Frederick of the Netherlands, who remained in front of the tribune while the lists were being arranged. Pillars with rings, targets, and Moors' heads were displayed, all encircled with white roses, and every time the shield was hit a white rose fell. The four sons of the King opened the tilting. First they rode with lances couched at the rings with the white roses, then at the Moors' heads, hurling their spears at the target, and finally attacking with swords the second rings. The other princes followed in succession, and forty knights closed these games.

At the close, the whole set of knights once more rode round the palace court twice, bending low before the tribune of the Empress as they rode past, and dismounting to escort the queen of the fête to the palace, whither the distant sounds of a choir summoned all to repair. The fête was now at an end for the public, the second portion being to take place in the interior of the palace. Although, like the first, intended to please the eye, it was not meant to be seen from any great distance. It represented dissolving views in a magic mirror. The entire hall received its light from a transparent wreath of roses running along the cornices of the upper gallery. The magic mirror embraced the whole theatrical scene, its surface was dark, and the frame alone bright with light, displaying in rich arabesques . white roses, and the forms of hovering genii. The obscure mirror only received light and life when the Empress looked into it, endowing it with the magic of her own eyes. Then came to life, on the surface of the mirror, pictures of memories both sad and bright. The representation had been intrusted to the members of the royal theatre, and the tableaux so arranged that one melted into another like a dream. The first was Berlin, the birthplace of the illustrious lady, with all the sweet remembrances of childhood and youth. Then came tableaux of Silesia, where she had taken the first steps into graver life; Moscow, the burning of which will ever be renowned in the history of Russia. But for Alexandra the sweetest of all incidents recalled to her memory was the birth of her son, the first meeting with her royal father after her marriage, and above all, the Imperial coronation. The Empress was not only touched but much agitated, especially as her health on that day had been more feeble than usual. As all eyes were fixed on the mirror, no one remarked that hers were filled with tears, and that her weakened frame could not stand so much pleasurable excitement. Her melancholy mood was heightened by the tableaux of Bellona, of the all-devouring Kronos; and although she could not withdraw at the third part, her heart remained unmoved. They all repaired to the Grotto Hall, where an orchestra hidden by bowers of white roses played, and twenty couples of the society danced in mediæval costume. Thus closed this fête, the most beautiful and intellectual of the century, the last reflection of the middle ages and its romantic customs on the present, overshadowed by dark clouds. The royal father was never seen to look happier than on that day. During the tournament he walked up and down behind the seats of his distinguished guests, entering at intervals into gay and playful conversation, and openly showing his paternal joy at being once more among his family. On the third day after the fête the Empress quitted Potsdam, in order to travel back to Russia. The happier the meeting had been, the more sorrowful was the parting.

Almost at the same period of these knightly games in Potsdam, the Russian troops were victorious in the Balkan, and were now pressing forward direct to Adrianople. In Europe as in Asia, Islam was yielding to the arms of the young Emperor, who in less than four years had written his name ineffaceably on the history of the world. Both in Court and elsewhere, another spirit breathed through the city and the country than in the time of Alexander.

END OF VOL. I.

EDINBURGH: PRINTED BY THOMAS AND ARCHIBALD CONSTABLE,
PRINTERS TO THE QUEEN, AND TO THE UNIVERSITY.